Challenges of Translation
in French Literature

Richard Bales (ed.)

Challenges of Translation in French Literature

Studies and Poems in Honour of
Peter Broome

PETER LANG

Oxford · Bern · Berlin · Bruxelles · Frankfurt am Main · New York · Wien

Bibliographic information published by Die Deutsche Bibliothek
Die Deutsche Bibliothek lists this publication in the Deutsche Nationalbibliografie;
detailed bibliographic data is available on the Internet at ‹http://dnb.ddb.de›.

British Library and Library of Congress Cataloguing-in-Publication Data:
A catalogue record for this book is available from The British Library,
Great Britain, and from The Library of Congress, USA

Cover design: Thomas Jaberg, Peter Lang AG

ISBN 3-03910-295-8
US-ISBN 0-8204-7221-2

© Peter Lang AG, European Academic Publishers, Bern 2005
Hochfeldstrasse 32, Postfach 746, CH-3000 Bern 9, Switzerland
info@peterlang.com, www.peterlang.com, www.peterlang.net

Printed in Germany

Frontispiece

PETER BROOME

Contents

Acknowledgements

I am exceptionally grateful to all who have contributed to this volume: they have shown the greatest helpfulness and enthusiasm at every turn. My particular thanks go to the five poets, who unhesitatingly offered exceptionally fine examples of their work. At Peter Lang, Alexis Kirschbaum has been the model editor: her efficiency and good humour are a constant inspiration. Queen's University has displayed considerable generosity in supporting this book financially, in the shape of grants from the Publications Fund and the School of Languages, Literatures and Arts. Lastly, thanks to Peter Broome for his translations, for keeping a low but helpful profile while this volume was being prepared, but above all for his magnificent example to us all over the years.

Belfast, March 2005

Notes on the essay contributors

RICHARD BALES is Professor of Modern French Literature at Queen's University, Belfast. His research is largely devoted to the work of Marcel Proust, the most recent volume being *The Cambridge Companion to Proust* (2001). He has also written on nineteenth-century authors (*Persuasion in the French Personal Novel*, 1997) and on Belgian Symbolism (editions of Georges Rodenbach (1999) and Grégoire Le Roy (2005)).

MICHAEL BISHOP is Emeritus McCulloch Professor of French at Dalhousie University. He has published widely in the field of modern and contemporary literature, art and culture. His most recent books include *Jacques Prévert: from Film and Theater to Poetry, Art and Song* (2002), *French Prose in 2000* (2002), *Contemporary French Poetics* (2002), *Altérités d'André du Bouchet* (2003), translations of Yves Bonnefoy: *L'Horizon/The Horizon* (2003) and *In the Lure of Language* (2003), and a translation of Gérard Titus-Carmel: *Jungle (non-lieu)/Jungle (unspace)* (2005).

JOHN CAMPBELL had the privilege of attending Peter Broome's inspiring lectures on poetry while an undergraduate at Queen's University. He is presently Reader in French at the University of Glasgow. A former editor of *Seventeenth-Century French Studies*, he has written a series of articles on French seventeenth-century literature, comparative literature, and contemporary France. His publications include *Racine's 'Britannicus'* (1990), *Questions of Interpretation in 'La Princesse de Clèves'* (1996), *Christine de Pizan 2000* (editor, with Nadia Margolis, 2000), and *Questioning Racinian Tragedy* (2005).

ANGELA CHAMBERS is Professor of Applied Languages and Director of the Centre for Applied Language Studies at the University of Limerick. She has also lectured at the University of Ulster and the Université de Lille-III. Her PhD thesis on the poetry of Aimé Césaire, supervised by Peter Broome, has given rise to a number of articles on Césaire. She has also edited books on aspects of language learning, and published articles in that area.

GRAHAM CHESTERS is Professor of French at the University of Hull. His first major publications (with Cambridge University Press) were jointly authored with Peter Broome. The main focus of his research has been on nineteenth- and twentieth-century French poetry, particularly Baudelaire (*Baudelaire: the Poetics of Craft*, 1988; an edition of *Les Fleurs du mal*, 1995). He is currently Director of the Institute for Learning at the University of Hull.

PAUL GIFFORD is Buchanan Professor of French and Director of the Institute of European Cultural Identity Studies at the University of St Andrews. Member of the Institut des Textes et Manuscrits Modernes (CNRS, Paris). Publications include: *Valéry: le dialogue des choses divines* (1989), *Reading Paul Valéry* (ed. with B. Stimpson, 1999), *2000 Years: Faith, Identity and the Common Era* (ed. with D. Archard, T. Hart and N. Rapport, 2002), *Love, Desire and Transcendence in French Literature. Deciphering Eros* (2005), and *Genesis, Intertext, Creation: Where are Genetic Studies Now?* (ed. with M. Schmid, 2005).

EDWARD J. HUGHES is Professor of Modern French Literature at Royal Holloway, University of London. He is the author of *Marcel Proust: a Study in the Quality of Awareness* (1983), *Albert Camus: 'Le Premier Homme'/'La Peste'* (1995), and *Writing Marginality in Modern French Literature: from Loti to Genet* (2001).

WALLACE KIRSOP has been attached to the Department of French (in its different guises) at Monash University since 1962. He was editor of the *Australian Journal of French Studies* from 1968 to 2002. Seven years into retirement his principal function is Honorary Professor in the School of English, Communications and Performance Studies and Director of the Centre for the Book.

ROGER LITTLE retired from the Chair of French (1776) at Trinity College Dublin in 1998. Active as a general editor (Critical Guides to French Texts, Autrement Mêmes...), his main research interests lie in modern French poetry and the portrayal of Blacks in French-language literatures. His books deal with Saint-John Perse, Rimbaud, Apollinaire, André Frénaud and *The Shaping of Modern French Poetry*, as well as *Nègres blancs* and *Black Man, White Woman in Francographic literature*. He has also edited several texts representing Blacks.

ROSEMARY LLOYD is Rudy Professor of French, Professor of Gender Studies, and Adjunct Professor of Comparative Literature and English at Indiana University, Bloomington. Her latest books are *Mallarmé: the Poet and his Circle* (1999), *Baudelaire's World* (2002), and *Shimmering in a Transformed Light: Writing the Still Life* (2005).

JOHN MCCANN studied French and Spanish at Queen's University. He became a lecturer in French at the Ulster Polytechnic, later the University of Ulster. Since 1987, he has been based at the Magee campus of the university. He has published on a range of authors, notably Laforgue, Camus and Baudelaire.

TERENCE MCMULLAN is Senior Lecturer in Hispanic Studies at Queen's University, Belfast, where his teaching interests include modern Spanish literature, pre-Civil War painting, and cinema. His research focuses mainly on early twentieth-century Spanish verse seen in relation to French culture and the visual arts. He has published essays on plays by Lorca and Buero Vallejo, and his articles on individual 1927 Generation poets have appeared in major journals. He is the author of *The Crystal and the Snake. Aspects of French Influence on Guillén, Lorca and Cernuda* (2002).

GERALD M. MACKLIN has been a Senior Lecturer in French Studies at the University of Ulster since 1996. He has published on Giraudoux and Verlaine, but principally on Rimbaud on whose poetry he has written a book and more than twenty papers. He is currently working on a book on Samuel Beckett on whose drama he has published four recent articles.

Les poètes se présentent

AUXEMÉRY. Une chose est très curieuse, lorsqu'on se mêle de poésie, et qu'on n'a pour ambition que de *revenir à la ligne* d'une certaine manière – qu'il faut inventer à chaque instant, sans perdre souffle: au détour de cette ligne-ci ou de celle-là, parfois, un lecteur attentif se signale, se présente, et finit par *faire signe*, à son tour, dans le parcours des mots vers leur destination.

De Peter Broome, j'ai su au premier mot que j'ai lu de lui dans une lettre, qu'il était ce lecteur qui guette et participe à la réalisation de ce qui doit être. Un scrutateur, un *traducteur* donc: quelqu'un qui suit les chemins de traverse des langues, et *fait passer*. Et si nous *autres*, nous faiseurs de poèmes, nous obstinons à suivre la pente qui nous mène, c'est en sachant que des lecteurs de cette sorte nous attendent, nous traversent, nous transmettent l'écho d'une parole qui, sitôt émise, peut-être se perdrait, sans eux.

Il a donc lu, avec le regard de la sympathie active, certains de mes livres, dont *Parafe*, et *Codex* (Flammarion). J'avoue m'être aussi livré à l'exercice de la traduction, parce que j'y trouvais un aliment nécessaire à mon propre accomplissement: Pound (la voix d'un siècle de fer), Reznikoff (la grammaire de l'horreur de ces temps), Olson (lui surtout, sismographe et bathygraphe), H.D. (notre Sappho, exilée en Egypte), W.C. Williams (fondateur, notre Hermès), ainsi que certains grands contemporains et amis: Clayton Eshleman, Nathaniel Tarn, Kenneth Koch...

MARIE-CLAIRE BANQUART. Professeur émérite à la Sorbonne, auteur de nombreux essais sur la prose de la fin du dix-neuvième siècle et sur la poésie contemporaine, j'ai publié une vingtaine de recueils de poésie, parmi lesquels *Énigmatiques* (Obsidiane, 1995). Je signale aussi une anthologie de mes poèmes, *Rituel d'emportement* (Le Temps qu'il fait/Obsidiane, 2002), et le recueil *Anamorphoses* (2003, au Québec). C'est sous les auspices du poète André Frénaud (sur lui, j'ai

16

organisé en 2000 un colloque à Cerisy), que nous nous sommes rencontrés, Peter Broome et moi. Son sourire et son talent ne pouvaient qu'attirer une sympathie qui bientôt s'est doublée de reconnaissance de ma part, avec sa traduction d'*Énigmatiques*.

LOUISE HERLIN. Née au Caire. Enfance et adolescence à Bruxelles. Etudes à l'université de Florence, puis à la Sorbonne. Traductrice à la BBC (Londres), aux Nations Unies (New York) et dans d'autres organisations internationales. Habite Paris depuis 1955. Son premier recueil de poésie, *Le Versant contraire*, paraît chez Gallimard, collection 'Le Chemin' en 1967. Suivent: *Commune mesure* (L'Âge d'homme, 1971), *Couleur de temps* et *Crayons* (Le Nouveau Commerce, 1981), *L'Amour exact* (Éditions de la Différence, 1990), *Le Poème inachevé* (Dumerchez, 1993), *Les Oiseaux de Méryon* (la Différence, 1993), *Synchronies* (Dumerchez, 1998), *Chemins de traverse* (la Différence, 2002). A traduit des poèmes d'Eugenio Montale.

VÉNUS KHOURY-GHATA. Née au Liban. Études de lettres. Mariée avec un médecin-chercheur scientifique mort jeune. A publié quinze romans et quinze recueils de poèmes. Lauréate des Prix Apollinaire et Mallarmé, et Grand Prix de la Société des gens de lettres. Sélectionnée pour le National Book Award pour son recueil *She says* publié aux États-Unis chz Graywolf. A obtenu le Prix Liberation de la Foire de Francfort pour son roman *La Maîtresse du notable*. Son œuvre est traduite en allemand, suédois, italien, anglais (États-Unis), coréen, turc, grec, arabe, néerlandais, russe, ukrainien, bulgare.

JEAN-CHARLES VEGLIANTE. Essayer de dire quelque chose, plutôt que rien. Pour quelqu'un et à partager si l'on veut (*Rien commun*, Belin, 2000)... Ecrire à partir de l'incompréhensible, voire d'une sidération devant la beauté et devant l'horreur – et comme repoussoir de l'ennui, d'où naît parfois la pensée, quand 'la Sorcière allume sa braise dans le pot de terre'. Sans jamais, croit-on jusque vers cinquante-cinq ans, d'*acquièscement* (j'ai un fils avec qui j'en plaisante).

Voilà en peu de mots, où je n'ai même pas signalé que je traduis beaucoup, mon sentiment du pourquoi. Réservant le 'comment', à Paris assez féroce; ainsi que le grand réservoir nocturne, où tout peut encore échanger et mentir; ou remonter à l'amont d'une langue perdue puis retrouvée (*Vers l'amont Dante*, L'Alphée, 1987), fleuve qu'à présent j'enseigne à l'université. En cette autre langue mienne, l'un des plus grands poètes contemporains a bien voulu me transporter: Giovanni Raboni (*Nel lutto della luce*, Einaudi, 2004).

RICHARD BALES

Introduction

Le devoir et la tâche d'un écrivain sont ceux d'un traducteur.

Proust's visionary dictum[1] sits well at the head of any book which concerns itself with translation. This is all the more true when, as here, a multiplicity of studies, all different in emphasis, are presented simultaneously. Proust gets a chapter of his own, but his words could stand as a motto for them all. If what he advocates is tantamount to an injunction, it is certainly not a set of instructions, rather a state of mind which can profitably be adopted. Of course, he is addressing the condition of an author, not a translator; but in his formulation, the definition of what constitutes a translator is almost as important as that of the writer. Both terms are left vague, but, employed pithily, they gain in weight, and what might have been considered the lesser activity – translation – acquires greater esteem by dint of being employed in just as powerfully syntactical a position as the traditionally more significant, 'respectable' occupation.

Much has subsequently been written about the technique(s) of translation, and whole theories elaborated;[2] but this is not the place to enter into the debate, if only because the essays which make up this volume cover such a wide field of subject-matter and entail the application of such different criteria that homogeneity, even if it were desired, would be impossible to obtain. Besides, the poems which punctuate this book throw up their own local difficulties of translation – another hint that uniform theory may not be as useful as pragmatic choice. So, instead of a proclamation of theory, what I propose in the

1   Marcel Proust, *A la recherche du temps perdu* (4 vols., Paris: Gallimard (Pléiade), 1987–1989), IV, 469.
2   For a convenient summary, see Susan Bassnett, *Translation Studies* (London and New York: Routledge, 1980 (2004)).

following pages is a brief meditation on the way in which, following the example of Proust, some authoritative twentieth-century voices have addressed central aspects of translation, in their varied attempts at pinning down a particularly elusive concept.

This intangibility is nicely highlighted by Walter Benjamin when he reminds us that 'there is no muse of philosophy, nor is there one of translation'.[3] In other words, there is no single, universally recognised authority to prescribe, or even recommend, a 'correct' manner of translating. In his famous essay 'The Task of the Translator', he abundantly demonstrates why dogmatism is misplaced if applied to the exercise. Taking the Proust maxim from the other end, as it were (intentionally, perhaps: Benjamin was Proust's first German translator), the gist of his essay constantly accentuates the creative role played by the translator: 'It is the task of the translator to release in his own language that pure language which is under the spell of another, to liberate the language imprisoned in a work in his re-creation of that work' (Benjamin, p.80). Nothing if not utopian in his ambition, Benjamin succeeds in turning to advantage the paradoxical situation of writing authoritatively about an activity which he believes should be free from authority. What in effect he addresses here is the primordial quality the translator ought to possess: it should be less one of technique than of vision,[4] the ability to perceive 'pure' meaning, perception which will permit the appropriate creative rendition in another tongue. The notion that meaning can exist in a putative ideal state is of course debatable; but it clearly enables Benjamin to give the requisite emphasis to what he views as the desirable driving force – that is, creativity.

Yet, as Paul Ricœur reminds us in a recent essay, we are dealing with a risky business:

3   Walter Benjamin, *Illuminations* (London: Collins/Fontana, 1973), p.77.
4   There is surely an echo of Proust again here: 'Le style pour l'écrivain, aussi bien que la couleur pour le peintre, est une question non de technique mais de vision' (Proust, IV, 474).

> Grandeur de la traduction, risque de la traduction: trahison créatrice de l'original, appropriation également créatrice par la langue d'accueil; *construction du comparable.*[5]

The gnomic utterances are a kind of summary reaction to the implications of Benjamin's enthusiastic advocacy of the creative mode. And if Ricœur would wish to share Benjamin's enthusiasm for it, he nuances the attitude somewhat. This he does in summing up what he sees as the three stages through which the translator necessarily passes, usefully organising his formulation as a mini-narrative which in itself encapsulates the dynamics of the act of translation:

> Nous avons suivi le traducteur depuis l'angoisse qui le retient de commencer et à travers la lutte avec le texte tout au long de son travail; nous l'abandonnons dans l'état d'insatisfaction où le laisse l'ouvrage terminé (Ricœur, p.15).

The key words here are scarcely encouraging; but if the end-result is dissatisfying, that is not the same as saying it is a failure. Like the Proust motto, the syntactical organisation encourages an egalitarian, positive interpretation. For, according to Ricœur, one needs to take a vital first step to 'renoncer à l'idéal de la traduction parfaite' (Ricœur, p.16). Decidedly more sober than Benjamin, he abandons the notion of 'pure' language; once one has done this, the compensations are considerable:

> C'est le deuil de la traduction absolue qui fait le bonheur de traduire. Le bonheur de traduire est un gain lorsque, attaché à la perte de l'absolu langagier, il accepte l'écart entre l'adéquation et l'équivalence, l'équivalence sans adéquation (Ricœur, p.19).

In shifting the emphasis from expectations of final perfection onto the act of translation itself, Ricœur is surely validating more than the utilitarian nature of the activity: the act acquires a nobility of its own, and the translator, whilst still an intermediary, becomes recognised as an individual who has to confront difficulties of the same order as the original writer is generally deemed to experience. In other words, he

---

5   Paul Ricœur, *Sur la traduction* (Paris: Bayard, 2004), p.66. Italics in the original.

has his own creative battles to fight. This will always be the case, according to Ricœur: for him, 'la traduction reste une opération risquée toujours en quête de sa théorie' (Ricœur, p.26). Another reminder, like Benjamin's, that there is no muse of translation.

Susan Sontag takes the 'dissatisfaction' aspect of translation a stage further, veritably embracing what might ordinarily be considered a drawback:

> Translation is about differentness. A way of coping with, and ameliorating, and, yes, denying difference – even if […] it is also a way of asserting differentness.[6]

This is a refreshing new credo, the more so as it enables Sontag to rehabilitate older meanings of the word 'translation', taking as a cue the etymology, which is 'to transfer, to remove, to displace. To what end? In order to be rescued, from death or extinction' (Ibid.). This represents more even than George Steiner had proposed, when he invaluably advanced the claim that 'inside or between languages, human communication equals translation'.[7] Communication: a notion more often than not taken for granted, but here usefully highlighted, and henceforth always implicit in Sontag's insistence on the *movement* inherent in translation:

> We retain only the sense of translation as the transfer or handing over or delivery from one language to another. Yet the older meanings expressed in the *tra-* and *trans-* words (welded to *-dere*, *-ducere*) remain as an underpinning. The fruitful affinities of etymology express a real, if subliminal, connection. To translate is still to lead something across a gap, to make something go where it was not (Sontag, p.340).

This is a dynamics which agreeably extends the normally envisaged field of translation, permitting the incorporation of ventures such as cultural transfers:

> The sense of physical or geographical separateness is still implicit, and potent. Languages are like separate (often antagonistic) communities, each with its own

6   Susan Sontag, *Where the Stress Falls* (London: Jonathan Cape, 2002), p.339.
7   George Steiner, *After Babel: Aspects of Language and Translation* (Oxford: Oxford University Press, 1975), p.47.

customs. The translator is the one who finds (identifies, formulates) the comparable customs in another language (Ibid.).

Perhaps Sontag's analysis takes little account of the anguish, struggle and dissatisfaction of Ricœur's translator, but it does possess the signal merit of opening out the act of translation beyond what is utilitarian, broadening its parameters in a manner which can only be helpful in maximising communicative power.

It is this sort of vision which some recent creative writers have exercised in launching investigations into areas of sensibility where the broad notion of translation is not only apposite but is explicitly named. Two works seem to me exemplary in this respect: Brian Friel's play *Translations* (1984) and Les Murray's collection of poems *Translations from the Natural World* (1993). In the former, complex situations of a topographical, socio-political, and personal nature arise when British officials survey 1830s Co. Donegal and re-name places. They all converge on a central notion, which is the very title of the play. At the heart of the issues raised is one which we have met before, but which is all the more telling for being articulated by one of the characters: Hugh, whose fondness for the bottle enables him to utter the occasional pregnant truth, allows a sober note to pierce through when he proclaims that 'words are signals, counters. They are not immortal'.[8] We are back to the riskiness of translation dealt with by Ricœur, but now, with Friel, the words about words take on wider implications than just translating place-names from Irish into English: a whole historical dimension is opened up, and who knows what the future will bring?

Less dramatically, Les Murray quite naturally (and literally: he apparently feels no need to explain his title) demonstrates that older connotations of the word 'translation' are happily not extinct, but can flourish again in a modern context. So, when he writes of his 'Yard horse' that 'his coat is a climate of mirrorings/and his body is the word for every meaning in his universe', the move into language

---

8   Brian Friel, *Translations*, in *Selected Plays of Brian Friel* (London: Faber and Faber, 1984), p.419.

could not more eloquently – or simply – reflect the multivalency of the term 'translation'.[9]

The essays contained in this book echo this breadth and sense of liberation, ranging as they do over a wide spectrum, from close-up studies of individual translations through cultural transfers to shifts of genre and translations of the self. And, being interspersed with examples of new poetry newly translated by the person from whom the present volume takes its inspiration and whom it seeks to honour, the reader is constantly reminded that translation is an unceasing activity which recreates itself on a permanent basis.

The first grouping of essays shows famous poets at work as translators of famous texts. John Campbell's close examination of Ted Hughes's and Robert Lowell's versions of Racine reveals not only an awareness of major local problems of translation, but also homes in on wider cultural and historical questions of transposition. Racine was, after all, already rendering a lost world for his audience. Philip Larkin, on the other hand, was being resolutely modern and personal; yet, as Graham Chesters subtly demonstrates, this 'poetry of multiple liberations' is largely built on intertexts and echoes of French symbolism. For his part, Derek Mahon, in tackling poets who largely issue from that school, is less concerned, as Roger Little convincingly argues, with the lure of perfection than with harnessing translation to his own creative purposes, regarding it as a 'servant'.

If the translators represented in the second section of essays are less famous, that is not to say the questions they raise are any the less pertinent. On the contrary, as Gerald Macklin shows to be the case with translations of Rimbaud, issues of hermeticism and untranslatability raise awkward questions to which there may be no answers. The case of Mallarmé, Rosemary Lloyd's chosen poet, may be even more extreme: how can translators achieve success in approaching areas of inaccessible meaning? Mallarmé was of course a direct antecedent of Valéry, and the problem for the translator here is capturing a specific mental-cum-spiritual attitude: what is required is

9   Les Murray, 'Yard horse', in *Translations from the Natural World* (Manchester: Carcanet, 1993), p.31.

detailed knowledge and poetic application of a cultural 'world' which foregrounds and cherishes metaphysical values. If Paul Gifford here *prepares* for the act of translation, then Michael Bishop, in his essay, shows the reverse motion: translation retroactively affects the tonality adopted by the translator/commentator and restarts the cogitative process.

At this point, with section three, the word 'challenge' in association with 'translation' acquires fresh connotations, yet, as Wallace Kirsop and Terence McMullan amply demonstrate, the vitality with which French poetry was made 'to go where it was not' (Sontag's gloss is especially apposite here): its reception and translation in Australia and Spain was quite remarkable, and very up to date. There may have been physical constraints and impediments from time to time, but these were always overcome, and boundaries impressively transcended.

The final section addresses those wider definitions which Susan Sontag so eloquently espouses, and which extend the realm of translation so imaginatively. John McCann's route is *into* his chosen poet Mallarmé, demonstrating how an ephemeral experience can be translated into a work of art: the challenge of what is trivial, no less. Richard Bales, though, shows a great writer – Proust – consciously theorising about translation, and effortlessly integrating this theory into the very fabric of his novel, notably advocating a cross-generic approach. The line which the last two contributors cross is a cultural one, and in doing so they extend the notion of translation to its fullest. Yet, as Edward Hughes and Angela Chambers constantly remind us, it is through the language of literary expression that one witnesses apparently new kinds of translation, whether they be within the hegemony of a colonial power or moving from colonial experience to the assertion of a new identity. Language, whatever its origins and whatever challenges it has to face up to, is forever being re-made, translated from one domain to another.

This conception of language on the move, language being shifted around, gainfully employed, could easily be characterised as central to the thought and activity of the person whom this book has been composed to honour. Peter Broome's academic career has always been concerned with making words meaningful. Following his studies at Nottingham, a first posting took him to Australia, where nearly five years at Monash were to provide a firm foundation for the rest of his career, which was entirely spent at Queen's University, Belfast. There, he was an inspiration to generations of students, especially adept at opening their eyes and ears to the marvels of French poetry. He moved rapidly through the ranks to Professor and directed innumerable Ph.D. theses. Several of his ex-students are now university teachers.

The roll-call of Peter Broome's publications is long and distinguished. If one were to attempt a single way of characterising them, it would probably be that they all privilege communicative power analogous to that which we have seen George Steiner and Susan Sontag give prominence to. So his first publication (with Graham Chesters) was a double volume whose avowed aim was to make French poetry accessible at various levels simultaneously: *The Appreciation of French Poetry 1850–1950*, together with its *Anthology*,[10] were to become, and have remained, major reference-points and inspiring textbooks for those wishing to get to the heart of the poetic experience. This desire for parallel investigation and communication was rapidly followed up by the twin volumes devoted to Michaux: the first comprehensive monograph on the poet, and an edition of *Au pays de la magie*,[11] in both of which a central concern was just the sort of probing which permits larger horizons to be discerned, a preoccupation which gave rise to a series of articles on Michaux which 'translate' the poet into pictorial and musical realms.

These works from the 1970s, seen in retrospect, clearly constituted archetypes, which would henceforth provide the model for works to come. Not that there has been any slavish repetition of methodology – on the contrary, Peter Broome's approach to each poet takes as its cue the unique poetic world which (s)he inhabits. Thus, his pioneering work on André Frénaud, in an impressive series of books and articles, succeeded in providing others with an in-depth ac-

10   Cambridge University Press, 1976.
11   *Henri Michaux* (London: Athlone Press, 1977); *Au pays de la magie* (London: Athlone Press, 1977).

cessibility to a 'difficult' poet. Not so difficult, after all, given this critic's desire and ability to move 'du lieu du poème à l'univers', to borrow one of his titles.[12] Broome's two Bloodaxe bilingual editions of Frénaud and Michaux are good examples of this desire for popularisation backed up by erudition: not just translation of the words, but also highlighting translation of another kind, the play of correspondences and coincidence between the languages of painting and writing.[13] Yet another manner of translation is attempted in *Baudelaire's Poetic Patterns: the Secret Language of 'Les Fleurs du mal'*.[14] Here, Peter Broome forges a remarkable new methodology by casting the book in the shape of a vast sonnet: readings of fourteen poems which 'translate' the sonnet form from the poetic object of study to that of overall critical framework.

The last few years have seen Broome concentrating more and more on contemporary poetry, with ground-breaking books devoted to Marie-Claire Bancquart, Louise Herlin and Jean-Charles Vegliante,[15] as well as work on Auxeméry and Vénus Khoury-Ghata: five poets who have enthusiastically wished to be associated with this volume. And since our focus is translation, it seemed appropriate to invite Peter Broome himself to provide a discreet yet exemplary presence in the shape of translations of poems which were written and contributed with him in mind. As will be seen, his formidable analytical powers permit the emergence of a subtle and elegant translator. In counterpointing the critical studies, these poems together with their trans-

---

12   *André Frénaud, 'Dans la crique': du lieu du poème à l'univers* (New York: Mellen, 1998). See also *André Frénaud* (Amsterdam: Rodopi, 1986).

13   Henri Michaux, *Déplacements, dégagements / Spaced, displaced* (Newcastle upon Tyne: Bloodaxe, 1992); André Frénaud, *La Sorcière de Rome / Rome the Sorceress* (Newcastle upon Tyne: Bloodaxe, 1998).

14   Amsterdam: Rodopi, 1999.

15   Chronologically: a bilingual edition of Jean-Charles Vegliante, *Les Oublies / Will there be promises* (New York: Mellen, 2000); *The Poetry of Louise Herlin: the Slow, the Fabulous Profusion* (New York: Mellen, 2003); a bilingual edition of Marie-Claire Bancquart, *Énigmatiques / Enigma Variations* (Halifax, N.S.: VVV Editions, 2004). The latter translation was awarded the *Prix de l'Ambassade* of the Irish Translators' and Interpreters' Association.

lations remind us not only that translation is a protean activity which points in many directions, but that with each fresh generation the challenges which it contrives are bound to be new and arduous; but tackling them is mandatory – and endlessly rewarding.

Auxeméry

Stone unto itself

At the edge of the route :

this stele
in all solemnity
defying gravity –

Standing between apportioned lands :

those nearby where bodies rose in rank and ran ;

the others, where repose itself made the spirit soar
at the end of the day's next stage of journeying.

Aspects to the winds :

some swept in from the plains
as we lolled to our horseback's easy gait ;

others, down from the mountain pass, and upwards to the heights

– we had shed our looks there,
our fatigue, our precious gift.

We, of no abode.

Wing of the book, outspread :

voice and silences, – laid bare ;

with the palm of the passer-by's hand
to smoothe out the characters,

but their printed outline stayed, and the onward march.

On this vertical tablet :

our name and erasures of that name –

rare joy of such a law,
beyond the tramp of empires, and of courts.

Then this, on the burning stone :

the forest of signs and lines ;
and this seal – fire, night entwined.

Finally one more step, to end all steps :

the *sîmurgh*'s feather,
language of the birds.

(translated by Peter Broome)

Stèle unique

Sur le bord du chemin :

    cette stèle,
    en toute gravité
    délivrée des pesanteurs –

Située entre les territoires :

    ceux-ci, où les corps se magnifièrent, & coururent ;

    les autres, où le repos les exalta –
    l'étape du jour étant accomplie.

Faces, à tous vents :

    les uns venus des plaines,
    quand nous suivions l'amble aisée de nos montures ;

    d'autres, descendus des passes, vers les sommets

    – nous y avions déposé nos regards,
    notre fatigue, notre richesse.

    Nous, sans demeure.

Aile du livre, ouverte :

    voix & silences, – exposés ;

    avec la paume de la main du passant
    qui lisse les caractères,

    l'estampe en est restée, & voyage.

Sur cette table verticale :

    notre nom & nos effacements –

    haute joie de cet édit,
    hors des marches des empires, & des cours.

Puis, ceci, sur la pierre ardente :

    la forêt de signes & de lignes ;
    & ce sceau – feu, nuit.

Enfin, ceci encore, qui conclut :

    plume du *sîmurgh*,
    langue des oiseaux.

JOHN CAMPBELL

The poetry of the untranslatable:
Racine's *Phèdre* confronted by Hughes and Lowell

Though amongst the major summits of world literature, it would be misleading to compare Racine's *Phèdre* (1677) to an Everest for the translator: Everest has been conquered. There have been, in the past fifty years, at least fourteen different attempts in English.[1] The following pages will seek to compare a recent translation, that of Ted Hughes (1998), with that of Robert Lowell (1961), in what can only be a short introduction to these three works, that might at least stimulate the desire to undertake a comparative reading.[2] The fact that these translations are from the pen of two of the past century's most distinguished poets in itself deserves the kind of attention we rightly give to Seamus Heaney's magnificent *Beowolf* or his versions of Gaelic poems.

---

1   This count is based on works cited in *The Encyclopedia of Literary Translation into English*, ed. O. Classe (London: Fitzroy Dearborn, 2000): others may of course have slipped through the net.

2   *Phèdre*, translated by Ted Hughes (London: Faber and Faber, 1998), and *Phaedra. Racine's* Phèdre, translated by Robert Lowell (London: Faber and Faber, 1961). Quotations from Lowell are from his introductory note, 'On Translating *Phèdre*', pp.7–8. Note the valuable article by D. Berry, '"Rough Magic": Ted Hughes's Translation of Jean Racine's *Phèdre*', in *French 'Classical' Theatre Today. Teaching, Research, Performance*, ed. P. Tomlinson (Amsterdam: Rodopi, 2001), which gives a valuable digest of critical reaction to the Hughes translation. On the general problems of translating Racine, a good introduction is K. Wheatley, *Racine and English Classicism* (Austin: University of Texas, 1965), but see also P. Swinden, 'Translating Racine', *Comparative Literature*, 49 (1997), 209–26, who concentrates on translations of *Phèdre*. The bibliographies of both works give details of previous efforts, and critical reaction to them.

Both Hughes and Lowell use the word 'translation', which supposes that their ambition is something other than the activity French Seventeenth-Century dramatists regarded as the mainstay of their creative work, the transposition of mythological stories, often via the works of classical dramatists such as Sophocles, Euripides and Seneca, into a version acceptable to contemporary taste, and answering to accepted theatrical conventions. The fact that Hughes and Lowell should have translated the masterpiece of France's greatest tragic poet allows us to focus on a series of problems that, while common to all poetry translation, occur in abundance here. For *Phèdre* is not just another poem. If we are looking for the finished article of that cultural production line called 'French classicism', then here it is, the hyperclassical text, packaged to perfection. This play, for George Steiner 'the keystone in French tragic drama' has always seemed an unassailably French peak of creative achievement.[3] As a recent critic has put it, 'There is an absolute quality about *Phèdre*: on its very own it represents an ideal of literary perfection'.[4]

For any translator the absolute nature of this identity is bound up with a series of thorny problems particular to the translation of French Seventeenth-Century tragedy. For example, it is impossible in English to replicate the alexandrine, regarded by some critics as inherently appropriate for the dignity of tragedy: Barthes even claimed provocatively that the actor in a tragedy by Racine did not need any particular talent for acting, but could let the verse do the job itself.[5] And it is true that in general the tragedy of the age has a consistently elevated tone, quite foreign to English-speaking audiences whose idea of 'tragedy' cannot exclude Shakespeare's gravedigger, porter or

3   G. Steiner, *The Death of Tragedy* (London: Faber and Faber, 1961), p.84.
4   B. Donné, edition of *Phèdre* (Paris: Flammarion, 2000), p.23 (my translation here). Quotations from the original play in the present article are from Racine, *Théâtre, Poésie*, ed. G. Forestier, Editions de la Pléiade (Paris: Gallimard, 1999).
5   R. Barthes, *Sur Racine* (Paris: Seuil, 1963), p.131. On the 'theatricality' of the Racinian alexandrine, see M. Bernard, 'Esquisse d'une théorie de la théatralité d'un texte en vers à partir de l'exemple racinien', in *Dramaturgies. Langages dramatiques. Mélanges pour Jacques Scherer*, ed. M. Corvin and others (Paris: Nizet, 1986), pp.279–86.

Fool.[6] There is also the abstract vocabulary, and the deliberate abstinence from reference to everyday things and their concrete reality. As Lowell points out, 'he is perhaps the greatest poet in the French language, but he uses a smaller vocabulary than any English poet – beside him Pope and Bridges have a Shakespearean luxuriance'. This leads Racine in particular to use few words, but to use them with killing exactness, in a tight syntax that can only be unwound with a sense that something essential has been lost. Added to this is the difficulty created by any attempt to translate the *précieux* love-vocabulary: how do we cope with terms such as *flamme* and *feu*, as descriptors of the love-experience, without quaintness or betrayal, or both? Some way must also be found of dealing with the mythological allusions, so difficult already for the French student of the play. An English translator hardly wishes to burden his text with the explicatory glosses necessary to understand these countless allusions in *Phèdre*, as any edition of the play would be required to do for the sake of simple comprehension.

Besides all of this, the translator is confronted with a crucial choice: whether to write a version intended for a stage production, or to see the task as primarily that of translating and therefore creating a piece of poetry. Can the poetic and the dramatic become one flesh, in the case of *Phèdre*? It might seem that we are just stating the obvious when we say, at the outset, that this dramatic masterpiece cannot be considered just as a poem, and that reading it is not enough. The fact is, however, that even in French Racine's plays are mostly read, and that in English this is overwhelmingly the case. We do not forget, in reading, that it is a play: we see it performed on the stage of our mind's eye, and are able to imagine, for example, the reaction of characters to words spoken. If the translator is writing for the stage, there will a natural bias towards the immediately comprehensible, with a concomitant avoidance of arcane vocabulary, contorted syntax and obscure cultural references: the danger here is a certain banality of

6   On what he calls the 'alien' nature of Racinian formality for English (or English-language?) audiences, see T. Yarwood, 'Staging Racine in England now: the Almeida's *Phèdre* and *Britannicus*', in *French 'Classical' Theatre Today...*, pp.229–47.

diction that betrays the spirit of the original. The 'poetry' option allows greater freedom, but by that very fact tempts the poet/translator into creating an artefact so culture-specific that the original seems a distant memory. Broadly speaking, it could be said that Hughes chooses the first option, understandably so, since the translation was for a performance of *Phèdre* by the Almeida company in the autumn of 1998, first at the Malvern Festival, and then in London, with Diana Rigg in the main role. Lowell, on the other hand, whose version was composed for a theatre anthology, addresses himself to the composition of a poem, and in his Preface expresses regret that neither Dryden nor Pope, famed translators of Homer and Virgil, did not try their hand at Racine's masterpiece.

There is, above all, the question of tone. The received wisdom about any translation work, that to be perfectly faithful is to be absolutely lame, certainly applies to Racine. For readers weaned on post-Augustan poetry, the mere replication of his formal patterns is the high road to monotony. However, the version that impresses through vibrant originality in the use of vocabulary and metaphor, syntax and rhythm, might by this very fact leave one feeling that the original has been forgotten. Past attempts to translate *Phèdre* have involved many different ways of avoiding the lameness of simple reproduction and the trap of 'elevated style': one thinks of Tony Harrison's *Phaedra Britannica*, a brilliant transposition of the setting from Ancient Greece to 19th century British India, or Edwin Morgan's Scots version, with that most falsely pellucid of lines, 'Le jour n'est pas plus clair que le fond de mon cœur' rendered as 'The core o ma hert's as bricht an trig as day'.[7] These examples show, however, that such solutions can themselves cause problems: the attempt to give the play roots in real living language and situations can also put some strain on the idea that translation should also be an attempt to render a particular otherness, a cultural otherness that in the case of Racine's *Phèdre* sits uneasily with anything colloquial or racy.

With these general considerations in mind, let us now compare some examples, firstly from the opening scene of the play, and then

7   Edwin Morgan, *Jean Racine's Phaedra: a Tragedy. A new verse translation of* Phèdre. (Manchester: Carcanet, 2000), p.52.

from the famous scene describing the death of Hippolyte, near the
end. The first will give us an immediate idea of the different translation strategies of the two poets, and of the two quite different
registers they adopt, while the second shows how one of these
strategies changes significantly, when faced with the challenge of
rendering the colourful death scene:

> Le dessein en est pris, je pars, cher Théramène,
> Et quitte le séjour de l'aimable Trézène,
> Dans le doute mortel dont je suis agité
> Je commence à rougir de mon oisiveté.
> Depuis plus de six mois éloigné de mon Père
> J'ignore le destin d'une tête si chère.
> J'ignore jusqu'aux lieux qui le peuvent cacher. (Act I, Scene 1, ll. 1–7)

Hughes	Lowell
I've made my decision.	No, no, my friend, we're off! Six months
It is six months now	have passed
And there hasn't been one word of my	since Father heard the ocean howl and
father.	cast
Somebody somewhere knows what's	his galley on the Aegean's skull-white
happened to him.	froth.
Life here in Troezen is extremely pleas-	Listen! The blank sea calls us — off, off,
ant	off!
But I can't hang around doing nothing	I'll follow Father to the fountainhead
With this uncertainty. My idleness	and marsh of hell. We're off. Alive or
makes me sweat.	dead,
I must find my father.	I'll find him.

The most obvious formal difference here is in the type of verse
employed. Unshackled by any requirement to produce a text for
performance, Lowell can base his choice on purely poetic criteria, as
he explains in his introduction:

> My meter, with important differences, is based on Dryden and Pope. In his
> heroic plays, Dryden uses an end-stopped couplet, loaded with inversions,
> heavily alliterated, and varied by short unrhymed lines. My couplet is run on,
> avoids inversions and alliteration, and loosens its rhythm with shifted accents
> and occasional extra syllables. I gain in naturalness and lose in compactness
> and epigrammatic resonance. I have tried for an idiomatic and ageless style, but
> I inevitably echo the English Restoration, both in ways that are proper and in
> my sometimes unRacinian humour and bombast.

Swinton rules out the possibility of using the rhyming couplet to
translate Racine, finding it 'fatally compromised [...] by its use as a
satirical instrument from Dryden and Pope onwards' (Swinton, p.217).
To this one might object that both Dryden and Pope produced
generally admired translations of the classics without transforming
them into satire. In its appropriation of a medium necessarily resonant
of the Augustan age, and in its desire not to be enslaved to received
ideas of the 'Racinian', Lowell's words are a striking proclamation of
the freedom to create. Hughes unfortunately provides no explanatory
introduction: but with the constraints imposed by the expectations of a
contemporary theatre audience, chooses to employ a blank verse not
too far removed from the rhythms of ordinary speech. He strikes a

tone of colloquial immediacy in the very first words, as though he wishes to signal to his audience that this was a play for the here and now, its expression that of everyday life. Syntax and vocabulary accompany what seems to be a deliberate banality of diction. Phrases such as 'there hasn't been one word of my father', or 'I can't hang around doing nothing', could come from a Home Counties drawing-room drama. Indeed, the line 'Somebody somewhere knows what's happened to him', for anyone over the age of forty, might even stir memories of an old Post Office advertising slogan. One can see all the reasons of simple immediacy why Hughes, faced with the problem of holding a live audience, found this an attractive option. By choosing the rather flat language of everyday experience, however, he does make it more difficult to recreate the experience of the *Phèdre* created by Racine. These opening lines certainly give us no clue that we are entering a mysterious world of light and dark, gods and monsters, in a dramatic action which traps human beings into engagement with the inescapable and the unavowable, and which in so doing explores the darkest sides of the problems of evil, freedom and human responsibility.

The contrast with Lowell could not be greater. From the outset he chooses high-colour metaphor, and risk. 'The Aegean's skull-white froth', 'the blank sea', 'the fountainhead and marsh of hell' transport us from the beginning into a harsh, dangerous world, one appropriate to primal and finally murderous emotion. On could task Lowell with creating a poetic medium too far removed from the restraint and dignity that characterises Racine's play: it is true that Racine was sparing of metaphor, and that Lowell's are pure inventions, if not intrusions. The American poet's response is written in the lines themselves, which deftly hint at depths below that 'blank sea', an appropriate liminal – or subliminal – metaphor for the apparent Aegean calm of the Augustan verse and patrician medium. The opening three bars, 'Off, off, off', are an inspired, Beethovenian device for conveying the excitement and urgency of a day that will soon end, though just begun, in a catastrophe that characters will desperately seek to prevent, though their actions are its cause. And any complaint that Lowell 'invents' here should be tempered by the thought that his 'inventions' are in fact anticipatory allusions. The howling, skull-white ocean looks forward not only to the emotional tempest soon to engulf the characters, but also to Hippolyte's death, a fact that gives all its irony to the son's desire to find his father 'Alive or dead', since it is the father, when he is found, who will kill him:

> Et dans quels lieux, Seigneur, l'allez-vous donc chercher?
> Déjà, pour satisfaire à votre juste crainte
> J'ai couru les deux Mers que sépare Corinthe.
> J'ai demandé Thésée aux Peuples de ces bords
> Où l'on voit l'Achéron se perdre chez les Morts.
> J'ai visité l'Elide, et laissant le Ténare,
> Passé jusqu'à la Mer, qui vit tomber Icare. (Act I, Scene 1, ll. 8–14)

Hughes
But where, my lord, would you begin to look?
We have done all we can to find him.
Our ships have searched both seas, they have gone
As far as the Acheron
Where it dives to the underworld, and nowhere
Can Theseus be found.
We have searched Elis, and on past Tenaros,
As far as the ocean
That drowned Icarus when he fell out of heaven.
We have searched every coast within reach
For news of the King and found nothing.

Lowell
Where, my lord? I've sent a host
Of veteran seamen up and down the coast;
each village, creek and cove from here to Crete
has been ransacked and questioned by my fleet;
my flagship skirted Hades' rapids, furled sail there a day, and scoured the underworld.

Comparing these translations and the Racine text, it does not take great deductive powers to conclude that Hughes amplifies where Lowell provides not so much a gist as a taste. Some of Hughes's repetition is undoubtedly felt necessary for a theatre audience that does not have the luxury of going back to read what has not been understood: this doubtless explains his final two lines here, which are not in the original, but usefully recapitulate. On the other hand, if priority is to be given to immediate comprehension by the audience on the night, it is slightly surprising that Hughes does nothing to remove or simplify allusions to the geography of Ancient Greece. Hughes is undoubtedly closer than Lowell to the text of the original, but paradoxically for that very reason creates potential difficulties for his audience. For what would they make of 'the two seas' (that Hughes for some reason amputates of the phrase 'que sépare Corinthe', used by Racine himself in explanation)? And how many, even in the most cultivated modern audience, could identify 'Elis' and 'Tenaros'? 'Acheron', too, is perhaps a more difficult term that Lowell's 'Hades', with its additional Joycean resonance. Indeed, it is Lowell who elides the precise geographical information, and, more boldly, even the reference to Icarus. Does he therefore lose in resonance? The answer might be that he creates his own. The veteran seamen, the ransacking, the flagship furling sail and the scouring of the underworld are all of his invention. His images evoke a world of vivid colour that radiate energy while suggesting mystery. These are qualities not immediately apparent in the Hughes version, where there is a strange coexistence between the memory of mythical events ('the ocean / That drowned Icarus when he fell out of heaven') and a flat, prosaic tone suited to a world where such things could no longer happen ('We have searched every coast within reach / For news of the King and found nothing'). Unlike Lowell, Hughes has very obviously opted for a strategy based on something approaching 'classical restraint', but without being able to recreate the sense of barely contained threat and pent-up emotion that this restraint only serves to amplify in a work such as *Phèdre*.

Not that Lowell refuses the challenge of the mythological allusion. As evidence, note the different versions of Hippolyte's admission that his life has changed since the arrival of his stepmother:

Cet heureux temps n'est plus. Tout a changé de face
Depuis que sur ces bords les Dieux ont envoyé
La Fille de Minos et de Pasiphaé. (Act I, Scene 1, ll. 34–6)

Hughes	Lowell
Everything has changed since the gods Decided to grace this palace With the daughter of Minos and Pasiphae.	Friend, this kingdom lost its peace, when Father left my mother for defiled bull-serviced Pasiphaë's child. The child of homicidal Minos is our queen!

Once again, the Hughes translation is the more 'faithful', but this fidelity means a simple transliteration of 'La fille de Minos et de Pasiphaé', one of the most famous lines in the tragedy, whose disturbing beauty no gloss has ever been able completely to explain, but whose potential is well illustrated by George Steiner: 'The line is superb not only for its exotic sonority; it opens the gates of reason to the night. Into the courtly setting, so clearly established by the formal notations and cadences of the neo-classical style, bursts something archaic, incomprehensible, barbaric' (Steiner, p.87). It thus seems important, for a contemporary reader or playgoer, that a translation should attempt to suggest some of the resonance of that densely-charged phrase. And it is exactly this that Lowell, in an almost pedagogical manner, has attempted to do. His inclusion in these few lines of what is a breathtaking amount of expository detail, concerning those closest to Phèdre, opens his version of the play up to the underground passions that we will see first possessing Phèdre, and then destroying her.

This is not an isolated case. In the third scene of the play, when Phèdre is confessing her love for Hippolyte to her nurse, she admits that 'Mon mal vient de plus loin' (269), which Hughes translates as 'My sickness began much earlier', perfectly acceptable as a translation of the French, in isolation from the rest of the play. Lowell, however, seemingly more alive to the idea that Phèdre's fatal love comes from somewhere beyond the immediate horizon of her consciousness, renders this as 'My evil comes from further off', which is invested with some of the disturbing ambiguity of the French *mal* and *loin*. A similar remark might be made with the translation, in this same confession-scene, of what is the most celebrated line in French tragic theatre, 'C'est Vénus tout entière à sa proie attachée' (306). Hughes renders this as 'Venus has fastened on me like a tiger', a reasonable enough translation of 'attachée', but the image is curiously static (and is this what tigers do with their victims?). Lowell renders the line less literally, but powerfully, as 'naked Venus was clawing down her victim', which coveys the impression suggested by *tout entière,* of raw energy totally focused on the kill.

This, however, is not the end of the story. Even in this briefest of comparative notes it is necessary to look at each poet's rendering of the scene, in Act V, where Thésée is told, in great detail, how his son met his death: a monstrous creature has emerged from the sea and frightened the horses into a wild gallop that ended only when Hippolyte's body was, in Lowell's version, 'a piece of bloody meat':

> […]
> Parmi des flots d'écume un Monstre furieux.
> Son front large est armé de cornes menaçantes.
> Tout son corps est couvert d'écailles jaunissantes.
> Indomptable Taureau, Dragon impétueux,
> Sa croupe se recourbe en replis tortueux.
> Ses longs mugissements font trembler le rivage.
> Le ciel avec horreur voit ce Monstre sauvage,
> La terre s'en émeut, l'air en est infecté,
> Le flot, qui l'apporta, recule épouvanté. (Act V, Scene 6, ll. 1515–24)

Hughes
And out of it,
The foam cascading from a colossal body,
Came a beast –
Up the sands, with the fury
Of a supernatural existence.
Its head was one huge monster all to itself,
Like a bull's head, with bull's horns.
But from the shoulders backwards
The whole body was plated,
Humped and plated, the scales greeny yellow,
A nauseating colour, that sickened the eye.
And beyond the humped bulk of the body
Came scaled and lashing coils. Half bull, half dragon –
Mouth hanging open, like a cavern,
And bellowing, like a heavy surf
Exploding in a cavern.
The earth trembled, the air was thick with horror.
We breathed a mist of horror

Lowell
Out of its fragments rose a monster, half dragon, half bull; a mouth that seemed to laugh
drooled venom on its dirty yellow scales and python belly, forking to three tails.
The shore was shaken like a tuning-fork, ships bounced on the stung sea like bits of cork,
the earth moved, and the sun spun round and round,
a sulphur-coloured venom swept the ground.

'Classical restraint'? Before even his play was published it was for the lack of restraint shown in this scene Racine was criticised. Though much of the imagery is inspired by Euripides, Virgil and Ovid, it was felt by some that a father could not plausibly listen impassively to such a long and detailed account of the putting to death of an innocent son he himself had asked the gods to punish. Some also judged that the flamboyant and even exotic quality of Racine's poetry here was at variance with the rest of the play, and indeed, with the accepted canons of taste he had until then followed.[8] Needless to say, such criticisms have subsided. From our narrow perspective, however, the energy and high colour of this passage is of particular interest, since it gives Hughes an opportunity to slip his self-imposed leash. We are suddenly transported into familiar Hughes territory, haunted by animal and myth, driven by fear and threat, a world of harsh, raw primeval absolutes uncharted by the human mind. This is Hughes coming into his own, his creative energy as though liberated, surging from a flat classical sea. In his introduction Lowell had quietly affirmed that his was a free translation, and he was as good as his word. But here for Hughes, extensively for the first time, Racine's text becomes inspiration more than template, as Virgil himself was for Racine, and his poetic genius uncoils with great power. He feels free to amplify and simply add, as in 'the fury of a supernatural existence' or 'A nauseating colour, that sickened the eye'. Equally, no translation is offered (and likewise with Lowell) for Racine's most daring line, which comes straight from Virgil, 'Le flot, qui l'apporta, recule épouvanté', nor for the epithets 'indomptable' and 'impétueux'. But despite what might seem an omission, the whole development of the monster image by Hughes expresses in other ways a sense of the violent, the unpredictable, the obsessive, the untamed. In phrases such as 'the humped bulk of the body', the 'scaled and lashing coils', 'the Mouth hanging open', 'bellowing, like a heavy surf', there is a disquieting suggestion of violent sensuality unleashed and beyond control, making this 'Half-bull, half-dragon' an apposite symbol for the monstrous rampaging passion that, when it surfaced in Phèdre's

---

8   For contemporary reactions to this scene, and the sources that underlie it, see the Forestier Pléiade edition, pp.1658–9.

incestuous passion and Thésée's jealous rage, destroyed Hippolyte and a dream of innocent love. In contrast one would have to agree with Swinton that there is a satiric undercurrent in Lowell's heroic couplets here that seems to militate against the expression of the tragic experience. There is certainly a notion of threat, conveyed in the 'python belly, forking to three tails', but also a sense of ironic distance, conveyed in the 'mouth that seemed to laugh' and in the 'bits of cork' rhyming with 'a tuning-fork'. The image of the moving earth and spinning sun does give us a larger perspective, but also seems to diminish the intensity of what Racine allows us to see happening in front of our eyes. In Lowell we have the bigger picture, but in Hughes we are close up, on the shore, breathing a mist of horror.

It would be rash to attempt to draw firm conclusions from what has only been a short introductory study that has cursorily examined a very small number of lines from these two works. Clearly, however, here as with any translation, the target audience does influence determining factors such as choice of vocabulary and syntax, the handling of cultural allusions and, in the case of poetry, the verse mode. We will never know whether Hughes, if he had not been writing for the theatre, would have chosen such a prosaic tone and sometimes colloquial register. And one must record the fact that, when the play was first produced using the Hughes text, critical opinion was overwhelmingly favourable, whereas not everyone has warmed to the Lowell version, Swinton even asserting with a surprising degree of vigour that it 'might be taken as a dreadful example of how not to do it' (Swinton, p.224). The opinion expressed here is therefore very much a minority one. It was, however, shared by two reviewers. In his comments on the Hughes version, Peter France confessed to missing 'the excitement of high formal poetry which can transfix a listener, and which gives *Phèdre* its exceptional place in the Racinian canon'. And Aleks Sierz's reaction has found an echo in these pages: 'Hughes's heroically mundane version only comes into its own at the end, [with] his magnificent description of Hippolyte's death.'[9] Lowell,

---

9   These and other views are recorded in Berry, pp.207–9, who chides France (and
      thus by implication the writer of this article) for his 'stereotypical reservations'.

we have seen, unconstrained as was Hughes, is always far from any suspicion of the mundane: his choice of the heroic couplet is guarantee enough of that. His images and rhythms are not those of everyday prose, since his subject is hardly an everyday experience, yet he manages to avoid the stilted and slightly patronising archaism sometimes used in translation in an attempt to replicate the ceremonial dignity and the quasi-liturgical tone of French high tragedy. He praises in Racine's poetry 'the glory of its hard, electric rage', and his own version shares something of that hard, electric quality: it crackles with creative energy, but is driven by a steady purpose and guided in every line by a vision of the play as a whole.

Lowell opens his introductory remarks in pithy self-deprecation: 'Racine's plays are generally and correctly thought to be untranslatable'.[10] However one understands this controversial term, few will regret that either Hughes or Lowell has made an attempt on the highest peak in the Racine range. The 'Racinian' must be supposed to exist, since we notice its absence. But until now it has proved inaccessible, because inexpressible. At altitudes such as this, 'translation' is not an outcome but a journey. We can only be grateful that we can accompany both Hughes and Lowell as, on different routes, they strike out for this ultimate summit for the literary translator.

An account of the production of *Phèdre* using the Hughes translation is given in Yarwood.

10   This statement is echoed by Swinton, p.224, who concludes: 'An examination of some translators' versions of *Phèdre* suggests that the best thing to do is to decide which of the essential but finally untranslatable features of Racine's verse must go, if others, equally essential but not so hopelessly untranslatable, are to remain.'

GRAHAM CHESTERS

Tireless play: speculations on Larkin's 'Absences'

Absences[1]

> Rain patters on a sea that tilts and sighs.
> Fast-running floors, collapsing into hollows,
> Tower suddenly, spray-haired. Contrariwise,   3
> A wave drops like a wall: another follows,
> Wilting and scrambling, tirelessly at play
> Where there are no ships and no shallows.   6
>
> Above the sea, the yet more shoreless day,
> Riddled by wind, trails lit-up galleries:
> They shift to giant ribbing, sift away.   9
>
> Such attics cleared of me! Such absences!

Larkin's *terza rima* is a rare seascape/skyscape from someone who is thought of as an essentially urban poet. 'Absences', were it not for that last line, might strike the reader as a peculiarly successful descriptive poem, attaining what Larkin called in an autobiographical fragment the 'fabulous bird' of 'positive objectivity'.[2] But the final exclamation, taking advantage of the special impact accorded to last lines of *terza rimas*, changes everything. It paradoxically asserts the absence of the self, whilst introducing the self in dramatic fashion. This eruption can be seen as a lyrical commentary on the preceding nine lines, washing the reader back to reassess the description not just as a description of sea and sky but very specifically of a scene which gains dizzying value from the fact that the poet is not there. But a re-reading might

1   The text of the poem is reprinted from *The Less Deceived* by kind permission of the Marvell Press, England and Australia.
2   Andrew Motion, *Philip Larkin: a Writer's Life* (London: Faber and Faber, 1993), p.139.

also perversely push one to colour the description more lyrically, tingeing the positive objectivity with a more personal symbolism. One might even see the changing skyscape (lines 7–9), with the clouds, first rain-bearing and then sun-infused, thinning as they recede into the distance, as a prefigurement of the clearing of the self; the 'sift away' from this perspective would culminate a reading (advocated by Andrew Motion) in which the poem mimes 'the processes of change and purgation experienced by the speaker'.[3] In other words, the scene described is far from neutral on re-reading but a subtle correlative of the poet's own mood (combining suggestions of weariness ['sighs', 'collapsing', 'drops', 'wilting'] and energy ['fast-running', 'tower suddenly', 'tirelessly at play']).

Without the last line, the poem would keep silent on the fiction of the observerless scene or provoke in the literal-minded reader some poet-figure, say, on the prow of a boat. The last line explodes the latter reading and appears to promote the observerless fiction to the key focus of the poem, suggesting that it is the absolute, raw freedom of the open sea and sky, liberated from the cluttering presence of the poet-observer, that excites. But we know that the observerlessness is a fiction, that each utterance has a self and that the self as speaker, once explicitly introduced, cannot even feign disappearance. Indeed, the intimation of the self as encumbrance or embarrassment ('cleared of me') suggests something more, a deeper self-criticism that goes beyond the play between objective and lyrical readings of descriptive text. Why should the poet celebrate so triumphantly his own exclusion? Is it his own tainted self that threatens the purity of scene? Is there something more in this last line than 'a joyous assertion of freedom' (Ibid., p.75)?

What, for example, are the resonances of the strange choice of the word 'attics'? On one level, it continues the metaphorical tasks assigned to 'floors', 'tower', 'wall' and 'galleries', all architectural reference points that seek to give manmade structure to natural phenomena and signal the limitations of depicting nature in its true rawness. But the anaphoric 'such', in tempting the reader to assume that the sea- and skyscapes are being compared to emptied attics, offers a

3   *Philip Larkin*, Contemporary Writers (London: Methuen, 1982), p.75.

startling compression of space from the vast, open vistas of lines 1–9. Can the towering seas and giant galleries of the sky really be re-described as attics? The shock may provoke another interpretation. The associations of attics with literary creation are part of the Romantic myth. If we accept the implications of the fact that (as we shall see) Larkin ascribes a certain Frenchness to 'Absences', then Baudelaire's 'Paysage' from the 'Tableaux parisiens' section of *Les Fleurs du mal* offers a straightforward intertext; the poet in his garret wilfully creates an imaginary poctic universe to escape from the tribulations of the everyday, a landscape from within the confines of a shuttered room.[4] The 'attics cleared of me' could point to the sweeping aside of such mythic self-portraits with their inevitable subjectivity. Or, bearing in mind other contemporary Larkin texts, such as 'Deceptions' (February 1950; *Collected Poems*, p.32) and 'Unfinished Poem' (1951; *Collected Poems*, p.60), one might view the attic as a place of sexual guilt, shame, disappointment and fear; in the first of these poems, 'fulfilment's desolate attic' represents emotional emptiness at the moment of expected satiation; in the second, 'that emaciate attic' is the speaker's chosen place to await death. These textual attics, whether a part of a myth-kitty or a tighter network of personal inter-texts, reinforce a reading of the final exclamation as the reflective poet's response to some inner revelation, a leap from the external models of infinity and purity to what would be his own emotional equivalent as poct. It is a realisation that literary places and poses might be swept clean by some yearned-for objectivity. There were, of course, real attics in Larkin's life. He lived in two in Leicester when, from 1946–1950, he was a sub-librarian at the then University College and gave 'romantically decrepit'[5] accounts of them in letters to

---

4   There are other Baudelairean echoes in Larkin's verse at this time. 'The Face', for example, replays the chance urban encounter of Baudelaire's 'A une passante'.

5   The phrase is Andrew Motion's in *A Writer's Life*, p.150. He cites two excerpts from Larkin's letters describing his first Leicester attic, the first written to Jim Sutton, the second to Kingsley Amis: 'It is a medium-sized attic, with carpet and bed, and I sit in a basket chair by a reading lamp with an electric radiator pointed cunningly up my arse and a brown rug over my shoulders', and 'I am established in an attic with a small window, a bed, an armchair, a basket chair, a

friends. So Larkin had witnessed at least two attics cleared of him before he left Leicester to become sub-librarian at Queen's University, Belfast in September 1950.

Larkin wrote 'Absences' soon after he arrived in Northern Ireland (but not at some attic desk – he lived in a hall of residence opposite the Queen's University in a room with 'the minimum of furniture in it'[6]) and published it for the first time in *The Less Deceived* (1955). According to Andrew Motion (*A Writer's Life*, p.203), it is one of seven poems that Larkin wrote between his arrival in Belfast and the end of 1950. The others were presumably 'The Spirit Wooed', 'No Road', 'Wires', 'Since the majority of me...', 'Arrival'[7] and possibly (because of its manuscript location in Larkin's *Workbook 2*,[8] p.110, surrounded by other early Belfast poems) a rough-hewn translation of a Verlaine poem, 'A Mademoiselle ***' taken from *Parallèlement*. Motion says of the poems (the Verlaine apart): 'Their overriding concern is with Ruth, and the struggle between love and self-preservation'. Ruth Bowman had been Larkin's fiancée before he moved to Belfast; they had known each other for seven years. The end of the engagement coincided with his move.

carpet, a reading lamp THAT DOESN'T WORK, a small electric fire THAT DOESN'T WORK and a few books, papers, etc. "Literary men" like us count ourselves *kings of a nutshell* when we have at hand the company of "the gentle Elia" or "rare Ben", eh?'. Motion (*A Writer's Life*, p.171) cites a further extract from a Jim Sutton letter, describing Larkin's second Leicester attic: 'Picture me in another garret – or no, garrets are supposed to be romantic; say a maid's bedroom – with a bed [...], a dressing table plus drawers, a fireplace plus gas fire *plus* meter, an armchair with a disconcertingly sliding seat, a small table (three and a quarter inches by one and three-quarter inches roughly) and hard chair, large cupboard and bookcase. The bed was very hard, like a dried-up watercourse'.

6   *Philip Larkin, Selected Letters 1940–1985*, edited by Anthony Thwaite (London: Faber and Faber), p.167.

7   For these six poems, see *Philip Larkin: Collected Poems*, ed. Anthony Thwaite (London: Faber and Faber, 1988), pp.46–51

8   Larkin's workbooks are held in the Larkin Archive of the Brynmor Jones Library at the University of Hull. Previously unpublished Philip Larkin material: copyright © 2005, the Estate of Philip Larkin. All citations from *Workbook 2* are reproduced by kind permission of the Society of Authors as the literary representative of the estate of Philip Larkin.

Motion identifies guilt and liberation amongst his dominant emotions at this time. Skeletally, such is the emotional background against which 'Absences' was written.

A sequential reading of Larkin's drafts of 'Absences', contained in his *Workbook 2*, throws light on the evolving drama of the poem. The variants are too complex to be reproduced here (there are, for example, thirteen versions of the opening two lines), so a brief narrative will have to suffice. The first attempts (found on p.109 of the *Workbook*) establish the *terza rima* pattern ('Rain patters on the sea, water to waters,/ A small sound in a huge afternoon,/ The heaving floors provoked to tiny craters.'), and continue on pages 111 and 112 to explore ways of capturing the seascape.[9] One version reads:

Rain patters on the sea, water to waters,
A small sound in a giant afternoon,
       (peopled with
A sighing floor (provoked to tiny craters;
       (speckled with

While
And rough winds rub the gloss off water-dunes
Running like walls, floundering to calm again –
     excitement ~~hollows~~ ,   ~~cursory brief~~
Shoreless ~~vivacity~~ , ~~lonely~~ ~~transient~~ ^ lagoons
       unobserved

The passage illustrates how Larkin re-uses in the final version words that had originally fulfilled a different function. For instance, 'giant' begins as a qualifier for 'afternoon' and survives to describe 'ribbing'; 'sighing' becomes a main verb ('a sea that tilts and sighs') and 'shoreless' serves eventually to describe the day rather than the more abstract 'excitement' or 'vivacity'. What does not survive however is the telling 'unobserved' – but its spirit does, specifically in 'Such attics cleared of me! Such absences!'. The earlier version allows the aporia of the observerless fiction to emerge explicitly in the first six lines. Resisting the provocation of the puzzle (however discreet) at this

---

9   Between pages 109 and 111, there is the translation of Verlaine's 'A Mademoiselle ***'.

point, Larkin will arrive at a much sharper, more dramatic, more clamorous statement of the paradox.

The compositional journey towards his final line is fascinating. The first appearance[10] of 'Such attics cleared of me! Such absences!' on page 113 is as an introduction to what looks like a concluding passage which compresses reflections on sky and sea:

> Such attics cleared of me! Such absences!
> ~~Such~~
> The ~~Those~~ many-plinthed and statue-crowded sky [skies]
> And   veracities
> The sea, unsnarling its ~~vivacities~~
>
> Merely in image
> Attain out there singular

There follow two pages of heavy editing of all the text (with the exception of the first three lines which have by now taken their almost final shape) but particularly of the prospective conclusion. Then something remarkable happens. Larkin, noting the date '28/11/50' in the margin, appears to begin on an entirely new conception:

> Such attics cleared of me! such absences!
> ~~is filling fills again, the case~~
> ~~But the courtroom [illegible]   restarts~~
> But here the courtroom fills, the case restarts,
> Dingy coughing, argument.

The turn of the poem is dramatic: 'But here the courtroom...' suggests the severest of contrasts with the 'there' of the empty, purified sea- and skyscapes. The apparently new movement is however the resumption ('the case restarts') of something suspended which predates the observerless description. An inner dialogue testing the conscience? An uneasy self-arraignment? On the following page 116 (where more

---

10   A caveat: it is not possible to be absolutely certain that the order of the text as it
      appears in the *Workbook* is actually the order of composition. On the other
      hand, it seems highly likely to be the case.

space is taken up with a return to the draft of another poem, 'Since the majority of me…'), Larkin writes:[11]

> Such attics cleared of me! such absences!
> We cannot leave the courtroom and the case,
> The stale and dingy coughing

What has weakened is the contrastive ('But here…') linkage with the sea- and skyscape; it is nevertheless still there, hinted at in the allusion to departure denied ('We cannot leave'), an attempt to escape from the spleen into the ideal. The loosened connection threatens the narrative (always tenuous) to the extent that one begins to wonder how Larkin envisaged the reworked text belonging to the same poem as 'Rain patters…'. The suspicion grows when 'Rain patters…' is never returned to and the courtroom scene itself disappears from the *Workbook* for twelve pages, re-emerging on page 128:[12]

> Such attics cleared of me! Such absences!
> Such courtroom consolations! for my case
> Is all dingy inaudibilities
>
> And, somewhere guilt. Thinking of any place
> I cannot cheapen lessens the disgrace.
>
> Such attics cleared of me! such absences!
> Such courtroom consolations in a case
> Made up of stale inaudibilities
>
> With somewhere guilt. The thought of any place
> Uncheapened by this vague drawn out disgrace

On its return, the courtroom text seeks greater integration with what precedes: the third exclamation ('Such courtroom consolations!') looks backward as part of the sudden reflection on the sea- and skyscape, as well as taking the poem forward into the new introspective drama. The whole narrative clarifies. The crafted musings on

---

11 The poet's editing of the draft on p.116 is so heavy that I am only reproducing text that is not crossed through.

12 See previous footnote. The same applies.

sea and sky are now presented as daydream consolations, relief from the anxiety of unfocused self-arraignment. The text here states openly both the purity of the natural which resists tainting ('any place/ I cannot cheapen'; 'any place/ Uncheapened') and the power of the imagined scene to provide a muting of the poet's inner shame.

With the *Workbook* offering no further drafts, one might assume that Larkin, unconvinced by the emerging broken-backed poem, moves radically to the final published version. Had this final version retained the courtroom drama, the exclamations would have been the place of articulation between exterior and interior, objective and subjective, descriptive and narrative. The hypothetical poem would have buttressed Motion's biographical view of the poet struggling with guilt and shame during his early days in Belfast. Instead, by jettisoning the 'stale inaudibilities' in an act of compositional cleansing, Larkin leaves us with a poem ending suggestively with an ambiguous line of exclamation which may indeed be 'a joyous assertion of freedom' as well as an oblique confession of inner guilt and dinginess. The draft presence of an alternative untitled poem also allows a reader appreciation of his decision to persevere with the *terza rima* (some of the text excised had cast doubt on how far the form would be sustained), to collapse the first two tercets into one block of text (so that the thinning from six to three to one line to blankness mimes the sifting towards absence) and to use the last word as an echo of the title, offering some kind of bulwark to the structure.

'Absences' remained one of Larkin's favourite poems,[13] celebrated as such in *Poet's Choice* (1962) where he explains why he chose it to represent his work:

> I suppose I like 'Absences' (a) because of its subject matter – I am always thrilled by the thought of what places look like when I am not there; (b) because I fancy it sounds like a different, better poet rather than myself. The last line,

---

13   For further evidence of his fondness for the poem, see *Selected Letters,* p.263, 'I... have a special affection for ABSENCES' or 'An Interview with John Haffenden', in *Philip Larkin: Further Requirements*, ed. Anthony Thwaite (London: Faber and Faber, 2001), p.61, where Larkin mentions 'Absences' as a candidate for his most typical poem.

for instance, sounds like a slightly unconvincing translation from a French symbolist. I wish I could write like this more often.[14]

The simple, personalised discourse and its stark refusal of any theoretical embellishment are typical of Larkin's (occasionally disingenuous) approach to talking about his own poetry. The simplicity should not deceive; it challenges those who would wish to draw a poetics from his words.

The first reason for Larkin's affection for the poem is, it is claimed, 'its subject matter', namely the vertigo of imagining places from which he is absent, whether they be the open sea or attics; this subject matter thrills him twelve years after the poem was written through a kind of revisiting. Larkin himself later said that the poem showed 'a desire to get away from it all'. If that formulation sounds too casual, too resonant of holiday brochures, then Larkin risks, unusually for him, a deeper wording: 'One longs for infinity and absence, the beauty of somewhere you're not'.[15] The poem's subject matter is one of Larkin's most enduring, whether it be expressed in the verse, or in spiritual language or more straightforward prose. And subject matter, for Larkin, is what matters.

In 'The Living Poet',[16] Larkin makes a distinction between, on the one hand, the impact of a poet's character and environment on what he writes and, on the other, the subject of the poems. The character and environment are fateful presences that the poet cannot ignore ('either one writes about them or to escape from them'). The subject of a poem, contrariwise, has the capacity to 'restore the balance and let in some fresh air', leaving behind the constraints of personality and place that surround the genesis of the poem. It clears the clutter of the contingent. Or rather it tries to. Larkin accepts that the subjects of poems too 'are chosen by our own natures... but blessedly the links are for the most part out of sight and the subjects free themselves to expand'. This liberation of the subjects from the 'pre-

14 From *Poet's Choice*, edited by P. Engle and J. Langland (New York: Dial Press, 1962), cited in *Further Requirements*, p.17.

15 'An Interview with John Haffenden', in *Further Requirements*, p.59.

16 'The Living Poet', BBC Third Programme, 3 July 1964; in *Further Requirements*, pp.79–91.

occupations that chose them' is itself an act which, over time, empties the poem of the poet. This emptying, for a poet revisiting a poem, has a particularly poignant thrill. Where has that self gone? Does the poem itself become a space that can touch the poet simply because he is no longer there? Or is the memory of the genesis inescapable?

Before I come back to the second reason for Larkin's affection for 'Absences' ('it sounds like a different, better poet...'), there is an irresistible exchange on the poem by Larkin and a well-meaning correspondent in 1961, a year before Larkin chose it to represent his work. It is irresistible because of the clash of perspectives. A marine biologist, Frank Evans, had written to Larkin:

> When I first read the poem... I thought: He's got his images wrong. Like so many people who walk along the shore and watch the breakers rolling in he thinks that waves in the open do the same. But it is only waves coming in to the beach that roll over and drop like a wall; offshore, no matter how big the waves are, when they break the water just spills down the front. It is the size and not the shape of deep-water waves that changes with the wind strength. Whether in storms or summer breezes makes no difference to the profile of breaking waves (*Selected Letters*, p.332).

This matter-of-fact intrusion into 'what places look like when I'm not there' could have been ignored by Larkin on grounds of poetic licence (although this excuse would scarcely have been consistent with his espousal of the real). Instead, he alludes contritely to Mr Evans's letter in his contribution to *Poet's Choice*:

> Incidentally, an oceanographer wrote to me pointing out that I was confusing two kinds of wave, plunging waves and spilling waves, which seriously damaged the poem from a technical viewpoint. I am sorry about this, but do not see how to amend it now.

And he had penned a reply to Mr Evans with his usual courtesy and humour:

> Thank you for your extremely interesting letter. It seems to me I was confusing two kinds of waves, for I was certainly thinking of 'spilling waves in deep water', as you call them. This makes nonsense of dropping like a wall, if they in fact never slope more than 1 in 7. I hope not too many of my readers are oceanographers. I suppose the only waves in deep water I have ever seen have

been from boats, which might themselves upset the water's behaviour, but I
certainly had the impression of waves playing about on their own like porpoises
(I've never seen a p. either) and was trying to reproduce it (*Selected Letters*,
pp.332–3).

The irony is directed at the self-deprecating portrait of the bookish
poet who knows the word better than the thing ('I've never seen a p.'),
an irony amplified by the hollowness of the authority that is supposed
to be at the base of all similes. But there is also a deeper reflection
hidden beneath the comment on the presence of the boat affecting the
water's behaviour, which can be viewed as a metaphor of the observer
changing what is observed, of the presence of consciousness upsetting
the thrilling fiction of unobserved, raw reality. What Larkin is
celebrating in 'Absences' is precisely the lack of the poet's presence,
the stripping away of Romantic/Symbolist notions of contemplation
and absorption of self into a land- or seascape (as pre-eminently in
Valéry's 'Le Cimetière marin', for example). He wants to reproduce
raw nature 'where there are no ships'; in trying to do so, he makes a
technical mistake which brings with it the traces of the very solipsism
he is seeking to avoid.

Larkin's second reason for liking 'Absences' is 'because I fancy
that it sounds like a different, better poet rather than myself'. He cites
as an example of that difference the last line, which 'sounds like a
slightly unconvincing translation from a French symbolist'. In *A
Writer's Life*, Andrew Motion refers to the poet's output in late 1950
after his move to Belfast: 'in two poems he wrote before the end of the
year, "Absences" and the unpublished "Verlaine", he adapted French
sources' (*A Writer's Life*, p.202). It is not clear which French sources
Motion had in mind for 'Absences'. The poem he refers to as
'Verlaine' is a robust effort at a direct translation of one of Verlaine's
ruder poems, 'A Mademoiselle ***' from *Parallèlement*. But there is
no equivalent original of 'Absences'. At most, it echoes (sometimes
faintly) seascapes found in Baudelaire ('Le Voyage'), Rimbaud ('Le
Bateau ivre', 'Mouvement') and Valéry ('Le Cimetière marin'). For
Larkin, the sense of the last line being a translation might have been
provoked by the structural (and thematic?) similarities with the last,
isolated line of Gautier's 'Terza Rima': 'Sublime aveuglement!

Magnifique défaut!' This latter poem is anthologised by Berthon in
Nine French Poets, a text that, according to Arthur Terry (cited in *A
Writer's Life*, p.202), was part of Larkin's extensive reading in his
early months in Belfast. One might note, in passing, that it also contained Gautier's 'Symphonie en blanc majeur' (the inspiration for
Larkin's title, 'Sympathy in White Major') and Baudelaire's 'L'Homme et la Mer' (with its last, split line, 'O lutteurs éternels, ô frères
implacables!' and direct reflections on the relationship between the
moods of man and sea).

Quite why Larkin should think that writing like a French symbolist is a reason for his liking 'Absences' is on the surface surprising.
His view of translations of poems was not favourable:

> Translations always perplex me. I frankly confess I cannot judge whether such
> lines as
>
> Blurring with flowers the eyes of human leopards,
> I've whirled Floridas none yet set eyes on

produce in me the emotion awoken in a French reader by:

> J'ai heurté, savez-vous, d'incroyables Florides
> Mêlant aux fleurs des yeux de panthères à peaux
> D'hommes!

Almost all poetic translations seem to me condemned to be poetic
zombies, assemblages of properties walking around with no informing
intelligence or soul.[17]

Mischievously quoting one of Roy Campbell's less happy renderings of lines from Rimbaud's 'Le Bateau ivre', Larkin makes an
important point. Why then should a 'slightly unconvincing translation
from a French symbolist' so commend itself? The answer must lie in
the power that Larkin attaches to being different from himself. Here
too, there is the temptation to read this distancing as a self-reflexive
enactment of absence, a paradoxical creation of a text from which the
writer's self is at one remove.

---

17   From Larkin's review of Roy Campbell's *Collected Poems* (*Guardian*, 25
     March 1960) in *Further Requirements*, p.225.

Is 'Absences' then a poem of multiple liberations? The poet liberated from his shame. The poem liberated from its genesis. The writer liberated from his style. If so, then the text takes on layered readings, a hermeneutic ribbing that nudges one from positive object-ivity to lyrical correlations to self-referentiality – and overwhelmingly to an enriching problematisation of the poem. Before one becomes too dizzyingly involved in the reflexivity and the tireless play of levels, it might be salutary to listen to Larkin's own caution on the limits of liberation. Having qualified, in 'The Living Poet', his definition of the most successful poems as those in which 'subjects *appear* to float free' (italics mine) and 'to exist in their own right, reassembled – one hopes – in the eternity of the imagination', Larkin immediately reels himself back in from the edge of literary fancy with an assertive 'But' and a cryptic anecdote:

> But I am frequently reminded of a story Forrest Reid tells about himself as a boy, lying in bed and watching the swallows nesting in the eaves of University Street, Belfast. Realising they had flown all the way from Africa, he was astonished that with the whole world to choose from they should have picked University Street, Belfast (*Further Requirements*, p.79).

In other words, the subject matter, having been set free from the poet, returns through some mysterious process to the place of its genesis and circumstance of its creation. For the poet revisiting his poem is akin to the swallow nesting again in attic eaves long vacated. So when Larkin chooses 'Absences' as a favourite poem, it might be because, paradoxically, its subject matter is recurringly present ('I am always thrilled...') but also because the subject born in the poet's desolate room in Belfast has the power to reconnect magically with a moment of creative triumph over shame and guilt.

Belfast, of course, is a city that Larkin looked back on with af-fection from his high windows in Hull. He is not alone in sensing that those who leave that magnetic city each carry swallows of memory.[18]

Such absences!

18 The author lived in Belfast between 1970 and 1972 when he was a departmental colleague of Peter Broome's. He left to join the Department of French at the University of Hull.

ROGER LITTLE

Poet and poet face to face: reflections on two recent translations by Derek Mahon

At fifteen months' distance, the fine poet and experienced translator Derek Mahon published in 2001 and 2002 his versions of Valéry's 'Le Cimetière marin' and Saint-John Perse's 'Oiseaux'.[1] His earlier translations from Philippe Jaccottet and several versions from seventeenth-century French plays by Molière and Racine have brought him a wide audience as translator and a considerable reputation in that field, to the point where one commentator has controversially suggested that his very being as a writer is as a translator rather than as a poet.[2] In the present paper, I propose to reflect on that contention in the process of examining some instances drawn from Mahon's two most recent translations from French poetry.

Saint-John Perse was amused to recall, as he stood on the roof of his colonial-style house at the point of the Presqu'île de Giens overlooking the Iles d'Hyères and the Mediterranean, that on the other hilltop stood the house of Comtesse de Béhague, to which Valéry would repair for relaxation and more. But beyond such an anecdote, Paul Valéry (1871–1945) and Saint-John Perse (pseudonym of René-

---

1   Derek Mahon, *The Seaside Cemetery: A Version of 'Le Cimetière marin' by Paul Valéry, with drawings by Fionnuala Ní Chiosáin* (Loughcrew, Oldcastle, Co. Meath, Ireland: Gallery Books, 28 June 2001); Saint-John Perse, *Birds: A Version by Derek Mahon* (Loughcrew: Gallery Books, 30 September 2002). Both are elegantly produced volumes, but neither, regrettably belying my title, contains the original French.

2   Kathleen Shields, following her book *Gained in Translation: Language, Poetry and Identity in Twentieth-Century Ireland* (Oxford: Peter Lang, 2000), argued this position at a seminar organised jointly on 13 December 2002 by the Translators' and Interpreters' Society of Ireland and Trinity College Dublin and held at the latter institution.

Marie Alexis Léger, 1887–1975) are indisputably twin peaks in the landscape of twentieth-century French poetry. However different their poetic styles, their poetry's high seriousness betokens their shared belief in the capacity of the art to rise above the anecdotal and explore the complexities of the intellect and of man's capacity for spirituality, doctrinally unaffiliated in both cases.

'Le Cimetière marin' is Valéry's best-known poem and, after appearing in the *Nouvelle Revue française* of June 1920, was published in his best-known collection, *Charmes*.[3] Its twenty-four six-decasyllable stanzas, tightly constructed both in form and in content, have given rise to a daunting mass of erudite commentary which threatens to overwhelm the poem. Does the translator feel impelled to familiarise himself with the work of the scholiasts? His is a critical analysis in another mode and by other means, no less illuminating in the best of cases, but throwing a different light by using a different angle. Every verse, every line, every word, every rhythm, every cadence, every echo, every phoneme must be weighed in his search for an appropriate equivalent for individual effects within the overall effect. If only all scholars were so painstaking! Many are content to substitute the grid of a predetermined position and inspissating jargon for empathetic analysis; many prefer self-serving opacity to the modesty of transparency.

If this is a danger for academic critics, it is also a danger for translators. And all the more so when the translator is a poet. The years of self-imposed effort to forge an identity as a poet, to create an individual style and voice are in many ways at variance with a position to which I cleave with what some would no doubt qualify as reactionary fervour: that to serve an original writer as translator, the only tenable posture is that of plate-glass. To be otherwise is to set oneself up as rival rather than as translator, to diminish the originality of the original, to place an ancillary art in a dominant position. Of course one has to admit that transparency is no more than an unachievable goal: no pane is without its flaws, and it has to be admitted that the imperfections of old hand-made glass are integral to the

---

3   Paul Valéry, *Charmes* (Paris: NRF/Gallimard, 1922); frequently reprinted and republished.

aesthetic pleasure that it can sometimes generate. They are faults and distortions nonetheless, something the glass-maker, like the translator, would normally seek to avoid. The position of poet as translator may appear so inherently paradoxical as to be untenable.

Is such a view too narrowly that of an academic seeking to inculcate in students a capacity for producing accurate translations from one language into another? My professional experience of translation is certainly in that field and if the charge is valid I must plead guilty. But I have also engaged in the translation of poetry as a regular hygiene for mind and pen: both a stimulating confrontation with frustration and a constant revelation of the poet's inspiriting exploration of linguistic resources. And while there is a recognisable difference in the degree of intellectual satisfaction between the varied challenges of attempting altruistically to translate a poem and the bread-and-butter business of selecting a range of texts to stretch a student's awareness of both source and target languages, the nature of the exercise is not intrinsically different. One starts from analysis and respect; one seeks by whatever means to produce a text which corresponds as closely as possible, in all respects, with the original, making an equivalent statement in equivalent ways to an equivalent reader. For this, mastery of both source and target languages (the latter often being woefully neglected by students of foreign languages) is imperative. What better master of a language than a poet in that language? The paradox we noted earlier is doubly paradoxical.

What can we possibly mean by 'an equivalent reader'? If translation transposes us in space, it also does so in time, in culture, in the shared assumptions of one society confronting the shared assumptions of another. Are we trying to produce a museum piece or a work of living literature? Let us assume the latter for present purposes, since in practice it predominates, even if the former has a specialised intellectual appeal. Should we expect the translator of poetry to discover more about the cultural climate of the society in which a poem is produced than what may reasonably be deduced from an intelligent reading of the poem? Would such labours not be lost if the poet's individual genius were itself lost in a welter of historical generalisations? If the poem is fully achieved, it will supply all the evidence we need. And primarily that deserves an attentive reader, sensitive to the verbal play of sound and pattern in its co-text of poem, collection and *œuvre* and, further, in their context of prosodic, cultural and social tradition. For a poem to stand alone and survive is to be an intimate part of that 'ecology'. As Mahon reminds us in his translation of 'Oiseaux', the mighty Genghis Khan's initially delicate gesture had extensive ramifications:

> The Mongolian conqueror who lifted a bird from its nest, and the nest from the branch, took up not only bird, nest and song, but the whole natal tree, ripped from its place with its population of roots, its sod of earth and its rim of soil – a portion of home 'topography' reminiscent of meadow, province, the very empire itself.

What I am arguing here echoes what Mahon writes in his prefatory note to the volume: '*Birds* is about birds, but also about the artistic vocation itself, Yeats's "lonely impulse of delight".' Creative solitude precedes shared enjoyment.

There are no formal constraints of versification on the passage just quoted, and while it is not strictly true to state as Mahon does that '[t]he original text (*Oiseaux*, 1962) was written to accompany a series of bird lithographs by Georges Braque', it is the case that words and pictures came together for the first edition in a particularly splendid example of the *livre d'artiste*.[4] 'Oiseaux' is a stand-alone text, though its relationship to Saint-John Perse's work is by no means that of 'Le Cimetière marin' to Valéry's. It is a relatively short late work without the heightened poetic stature of *Anabase*, *Exil*, *Vents* or *Amers*; more

---

4   Saint-John Perse, Georges Braque, *L'Ordre des oiseaux* (Paris: Au vent d'Arles, Société d'édition d'art, 1962). 130 copies in all, on hand-made paper, in 54 x 42 cm oblong format in a silk-covered slip-case decorated by Braque, with 12 lithographs by him. A luxurious edition at a luxury price! For all subsequent separate editions, the title was reduced to *Oiseaux*. Poet and painter were working independently on the bird-motif (on which Saint-John Perse had written a long early poem, 'Cohorte') when a common friend, Jean Paulhan, brought them together. They hit it off splendidly. The publisher Jeannine Crémieux acted as impresario for the joint publication. It may be noted that the dust-cover of Mahon's translation is enhanced by the photograph of an elegant sculptural work by Eilís O'Connell, somewhat reminiscent of Brancusi, taking the abstraction of birdness a step further than Braque.

loosely textured than they, it is, because of the explicit references to Braque in the published version, more overtly circumstantial. If shortcomings are found in the translation, it seems fair to be more severe. Not having to worry about tackling rhyme means that correspondingly more attention can be paid to accuracy, even if many other criteria for judgement, such as matters of sonority and rhythm, remain firmly in place.

To consider the verse (or paragraph: terminology will always be a delicate matter in relation to poetry in prose) already quoted, let us first remind ourselves of the French:

> Nous connaissons l'histoire de ce Conquérant Mongol, ravisseur d'un oiseau sur son nid, et du nid sur son arbre, qui ramenait avec l'oiseau, et son nid et son chant, tout l'arbre natal lui-même, pris à son lieu, avec son peuple de racines, sa motte de terre et sa marge de terroir, tout son lambeau de « territoire » foncier évocateur de friche, de province, de contrée et d'empire...[5]

Many of the transpositions in Mahon's translation are entirely acceptable: the altered presentation of the story, which we no longer 'know' and are therefore told; the minor variation in the listing of items taken. Other alterations seem less legitimate: the slippages of register and semantics in *natal* / 'natal', from *ravisseur* to 'who lifted' (without the sense of ravishing, even raping), from *marge de terroir* to 'rim of soil' (too small a scale), from *friche* (wasteland, now the EU's 'set-aside') to 'meadow'. For one addition ('very') there are several omissions: *lui-même*, *tout*, *de contrée*, some commas and the final

---

[5] Saint-John Perse, *Œuvres complètes* (Paris: NRF/Gallimard, Bibliothèque de la Pléiade, 1972 (1978)), p.412. The printing history of the poem and details of four existing translations into English (including my own) and of several into other languages may be found on pp.1367–9. Further references to this volume will be given as *OC*. To lay my cards on the table and leave myself open to similar scrutiny, I like to present my own proposal for the passages I analyse:
We know the story of that Mongol Conqueror who ravished a bird from its nest, and the nest from its tree, who brought back, with the bird, both its nest and its song, the whole native tree itself, taken from its location, with its population of roots, its clump of earth and its margin of land, all its strip of home 'territory' reminiscent of prairie and province, country and empire...

suspension points.[6] Small losses, one might say, for the benefit of being given privileged access to a foreign text.

Yes and no. As always with translation, the devil is in the detail. Resonances will often disappear in the process, and the bilingual reader will impotently grieve their going. But small things add up: behind the simple word *lieu* 'place' lies the more technical 'locus' for which the identical French word is used. We know that Saint-John Perse was familiar with it: he refers elsewhere (*OC*, p.551) to the '«lieu géométrique »' which the French language represents for him. The rarer, nobler word seems more apposite here, given the grandeur of the evocation and the expansiveness of the vision. Did Mahon judge it too technical? We may never know. As to the closing suspension points, unusual as a form of punctuation in English but used more in French and one for which Saint-John Perse shows particular fondness, Mahon does not disdain them in section IX of the poem.[7] Why does he not use them here, where their emphasis on the open-endedness of the list of ever-wider reaches is of some significance? And while the practice of using commas is different in French and English, a poet's disposition of them is never innocent. Mahon's reduction of them from eleven to eight must be in response to the dictates of his ear.

Does this mean that we can have no critical purchase on the product when a poet turns to translation, that anything goes, in short, in some dragomanic equivalent of Romantic submission to the Muse? One has only to ask the poet if he or she would be happy to know that a translator had been cavalier with his or her text. The more responsible and rigorous the poet, the unhappier s/he would be. If we cannot credit a poet with responsibility for the written words, how can we formulate any serious criticism and go beyond the mishmash of biographical irrelevancy and unanalysed emotionalism which still sometimes pretends to that title? And if any poets were rigorous,

---

6   Inexplicably, Mahon also omits the poem's epigraph from Aulus Persius Flaccus (*OC*, p.407): ... *Quantum non milvus oberret.* / '... More than a kite can fly over.'

7   Even if he changes them to dashes at the end of section II and the beginning of section III.

Valéry and Saint-John Perse are they, not far below the pinnacle of rigour represented by Mallarmé.

Although Saint-John Perse inscrutably masks his mastery of the traditional art of prosody and metrics under the appearance of longer lines,[8] it is Valéry who espouses the French tradition of syllabic regularity more obviously. While Saint-John Perse subsumes elements of predominantly six, eight and twelve syllables in his *versets*, generally eschewing the ten-syllable unit because, he felt, it does not correspond to any rhythm adopted by a horse, it is precisely the decasyllabic line that Valéry uses in 'Le Cimetière marin'. That Valéry should in addition espouse traditional rhyme presents a further problem for the translator.

In the history of French prosody, translation played a crucial role in two major developments, and it did so because of the practical difficulties of translating rhyme by rhyme. First the prose poem emerged in the eighteenth century under this impulse, then, towards the end of the nineteenth, *vers libre* also had its earliest manifestations in translated works. The precedents are therefore more than honourable. But to rise to the challenge of matching rhyme by rhyme is a singular temptation for a master technician. For his translation of 'Le Cimetière marin', Mahon has chosen a middle way: instead of strict rhyme in the order Valéry chose (aabccb), he varies the order to suit his needs and further accommodates them by using a flexible mixture of full rhyme, half-rhyme, eye-rhyme, pararhyme, assonance and distant echo. The result is generally pleasing, particularly to ears no longer attuned or sympathetic to the regular gong of full rhyme.

The celebrated opening stanza:

---

8   See notably Saint-John Perse's comments in his letter to Katherine Biddle of 12 December 1955 (*OC*, p.922): 'Nous parlerons une autre fois de cette question de métrique interne, rigoureusement traitée dans la distribution générale et l'articulation de grandes masses prosodiques (où sont bloqués, par strophes ou laisses, dans une même et large contraction, avec la même fatalité, tous éléments particuliers traités comme vers réguliers – ce qu'ils sont en réalité). Il est facile, évidemment, au lecteur étranger de se méprendre sur cette économie générale d'une versification précise encore qu'inapparente [...]. (D'où une difficulté encore accrue pour le traducteur étranger.)'

> Ce toit tranquille, où marchent les colombes,
> Entre les pins palpite, entre les tombes;
> Midi le juste y compose de feux
> La mer, la mer, toujours recommencée!
> O récompense après une pensée
> Qu'un long regard sur le calme des dieux!

is rendered as:

> A tranquil surface where a spinnaker moves
> flickers among the pines, among the graves;
> objective noon films with its fiery glaze
> a shifting sea, drifters like pecking doves,
> and my reward for thought is a long gaze
> down the blue silence of celestial groves.[9]

Mahon opts for a fluid adaptation of the iambic pentameter. Not only is this the most familiar metre in English but it basically contains the same ten syllables as Valéry's line. Is it appropriate as an equivalent? One might reasonably argue that in French it is rather the alexandrine which is the cultural equivalent to our iambic pentameter, since it predominates massively in French literature from the seventeenth century to the nineteenth and beyond. It remains, as does the iambic pentameter for the English ear, the undisputed point of metric reference. Even its avoidance in good prose remains a principle that every French student learns, sure proof of its power within the language. The generally more concise phrasing of English compared with French might argue in favour of using an eight-syllable, four-foot line (as I have done, but could I sustain it over twenty-four stanzas?). The French decasyllable contains a variable number of feet but usually three or four, and this corresponds more closely to a tetrameter than to

---

9   Again, fully recognising the ultimate impossibility of the task, I present my
     suggestion without further comment for others to judge:
         This tranquil roof where doves parade
         Throbs among pines, among the graves;
         Impartial noon makes up with fire
         The sea, the ever-endless sea!
         O rich reward for an idea
         This long gaze at the gods' calm stare!

a pentameter. If rhythm determines the choice (and rhythm is independent of syllable-count in French versification), then this would seem preferable. But whatever the decision, the transposition from the arithmetic of syllable-count in French to English feet represents an unavoidable sea-change.

The three eye-rhymes (moves – doves – groves) of Mahon's version, and their corresponding half-rhyme (graves), interspersed with the two full rhymes (glaze – gaze), establish from the outset a sense of tightly organised verse and this is important. Is the cost too high? The opening demonstrative adjective commands attention and gives a feeling of immediacy lost in the indefinite article of the English. The word 'surface' deprives *toit* of something of its sense of everything that lies beneath it. But an eyebrow rises involuntarily like a seagull on a thermal when a spinnaker makes its appearance in the first line, explicating the metaphor which in the original is not fully clarified until the very last line of the poem: 'Ce toit tranquille où picoraient des focs'.[10] To call noon 'objective' approaches one sense of the word *juste*, namely 'impartial' (but in that case, why not use 'impartial', with the same rhythm as 'objective'?), but one has to recognise that no single English word conveys the full meaning and resonances of *juste* in this context: noon is not only equitable, it has undertones of accuracy as well as fairness. And to be fair, Mahon compensates for losing the first line's reference to *colombes* by having them heave into view as 'doves' in line 4. Yet they are pecking, and do not peck in the original until the final verse when they are revealed as a metaphor for jibs. Such conflation can no doubt be argued, but it remains undeniable that the order in which the reader discovers the scene in Mahon's version is not the same as in the original. Nor is the exclamatory tone, indicated by two exclamation marks in the French, in any way sustained in this translation. Yet by and large the tonal range of Valéry's poem is matched by Mahon's: even if there are

10   Internal consistency is at least maintained by Mahon translating this last line: 'this shifting surface where the spinnaker flocks.' The semantic inaccuracy of the last word can be justified only by the demand for rhyme. As to 'spinnakers' for *focs*, properly 'jibs', landlubbers would consider any objection pedantic.

displacements, there are none of the unwarranted vulgarities that jar and occasionally mar his earlier versions of Jaccottet.[11]

These are perhaps avoidable difficulties. But how can a translator suggest that a line of verse has passed into common currency? How often does a cultured person, sighting the sea, repeat Alexander's cry 'Thalassa, thalassa!'? In English, in homage to Keats, one might stand 'silent upon a peak in Darien'. In French, 'La mer, la mer, toujours recommencée', itself an echo of Alexander, is what comes immediately to mind. This is scarcely captured by 'a shifting sea', even if 'drifters' provides a nice echo of the phrase. Each reader must judge whether such alert phrasing, so pleasing to the ear, is sufficient compensation for a reduction in accuracy and a loss of cultural resonance. In short, the precise balance between creative poet and sensitive translator is not a matter for legislation but for individual sensibility.

The workaday translator who has no pretensions to fully fledged creative writing is bound to privilege accuracy of meaning over any consideration of the signifier. But where poetry is concerned, the signifier is an integral part of the effect and so ultimately indistinguishable from meaning. The conundrum remains intact! The tension for a poet-translator stems from the fact that his or her particular balance between these forces is unlikely to correspond exactly to that of the source-poet. Elective affinity may prompt a sympathetic choice where s/he has a free hand, but in the (rare) event of a more or less formal commission no such predisposition can be assumed, and the reader is not necessarily privy to such paratextual information. The high degree of competence in the native language ascribable to a poet who embarks on translation, eminently desirable in any translator, is by definition taken to an extreme of individual efficacy which runs the risk of overwhelming the voice of the original poet.

Why then should available translations of poetry so often be by poets? Firstly, because poets are drawn to poetry and properly want to have access to poets in languages other than their own. How better to

---

11 I think for example of *ordure* appearing repeatedly as 'shit' (a word unimaginable in Jaccottet's vocabulary) in a poem from *Leçons*: see Philippe Jaccottet, *Selected Poems*, selected and translated with an introduction by Derek Mahon (Harmondsworth: Penguin Books, 1988), p.109.

'possess' a foreign poet's work than to translate it and so discover its most intimate mechanisms. It is an approach I have long recommended to students as one of the best ways to engage with a French poem as part of an analytical and critical process. Secondly, because such a demanding task brings no monetary reward: it is a labour of love in the strictest sense. A professional translator might undertake the translation of a poem as a busman's holiday, but none could make a living from that activity alone: the rewards are purely intellectual – linguistic and perhaps spiritual. The disproportion between the multi-faceted competence required and the financial recognition is grotesque. The compensations, like the activity itself, are intangible but real, in introducing a few solitary and privileged readers to a foreign voice and so nurturing a dispersed community of sensitive souls. The third reason, less noble, is that hard-nosed publishers need a name to sell poetry in translation.

As to critical attention, the translator of poetry can expect either a brief gush of often ill-informed emotion or, from the closer critic, carping, quibbling and nit-picking as evidenced above. Scarcely in either case a satisfying acknowledgement of dedication and altruism. And the extent to which the very process and act of translation feeds into the poet's original writings is usually forgotten, to the point where studies of poets' work most often ignore or, at best, treat separately any translations undertaken. The pointedly titled *Gained in Translation*, the book by Kitty Shields to which I referred earlier, represents a welcome corrective to that familiar disdain. She emphasises that for several major modern Irish poets translation is integral to their creative process and prompts the reflection that 'all poetry is metaphorically written in a foreign language and that if it were not it would not be poetry. It requires special attention and feats of interpretation.'[12] Of Michael Hartnett, Shields writes (p.128) that 'his natural home is in translation where he can exist as a linguistic and cultural hybrid and rejoice in the lack of an end point' and this too is where she would situate Mahon who, in her view, 'wants his

---

12   The reflection is my own: see my review of *Guined in Translation* in *Translation Ireland*, 15, 2 (Summer 2001), 24–5.

English-speaking readers to be aware that they are reading a text which has been translated out of another language' (p.157).

In a student's work, this would be berated as linguistic incompetence. What mysterious sophistication transforms it into a higher form of competence in the work of a publishing translator? The argument has it that the reader should be reminded of the foreignness of the work being read. As if there were not already enough reminders of the fact: paratextual indications of all sorts. And as if there would not always be enough inevitable signals in the translation itself – like the flaws in my metaphorical pane of old glass – that its origins lay outside the reader's native culture. To make a virtue of incompetence might strike one as singularly perverse, yet the long tradition of *belles infidèles* is a manifest refutation of such a view. Has the erection of accuracy into a dominant principle of translation over the last century in fact represented a diversion from the mainstream only now being rediscovered? For all the modern translations of the Bible, is it not the phrases and cadences of the less accurate King James' version that still re-echo in our minds, woven as they are into the very fabric of English? Will Terence Kilmartin or, most recently, a team of academics ever oust our nostalgia for Scott-Moncrieff?

The quandary remains. It is all very well to dream of an ideal capacity to learn and master a foreign language and then another and another: there are limits. Is it better to make do with translations from languages we do not know or to close one's mind to such cultures because of the imperfections of the medium or the messenger? If the translator is a poet, something will be gained, not only by him or her but by the reader. And yet I cleave to transparency. However important the function of translating is, it is primarily the servant of a pre-existing original. It can never reverse those roles, determined by time and circumstance. And so, whatever its importance, translation necessarily remains a secondary art, however fashionable it is in some circles to suppose otherwise.

What, one might ask, of the approaches adopted by Ezra Pound, Louis Zukofsky or Robert Lowell? In part, they provide the answer to the question themselves: they are engaged in imitation, not translation. Certainly a foreign text inspires their work, but they adopt it as a springboard to an exercise quite different from translation in any strict sense that I can recognise. Some might argue that the word 'translation' should not be so rigidly circumscribed as to exclude imitation, but that would be to adopt Humpty-Dumpty's view of language, and we all know what happened to him.

So bully for Derek Mahon. He has dared and, with some reservations, he has won. Won for his own creative purposes. Won for us readers who, thanks to his undertakings, become more alert to a particular set of linguistic challenges. Won for Valéry and Saint-John Perse and for French poetry in general a new readership, a renewed attentiveness. Of course, as T. S. Eliot observed, 'every attempt is a different kind of failure'. But Beckett's ardent recommendation blazes through his work: 'Fail again. Fail better.'

Marie-Claire Bancquart

A Woman's hue

On the tautness of space
head like Orpheus
between the flames of sun and the rock's sterility.

Voice backwards and forwards
Euridice
in the teeth-bite of the trees.

Their secular sun
persists at the fringes of the sky.

Orpheus would still identify our flowers our animals
the gathering of shadows over our memories.

It hasn't gone, the mystery of that greeting to the souls
of the unfulfilled
nor the call to resist the insects nibbling from
the depths at a woman's hue.

The world of a lightness such
that one could slip it whole beneath the female dead.

(translated by Peter Broome)

Couleur des femmes

Sur un étroit espace :
tête d'Orphée
entre les flammes du soleil et la stérilité du roc.

Voix qui passe et repasse :
Eurydice
entre les dents des arbres.

Le soleil de leur millénaire
n'a pas disparu des lisières du ciel.

Orphée reconnaîtrait nos fleurs nos animaux
le rassemblement des ombres sur nos mémoires.

C'est toujours le mysterieux salut aux âmes qui n'ont pas
comblé leurs vœux,
et l'appel contre les insectes, rongeant du plus bas la
couleur des femmes.

Le monde est si léger qu'il peut tout entier glisser sous
les mortes.

A notebook headed : 'Save our bears !'

And under the title the cover states 'Made from recycled paper'.

Jottings inside on Kafka,
how he loved the sound of a resonant F sharp bell,
crossed-out lists, times of meetings, shopping reminders, addresses
where the tight-lipped
urgency
of human fate which thrives on the secretive
brings to the fore a hotel name : *Hotel*,
quite simply, as one might speak of Beauty or of God.

Encounters, washrooms, ever-changing bodies,
all are here in digest form.

Hotel. Who is it that comes and goes ? Save our bears
amidst these vestiges, for Kafka's days were numbered.

(translated by Peter Broome)

Carnet : 'Sauvegardons les ours !'

La couverture affirme 'En papier recyclé' sous ce titre.

À l'intérieur, des notes sur Kafka,
l'amour d'une pénétrante cloche en fa dièse,
des listes raturées, rendez-vous, courses, adresses,
où l'urgence
muette
du destin qui n'aime rien tant que le tapinois
laisse apparaître un nom d'hôtel : l'Hôtel,
tout court, comme on dirait le Beau ou Dieu.

Rencontres, lavabos, corps jamais les mêmes,
les voici en compact.

L'Hôtel. Qui va, qui vient ? Sauvegardons les ours
parmi ces vestiges, car les jours de Kafka furent éphémères.

GERALD M. MACKLIN

'Je réservais la traduction':
decoding Rimbaud's 'Dévotion'

> Je réglai la forme et le mouvement de chaque consonne, et, avec des rhythmes instinctifs, je me flattai d'inventer un verbe poétique accessible, un jour ou l'autre, à tous les sens. Je réservais la traduction ('Délires II'/ 'Alchimie du verbe'–*Une saison en enfer*).

Any endeavour to translate Rimbaud must take account of his avowed intention to create a new poetic language, an idiom paradoxically 'accessible... à tous les sens'[1] and yet resistant to all readings and interpretations. Indeed, when one considers not only the poems themselves but equally some of Rimbaud's assertions in both the 'Lettre du voyant' and 'Délires II' in *Une saison en enfer*, one might very well arrive at the conclusion that any attempt at decoding or translating the Rimbaud corpus is to do violence to work that, even in the original French and to the French reader, is characterised by its cryptic and enigmatic quality. The letter of the 15 May 1871 argues that the real poet has never existed, that the *voyant* must undergo torture which is 'ineffable' and that his Promethean programme necessarily sets him and his select band of confederates apart from everyone else. The paradox follows immediately in that the same letter underscores the necessity of developing a 'langage universel' whereby the poet can respond to the imperative to 'faire sentir, palper, écouter ses inventions'.[2] One notes, however, that this urge to communicate the 'inconnu' – new forms to communicate new ideas – is not couched in terms of verbal or semantic understanding but rather as transmission

---

1   Rimbaud, *Œuvres*, éd. Suzanne Bernard and André Guyaux (Paris: Garnier, 1983), p.228. It is this Bernard/Guyaux version of 'Dévotion' that I refer to in this chapter.

2   From the 'Lettre du voyant', *Œuvres*, p.349.

on a sensual, tactile and auditory level. In 'Délires II' we find the poet recalling his audacious plan to give colours to the vowels and then this key sequence:

> Je réglai la forme et le mouvement de chaque consonne,
> et, avec des rhythmes instinctifs, je me flattai d'inventer
> un verbe poétique accessible, un jour ou l'autre, à tous
> les sens. Je réservais la traduction (*Œuvres*, p.228).

Here again we encounter the idea of a poetry that speaks, not on the level of verbal meaning, but rather as an appeal to all the senses. In fact, Rimbaud asserts his right to reserve meaning, ideas and any possible translation. He immediately establishes the quality of his writing by saying 'J'écrivais des silences, des nuits, je notais l'in-exprimable'. What he will later in 'Délires II' term 'l'hallucination des mots' (*Œuvres*, p.230) emerges here as a language unlike any other and so not susceptible to the probings of interpreters, translators and code-crackers. And yet there is a repeatedly teasing quality to Rimbaud's work[3] whereby he seems to invite us to try anyway and establishes a relationship with his reader which involves himself as the sphinx-like and inscrutable intellectual, superior to a reader desperately attempting to keep up.[4] A provocative poet who can calmly write 'c'est oracle ce que je dis' ('Mauvais sang' in *Une saison en enfer*, *Œuvres*, p.214) would seem to invite decoding and, of course, this is precisely what has happened over the years. Not-withstanding all the caveats listed above, there have been repeated attempts to translate Rimbaud and it is the specific purpose of this chapter to investigate the particular exigencies of any project to translate the apparently hermetic texts that make up the *Illuminations* with particular reference to 'Dévotion'.[5]

---

3   G. Macklin, 'Rimbaud mystificateur', *French Studies Bulletin*, no.56 (Autumn 1995), 12.
4   One might think here of how the Vierge folle utterly fails to comprehend the thinking of the Epoux infernal in 'Délires I' in *Une saison en enfer*: 'j'étais sûre de ne jamais entrer dans son monde' (*Œuvres*, p.225).
5   This predilection for teasing is apparent in many of the *Illuminations*. The ending of 'Vies I' is a fine example where Rimbaud writes: 'Ma sagesse est aussi dédaignée que le chaos. Qu'est mon néant auprès de la stupeur qui vous

Since we are here dealing with Rimbaud's prose poems, it is appropriate at this stage to identify rapidly some of the stylistic features of the *Illuminations* which problematise the task of any aspirant translator. These features are illustrative of the broader theoretical difficulties outlined above but it is at least arguable that the fluidity and plasticity of Rimbaud's prose poems render translation even more difficult than do the early verse poems or even the *Derniers vers*. It is extremely difficult to pin down the nature of the Rimbaldian prose poem but a significant body of evidence exists to suggest that Rimbaud envisaged this form as a liberation from the strait-jacket of rules and regulations associated with prosody and that for him the prose poem came to represent the emancipation of language to permit a free play of associations, juxtapositions, verbal formulae, fragments and so on.[6] Some strikingly frequent and specific features immediately come to mind. In the *Illuminations* Rimbaud develops a quite alien lexicon, a vocabulary that is characterised by large numbers of neologisms, foreign terms and other linguistic idiosyncrasies. Thus any one of the prose poems at any time is able to startle the reader with the sudden appearance on the page of a term that baffles us or disorientates us or makes us query its obscure provenance or etymology.

A memorable illustration, and one that has given rise to much debate and exegesis is the celebrated term 'Baou' which seems to be lobbed into 'Dévotion' like a *pétard*.[7] Later in this chapter we will be considering in depth the problematics of translating 'Dévotion' and assessing three recent attempts to decode this enigmatic text. At this point we may simply note how 'Baou' abruptly disorientates the

---

attend?' (*Œuvres*, p.264). Here we have a mixture of superiority, mystification and menace.

6   André Guyaux entitles one of his works on the poet *Poétique du fragment. Essai sur les 'Illuminations' de Rimbaud* (Neuchâtel: Editions de la Baconnière, 1985) while Michel Murat deals with the fragment in Rimbaud's prose poetry in the second part of his book *L'Art de Rimbaud* (Paris: José Corti, 2002).

7   In terms of the word 'Baou' one recalls the celebrated debate in the pages of *French Studies* between Roger Little and J. Hiddleston. See vol.XXXV, nos.2, 3 and 4. See also R. Little, 'Light on Rimbaud's "Baou"', *French Studies Bulletin*, no.7 (Spring, 1984), 3–7.

reader, appears not to connect with what precedes and follows it and may well represent an example of a language that operates on the level of sound and sensual appeal rather than on a strictly semantic level. It also appears to substantiate one's sense of the *Illuminations* as a text which liberates the individual word, allowing it to float freely as an independent unit not necessarily assimilable to any broader verbal structure or formula. Connected to this is the wholesale deployment in the collection of proper names which are not immediately recognizable to the reader: Eucharis, Hottentots, Molochs, Mabs, Hélène, Solymes, Méandre, Ossian, Guaranies, Elle, Béotiens and many more. These proper names ensure that, in a sense, the *Illuminations* become a compendium of names or a kind of index or directory which poses all sorts of problems for the decoder who is keen to discover sense or meaning. Cumulatively, all of these ingredients seem designed to create a language that resists decoding, interpretation, translation. One is reminded of Rimbaud's words in the letter to Izambard of 13 May 1871: 'Vous ne comprendrez pas du tout et je ne saurais presque vous expliquer'.[8] Rimbaud seems wedded to a sense of the poet as impassive and inscrutable prophet, the zealous guardian of privileged insights and consequently the prose texts of the *Illuminations* dramatise the tension between the need to lead and inform and the impulse to alienate the reader and keep him at arm's length. The use of neologisms is another factor which appears to contribute to the collection's impenetrability and to complicate the task of the translator. 'Accidences' ('Veillées II'), 'opéradiques' ('Nocturne vulgaire'), 'Palais-Promontoire' ('Promontoire'), 'clarteux' ('H'), are just some illustrations of how the lexicon used in the collection can puzzle, estrange and arrest the unsuspecting receiver.

Another significant feature of the collection that complicates the task of the translator is the revolutionised function of punctuation developed by Rimbaud. Even a cursory reading of these poems reveals how punctuation has been released from its traditional role as prop or support system for syntax, grammar and meaning and has been reimagined as a dynamic, pulsating presence in the heart of many poems. Quite apart from the proliferation of capitalization, one is

8   In the letter to Georges Izambard of 13 May 1871 (*Œuvres*, p.345).

struck above all else by the multiplicity of dashes that occur and by the many and varied functions that they have. Many vivid examples come immediately to mind, ranging from the telegrammatic effect created by the *tirets* in the penultimate paragraph of 'Après le déluge' to the pre-climactic dash found in the finale of 'Les Ponts' and from the numerous dashes in 'Nocturne vulgaire' which affect rhythm, continuity and structure and seem like some form of musical notation to those in 'Barbare' which contribute to 'la musique' which that text seems to distill. However, perhaps the most compelling example is found in the second paragraph of 'Angoisse':

> (O palmes! diamant! – Amour, force! – plus haut que toutes
> joies et gloires! – de toutes façons, partout, –Démon, dieu, –
> Jeunesse de cet être-ci: moi!) ('Angoisse', *Œuvres*, p.289).

Clearly the dashes in this excerpt are every bit as much an integral component of the language as are the words themselves. They carve up expression into brief and energetic spasms and, of course, they are linked here to other features of punctuation. The exclamation marks, the capital letters and the parentheses combine with the dashes to convey powerfully to the reader the visual impression of a new idiom that responds to different laws from those of conventional expression. All of this has evident implications for anyone setting out to translate the passage. Indeed one might suggest that the traditional notion of translator is here challenged in the sense that this liberated and dynamically charged punctuation seems to propose a task more in the field of decoding than translating in the normal sense of the term. The language on show here seems to be characterised by a high number of ciphers and this would coincide with the sense of encountering a secret method of communication that will exclude many more than it will embrace. The implications for the would-be translator are not hard to define – any attempt to translate these texts must involve not just a basic rendering of 'meaning' but a willingness to seek an English idiom that will be as fluid and mobile as the original allied to a sensitivity to the musicalisation of text that the *Illuminations* represent.[9]

Clearly, the *illisibilité*[10] of the *Illuminations* is well advertised in the author's Parthian shaft at the end of 'Parade' where he writes 'J'ai seul la clef de cette parade Sauvage', and again in the final italicised word *'Assassins'* in 'Matinée d'ivresse' which is calculated to emphasise the gnomic and impenetrable nature of the writing.[11] Another key feature of the collection relevant to one embarking upon translation is the rich reservoir of accelerations and decelerations it contains. There are all sorts of gear-changes in the *Illuminations*, switching tempos and alternating rhythms which occur unpredictably. This is central to the Rimbaldian conception of the prose poem, leaving behind stabilizing agents such as stanza, metre and rhythm and liberating a mysterious artistic intuition. As Todorov has pointed out, an inherent trait of the collection is 'la discontinuité en règle fondamentale'.[12] Paule Lapeyre has also emphasised this characteristic of the *Illuminations* in her perceptive study.[13]

Having laid down some of the theoretical and very real obstacles in the way of successful translation of the *Illuminations*, we are now in a position to attempt to consider these in the form of what may prosaically be called a 'case-study'. For this purpose, I have selected the poem 'Dévotion' and I now propose to analyse it carefully with the challenge of translating it into English as my focus. As well as looking at the poem itself, I propose to refer to three recent trans-

9   In terms of musicalisation of texts in the *Illuminations*, see the collected essays of Sergio Sacchi, *Etudes sur les 'Illuminations' de Rimbaud*, textes recueillis par Olivier Bivort, André Guyaux et Mario Matucci (Paris: Presses de l'Université de Paris-Sorbonne, 2002), where the issue is treated regularly.

10   A. Kittang (*Discours et Jeu. Essai d'analyse des textes d'Arthur Rimbaud* (Bergen et Grenoble: Presses universitaires de Grenoble, 1975)) is the key text for discussion of *illisibilité* in Rimbaud.

11   'Chaque mot poétique est ainsi un objet inattendu, une boîte de Pandore d'où s'envolent toutes les virtualités du langage' (Roland Barthes, *Le Degré zéro de l'écriture* (Paris: Editions du Seuil, 1972), p.38).

12   T. Todorov, 'Une complication de texte: les *Illuminations*', *Poétique*, 34, avril 1978, 241–53.

13   Paule Lapeyre, *Le Vertige de Rimbaud. Clé d'une perception poétique* (Neuchâtel: Editions de la Baconnière, 1981).

lations of it: from James Lawler in his *Rimbaud's Theatre of the Self* (1992), Mark Treharne in *Arthur Rimbaud: A Season in Hell and Illuminations* (1998) and Martin Sorrell in *Arthur Rimbaud: Collected Poems – New Translations with parallel French text* (2001). As a *modus operandi*, I shall reproduce the poem itself, identify key areas of difficulty for the translator and then compare and contrast the approaches of Lawler, Treharne and Sorrell:

'Dévotion'
A ma sœur Louise Vanaen de Voringhem: – Sa cornette
bleue tournée à la mer du Nord. – Pour les naufragés.
A ma sœur Léonie Aubois d'Ashby. Baou – l'herbe d'été
bourdonnante et puante. – Pour la fièvre des mères et des
enfants.
A Lulu, – démon – qui a conservé un goût pour les oratoires
du temps des Amies et de son éducation incomplète. Pour les
hommes! A madame ***.
A l'adolescent que je fus. A ce saint vieillard, ermitage ou
mission.
A l'esprit des pauvres. Et à un très haut clergé.
Aussi bien à tout culte en telle place de culte mémoriale et
parmi tels événements qu'il faille se rendre, suivant les aspirations du
moment ou bien notre propre vice sérieux,
Ce soir à Circeto des hautes glaces, grasse comme le poisson, et
enluminée comme les dix mois de la nuit rouge, – (son coeur ambre et
spunck), – pour ma seule prière muette comme ces régions de nuit et
précédant des bravoures plus violentes que ce chaos polaire.
A tout prix et avec tous les airs, même dans des voyages
métaphysiques. – Mais plus *alors*.

Let us first identify some key features. Clearly the poem is based on some conception of anaphora and this would seem to be the litanical format that underlies traditional prayer. Thus we have an 'à'/'pour' structural network with 'à' designating addressees who are being approached on behalf of beneficiaries designated by 'pour'. However, even a cursory inspection of the text reveals that this litanical pattern is subverted and breaks down suggesting that

Rimbaud may very well be embarking upon a parody of prayer.[14] So any attempt to translate 'Dévotion' will necessitate a negotiation of this phenomenon of a text that sets up a structural pattern only to negate it and disengage from it, so becoming a very different text from what it initially promises to be. Many specific challenges arise in the text. While the proper names can obviously be rendered as such (Louise, Léonie, Lulu), their mysterious and enigmatic nature is a strong indication of the cryptic nature of the language in the poem as a whole. The term 'Baou' has already been mentioned as an example of how decoding is invited here and later in the poem we have the term 'spunck' which could have many possible significances and then the very last word in the text *'alors'* which in its italicisation and vague semantic value concludes 'Dévotion' with yet another problem for the translator.

Apart from these individual terms that baffle and confuse, we must also draw attention to the rhythmical patterns at work in the poem which are intimately linked to the structural complexities already alluded to. While the opening three fragments seem to correspond to some stately and measured rhythm – perhaps that befitting prayerful reverence – this pace is altered and quickened in sections four and five which are briefer, less reverent and more throwaway in tone. Section six is altogether different once again since it is a larger block paragraph with an internal logic all of its own. For the first time the devotional 'à' loses its place as first word in the sequence and is absorbed into the body of the paragraph and the dedication here seems to lose much of the specificity of earlier dedications in the poem. It is as if the litany is running out of momentum, as if this prayer is now losing force and direction. There is indeed a casual, throwaway feel to this section as evidenced by the vagueness of 'telle place', the repetition of 'culte' and the loss of a specific person or addressee replaced by more abstract and indeterminate terminology. And yet, the seventh phase of 'Dévotion' brings another switch of tempo and direction as the precise temporal reference 'Ce soir' seems to provide a much needed and temporarily lost focus, and the proper name

14   G. Macklin, 'Prayer and Parody in Rimbaud's "Dévotion"', *French Studies*, LI, no.3 (July 1997), 281–92.

Circeto (be it an individual or a place) heralds a newly found sense of urgency.

One senses that Rimbaud has used this poem to deride conventional systems of prayer and devotion and to arrive in these closing stages at some definition of his own prayer and spirituality ('ma seule prière muette'). The heavy sibilance ('glaces' ... 'grasse' ... 'poisson'), the illumination and colour ('illuminé' ... 'rouge'), the introduction of Rimbaud's cherished polar location,[15] the scatalogical 'spunck' – these are just some indicators that we have arrived at a more significant sequence of image and language, at the evocation of some vision or reality to which true devotion may be justified. As a final sting in the tail, the closing lines play again with 'à' in the expression 'à tout prix' and then confront us with the pithy and enigmatic three word formula by way of closure: '– Mais plus *alors*.' In summary, then, 'Dévotion' stands as a complex, multi-layered and ludic text[16] with multiple changes of pace and tempo, enigmatic shifts of emphasis and a clear intention to experiment with the litanical format of conventional prayer.

Henri Meschonnic writes: 'Traduire un poème est écrire un poème et *doit* être cela d'abord'.[17] How might the translator achieve this aim in engaging with such a difficult text? How, specifically, have Lawler, Treharne and Sorrell measured up to the Meschonnic criterion and dealt with the problems posed above? If we look at the Lawler translation first[18] we find a number of striking elements. He renders 'Baou' as 'Lo-ve-ly' and suggests that 'Baou' is 'beau' pronounced *à l'anglaise*, after a fashion that seems to have been characteristic of Verlaine (Lawler, p.194). He sees the term as evidence of word-play common to Verlaine and Rimbaud and, in particular, their playful approach to English pronunciation. Lawler also suggests that 'Baou' might correspond to '-baud' in Rimbaud and that 'Dévotion' may well

15   Rimbaud's interest in the polar regions is advertised across the *Illuminations*: in 'Après le déluge', 'Métropolitain' and 'Barbare'.
16   Once again it is to Kittang that one should turn for an exposition of the ludic dimension of Rimbaud's writing. See note 10.
17   Henri Meschonnic, *Pour la poétique* (Paris: Gallimard, 1973), p.355.
18   James Lawler, *Rimbaud's Theatre of the Self* (Cambridge, Mass. and London: Harvard University Press, 1992), p.192.

contain hidden references to both names – Verlaine and Rimbaud – and so supports the concept of poet-as-lover within this text. Lawler recognises the hermetic nature of this piece and sees it as 'the poem of fidelity to a commitment' (Lawler, p.191). He also follows a sexual code through the poem, highlighting its allusions to homosexual activity and to scandalous sexual behaviour in the Circeto section. In connection with the final formula '– Mais plus *alors*', Lawler points out that we do not get the 'pour' that we might have expected in line with patterns established earlier in the poem and instead find ourselves confronted with a statement of harsh and absolute refusal. He concludes that 'Dévotion' has the force of a pledge that is ordered with a view to a climax, then to a sudden astonishing and brutal anti-climax (Lawler, p.198). He feels that it is 'a text as intense as it is witty, as lived as it is mysterious, as scatalogical as it is religious, as rich as it is severe' (Ibid.). What emerges very forcefully here, one feels, is the extent to which translation of the poem is informed by a particular interpretative approach to it. To translate is to interpret in many senses and with Lawler we see a critic whose rendering of the poem into English is contingent upon his reading of the text in terms of its meaning, patterns of illusion and structural development. The problem, of course, is that 'Dévotion' (like so many other Rimbaud prose poems) is susceptible to so many different readings and so, by extension, to a wide range of translations.

Turning to Treharne,[19] we find subtle and suggestive differences in the translation of the text. Where Lawler chooses 'cornet' for 'cornette', Treharne selects 'coif'. Treharne does not even attempt to translate 'Baou' but leaves it untouched in translation. Is this a failure to engage with the term, an evasion of the responsibility to attempt some decoding of this bizarre item? Or is it perhaps to be seen more positively as a recognition that the word lies beyond translation and should be left untouched to reverberate in all its strange sonority and otherness? Switching to the end of the translation and to the vexed problem of how to deal with '– Mais plus *alors*', we discover that Treharne goes for '– But an end to *and then*' which is rather different

---

19   *Arthur Rimbaud: 'A Season in Hell' and 'Illuminations'*, new translation by Mark Treharne (London: Dent, 1998).

to Lawler's '– But no longer *then*' and suggests a somewhat different reading of the finale. It should, of course, be pointed out here that whereas Lawler includes translations of poems as a prelude to his critical exegesis of them, what Treharne offers is a series of translations of the poems of *Une saison en enfer* and the *Illuminations without* commentaries on the texts themselves. There are other variations between the two versions. Lawler refers to the 'wit' of the poor, Treharne to their 'spirit', Lawler alludes to 'Les Amies' while Treharne refers to 'Girlfriends', Lawler writes 'To every prize, and with all melodies', while Treharne speaks of 'At any cost and in any guise'. Significantly, Lawler chooses the title 'Devotion' while Treharne selects 'Devotions'. While Treharne's work is a book of translations with no pretension to be a critical study of the prose poems, he does provide an introduction to his work in which he acknowledges how Rimbaud's poetry 'resists orthodox interpretation' (Treharne, p.xx) and confirms its elliptical and enigmatic nature. He works from the principle that Rimbaud's idiosyncratic style with its drift of syntax, strange punctuation and irony and equivocation is predicated upon the repudiation of an existing canon and set of conventions. Rimbaud's work, Treharne reminds us, is plurivocal and open-ended, open to questioning and with a particularly modernist slant:

> All of this suggests a decentred and plurivocal discourse subversive of any convenient assumption a reader might be tempted to make about a piece of writing. Functioning as a strategy of defamiliarisation, the prose poem invites a reading that will ideally always start from scratch without predisposition or any sort of reliable expectation (such as that conferred very often by a title). 'Inventions of the unknown demand new forms', as Rimbaud put it in 'Les Lettres du voyant' (Treharne, p.xxviii).

This is very useful as a reminder that the Rimbaldian prose poem represents a singularly elusive target for the reader, exegete and translator. 'The overall optic of the work is variously fragmented, contradictory, decentred, hallucinatory, distorted', argues Treharne (Ibid.) and if we accept this characterisation of the *Illuminations* then a piece like 'Dévotion' is resistant to rendering in another tongue. No single translation might be capable of capturing all the poem's mystery, enigma and multiplicity of implied meaning. Treharne is right to

assert that Rimbaud's prose poems move us away from the concept of
a single poetic voice and towards 'his view of self as a plurality of
voices' (p.xxx). In his concluding remarks, Treharne argues that these
texts insist on the 'here and now' of the poetic text, on the very act of
construction of the text through language in all the immediacy of that
process. He humbly states that he can only offer 'provisional translation' since any translation is an 'implied act of criticism and
selective judgement' (p.xxxi). So Treharne's 'Devotions' can be seen
as just one attempt to capture 'Dévotion' in English, a 'translation'
that cannot be definitive but which continues a series of endeavours
and invites others to add their 'version' to the list. Indeed, scarcely can
the French term *version* have seemed more appropriate since it implies
one possibility among countless others.

We come now to the third of our three translators, Martin
Sorrell.[20] Like Treharne, Sorrell does not offer any textual commentaries since his objective is translation rather than criticism. Yet
he too makes some interesting remarks in his introductory statement.
He describes the writing in the *Illuminations* as dancing 'on a tightrope between coherence and chaos' and says that in it 'there comes
into being a bedazzlement of events and moments, people and
apparitions, dissolving as quickly as they appear, as if each illumination was like a waking dream' (Sorrell, p.xxiii). For Sorrell, the
Illuminations raise the issue of authorship and he contends that they
represent the achievement of Rimbaud's long-held ambition to
produce objective poetry. As he puts it: 'it is as though the vision were
in the beholder, and the beholder *in* the vision' (Ibid.). He concludes
that Rimbaud's most important artistic influence is on Surrealism in
that his poetry subverts syntax, grammar, form and image. Appropriately, Sorrell acknowledges 'the legion of earlier translators of
Rimbaud' (p.xxviii), asserting that the quality of translation of his
poems has been uneven. He warns against the pedestrian effect of too
faithful a translation: 'where Rimbaud flies, the translator will walk,
counting steps' (Ibid.). At the 'non-faithful' extreme he finds impressive if startling results in the many 'versions' that such translators
have produced of Rimbaud's texts. He comments that he has tried to

20   *Arthur Rimbaud: Collected Poems* (Oxford University Press, 2001).

give his own readers 'a feeling of the vigour of Rimbaud's poetic voice, its explosive force, its brilliance, and its poignancy and delicacy too' (Ibid.).

While Sorrell sees *Une saison en enfer* as particularly resistant to secure, convincing translation, he remarks that the *Illuminations* are full of traps and thanks Treharne for helping him avoid these. It is now time to consider his own translation of 'Dévotion' (Sorrell, p.309) and to assess how he has dealt with the many problems already identified in our observations on Lawler and Treharne. He too goes for the pluralised 'Devotions' as his title and follows Treharne in rendering 'cornette bleue' as 'blue coif'. He endorses Treharne's decision to allow 'Baou' to speak for itself rather than attempt to give it an English form but for 'l'herbe d'été bourdonnante et puante' he gives 'the buzz and stench of summer grass', whereas Treharne offers 'buzzing stink'. For 'conservé' he offers 'preserved' (Treharne gives 'kept') and for 'très haut clergé' he suggests 'a very high clergy' where Treharne proposes 'very high-ranking'. Despite these minor divergences, however, one is struck by the near identity of the two translations up to this point. They are also remarkably convergent in their rendering of the Circeto paragraph even though Sorrell translates 'hautes glaces' as 'heights of ice' while Treharne goes for 'icy heights' and the former renders 'bravoures' as 'deeds of daring' while the latter selects 'exploits'.

However, there are some suggestive and interesting differences in how they deal with both section six (beginning 'Aussi bien à tout culte...') and the concluding paragraph of the poem. Section six is fascinating since it seems to deviate from the litanical format and to introduce a new tone into the piece:

> Aussi bien à tout culte en telle place de culte mémoriale
> et parmi tels événements qu'il faille se rendre, suivant
> les aspirations du moment ou bien notre propre vice sérieux,

Sorrell offers this version:

> Equally to all denominations in whatever place of memorial
> worship and among whatever events it might be necessary to

> witness, depending on the aspirations of the moment or our
> own major vice,

Treharne's translation reads:

> Also to all worship in any place of memorial worship and
> among any events it may be necessary to attend, depending
> on the aspirations of the moment or indeed our own important
> vice,

There are certainly more discrepancies here than in any other area of the two respective translations. One might very well feel that this section of 'Dévotion' is designed to capture the breakdown of the anaphora, the traditional litany of devotional prayer that the poem had seemed to espouse. There is a desultory, irreverent tone in this section and there is a sense of language petering out into insignificance before the poem seems to galvanise itself with the new focus on Circeto in the penultimate section.

Finally, it is important to add some comments on how the three translators deal with sections seven and eight at the end of 'Dévotion'. One feels that Rimbaud injects a fresh sense of urgency into the poem at this point, a sharpened focus in the specific reference to 'Ce soir' and arguably a redefined meaning of prayer itself. Treharne and Sorrell converge remarkably closely in their rendering of section seven but Lawler opts for 'ambergris' rather than 'amber' and prefers 'mute' to 'silent' in endering the locution 'ma seule prière muette'. For 'bravoures', Lawler gives us 'bravuras', Sorrell 'deeds of daring' and Treharne 'exploits'. However, there are more interesting divergences in the three translations where the highly ambiguous closing section is concerned. It reads:

> A tout prix et avec tous les airs, même dans des
> voyages métaphysiques. – Mais plus *alors*.

It is this last section, and particularly the three words after the dash, that have always given most trouble to those attempting a definitive exegesis of 'Dévotion'. I now give the three translators' versions of this sequence:

To every prize, and with all melodies, even in metaphysical
excursions. – But no longer *then* (Lawler).
Whatever the cost, whatever shape or form, even on
metaphysical journeys. – But no more *then* (Sorrell).
At any cost and in any guise, even on metaphysical
journeys. – But an end to *and then* (Treharne).

One notices instantly that Lawler goes for a more literal rendering of
'prix' and 'airs' than the other two and this divergence crucially raises
the question of what Rimbaud is up to in this finale. Does the
expression 'A tout prix...' necessitate a literal reading in line with all
previous dedications in the poem or is he not here playing with the
prepositional 'à' of dedication and at the same time signposting a new,
more fluid form of prayer? The translating of 'avec tous les airs' as 'in
any guise' or 'whatever shape or form' would be consonant with a
project to disrupt the original litany and to create a redefinition of
prayer. Bernard and Guyaux have written of Rimbaud as a 'poète
ludique, jouant avec son lecteur comme le chat avec la souris, sans lui
donner accès au sens de ce qu'il écrit' (*Œuvres*, p.249).

Also interesting is a consideration of the three renderings of
'– Mais plus *alors*'. Sorrell opts for '– But no more *then*', Treharne's
version is '– But an end to *and then*', and in Lawler we find '– But no
longer *then*'. Treharne's rendering stands out here in that he chooses
'*and then*' for '*alors*' whereas the other two translators go for '*then*'.
However, what may well be more intriguing in Treharne's case is that,
whether by accident or design, he manages to include the preposition
'to' in his version of the finale. This strikes one as particularly
felicitous since 'Dévotion' is a text that has been predicated upon the
use of 'à' as the preposition of dedication in conventional prayer and
the subsequent ludic displacement of this preposition as Rimbaud
seems to move from the traditional litany to a reinvention of prayer in
the latter stages of the text. Incidentally, this is a kind of structural
development replicated many times over in differing contexts in the
Illuminations. It might very well be that Rimbaud broke the term
'*alors*' down in his mind to 'à' and 'lors' with not just a ludic
intention but with the serious notion of dispensing with traditional
forms of worship. This would be consonant with his thinking in poems
from 'Les Pauvres à l'église' and 'Les Premières Communions' to

'Matin' where he calls for an end to superstition and 'Génie' where he speaks of an end to 'les agenouillages anciens'. However, irrepective of the poet's thematic intentions, Lawler, Treharne and Sorrell are three among many confronted with a linguistic audaciousness that arguably lies beyond translation. The *traduttore* of 'Dévotion' may well inevitably be a *traditore*.

ROSEMARY LLOYD

The parts translators try to reach

In the 1970s the Heineken Beer Company ran a long, witty, and inventive series of advertisements claiming (indeed showing) that their beer reached parts inaccessible to other beers. Any translator might wish to acquire some blend of malt and yeast that reached those parts of a text that seem resistant to translation, which almost by definition are the very parts that make one want to translate them. Guy Lee, introducing his brilliant version of Ovid's *Amores*, puts the point powerfully and succinctly:

> Seven years ago I thought I could do a fairly literal translation of the *Amores* into modern English, but a long struggle with the first few poems convinced me that the letter kills. Literal translation can be totally misleading. Usually the tone is all wrong. Take the opening couplet. H. T. Riley in 1896 thought the literal 'meaning' was this: *I was preparing to write of arms and impetuous warfare in serious numbers, the subject-matter being suited to the measure.* But it is inconceivable that this is what the poet 'means'. He means he meant to write an epic, in hexameters, the regular epic metre from Homer onwards, but he does not mean it seriously. He means the reader to think of the *Aeneid*. He means to sound grandiose, undercutting epic dignity by the dactylic movement of the whole couplet.

And after magisterially unpeeling a few more layers of suggestion Lee concludes: 'And when all this has been said his poetic "meaning" is still not exhausted. No translator has a hope of getting it all in.'[1]

Part of what proves so difficult to 'get in' for translators of poetry is the element to which Baudelaire alludes when he explains his refusal to add translations of Edgar Allen Poe's verse to his brilliant versions of the short stories: 'Tout vrai amateur de poésie reconnaîtra que [...] ma très humble et très dévouée faculté de

---

1   Guy Lee, *Ovid's 'Amores'* (London: John Murray, 1968), p.199.

traducteur ne me permet pas de suppléer aux voluptés absentes du rythme et de la rime.'[2] Octavio Paz is much more reassuring, but he is also far more bland: 'Everything we do is translation and all translations are in a way creations', he affirms, although he blithely contradicts himself elsewhere in asserting that 'Originality in a given translation is untrue in that no text is entirely original because language itself, in its essence, is already a translation'.[3] Other translation theorists can also offer affirmations and strategies that, however much their essays might command respect on a theoretical and intellectual level,[4] are not entirely bereft of ambiguity when applied to the praxis of what is often considered the invisible work of translation.[5] Such is the case for both Walter Benjamin, basing his support for literal translations on his belief in a suprahistorical kinship of languages, and Emanuel Levinas revealing his optimistic conviction that communication occurs despite apparently insurmountable barriers between languages and across time.[6] Roland Barthes offers a more pragmatic solution in arguing that translating a text is not an act of conferring meaning but rather an evaluation of the plurality of the text's meanings.[7] Clive Scott, probably the best metrician of French verse currently writing in English, proposes an ambitious and intimidating programme anchored by the need to find parallel sound

2   Charles Baudelaire, *Œuvres complètes*, edited by Claude Pichois (Paris: Gallimard, 1976), II, 347.

3   Quoted in Willis Barnstone, *The Poetics of Translation* (New Haven: Yale University Press, 1993), p.5.

4   In this regard they recall certain illustrious writers of recipes: in regard to Elizabeth David's command to 'melt the tomatoes' for example see Julian Barnes's essay 'The Land without Brussels Sprouts' in *Something to Declare* (London: Picador, 2002).

5   This is the title of E. Kristal's recent study focusing on Borges and translation. In using it I am thinking of those many translations where the translator's name is absent or buried in the front matter.

6   Walter Benjamin, 'The Task of the Translator', in *Illuminations. Essays and Reflections* edited by Hannah Arendt, translated by Harry Zohn (New York: Schocken, 1969) and Emmanuel Levinas, *L'Autrement qu'être ou au-delà de l'essence* (The Hague: Martinus Nijoff, 1974).

7   See Roland Barthes, *S/Z*, section II (Paris: Seuil, 1976).

groupings.[8] Finding a translation of, say, Ovid's opening couplet that comes close to suggesting what the poet might have meant demands something more than belief in suprahistorical kinships and mystic communications, something closer to the programme implicit in the writings of Barthes or Scott, but that is basically a question of trial and error, and a great deal of luck.

In pondering translation, its limits, and its possibilities, it is often illuminating to explore what other translators have achieved, comparing their versions of a specific text, as William Gass does, brilliantly and revealingly, for Rilke in his 1999 study entitled *Reading Rilke. Reflections on the Problems of Translation.*[9] Adopting this approach to the works of the French symbolist poet, Stéphane Mallarmé, whose dense, multi-layered work is among the most resistant to translation, provides yet another indication of the extent to which his poetry exemplifies his conviction that:

> Le vers qui de plusieurs vocables refait un mot total, neuf, étranger à la langue et comme incantatoire, achève cet isolement de la parole: niant, d'un trait souverain, le hasard demeuré aux termes malgré l'artifice de leur retrempe alternée en le sens et la sonorité, et vous cause cette surprise de n'avoir ouï jamais tel fragment ordinaire d'élocution, en même temps que la réminiscence de l'objet nommé baigne dans une neuve atmosphère.[10]

8   See his *Translating Baudelaire* (Exeter: University of Exeter Press, 2000).

9   William Gass, *Reading Rilke. Reflections on the Problems of Translation* (New York: Alfred A. Knopf, 1999). In making such comparisons I will do my best to follow Barnstone's advice: 'Don't eat a prickly pear for a peach and make unfriendly faces' (p.270).

10   Mallarmé, *Œuvres complètes*, edited by Henri Mondor and G. Jean-Aubry (Paris: Gallimard, 1945), p.279. For recent studies of the question of Mallarmé and translation see for instance Toby Garfitt, 'A Plural Approach to Translating Mallarmé', *Forum for Modern Language Studies*, 34:4 (Oct. 1998), 345–52; Judd H. Hubert, 'Mallarmé and Critic-Friendly Translators' in Robert Greer Cohn and Gerald Gillespie (eds) *Mallarmé in the Twentieth Century* (Cranbury, NJ: Associated UP, 1998), pp.159–66; David Mus, 'Should I Transliterate...', *Po&sie*, 85 (1998), 159–68; Serge Gavronsky, 'Mallarmé in the USA', *Talisman,* 20 (Winter 1999–2000), 8–14; Henry Weinfield, 'A Test of Translation: "Donner un sens plus pur aux mots de la tribu..." (A Reply to Serge Gavronsky)', *Talisman,* 20 (Winter 1999–2000), 15–17, and also his 'Ceding the Initiative to Words: Mallarmé, Lyric Poetry, and the Problem of

The challenges of seizing even some of these aspects of Mallarmé's poetics in an English translation are brought sharply to light through comparing selected translations of his beautiful sonnet 'Le Cygne'. In this sonnet, a swan, trapped in ice, struggles to break free, knowing that even if it succeeds in liberating itself, it will be sullied by contact with the mud. Irrevocably trapped, the swan dies, to be metamorphosed into the constellation we call Cygnus, the Swan. The quatrains capture the swan's final efforts to escape:

> Le vierge, le vivace et le bel aujourd'hui
> Va-t-il nous déchirer avec un coup d'aile ivre
> Ce dur lac oublié que hante sous le givre
> Le transparent glacier des vols qui n'ont pas fui!
>
> Un cygne d'autrefois se souvient que c'est lui,
> Magnifique mais qui sans espoir se délivre
> Pour n'avoir pas chanté la région où vivre
> Quand du stérile hiver a resplendi l'ennui.[11]

While the meaning of these dense and evocative quatrains might not immediately leap off the page, several elements that the translator needs to capture are instantly clear. First, it is indisputable that Mallarmé, in creating for this sonnet that 'new atmosphere' in which his subject bathes, does not resort to archaisms, erudite words, or unusual terms. Words may not always appear in the traditional order – of the three opening adjectives, for instance, only 'bel' would normally precede the noun – but while this confers on these words possibilities beyond those normally associated with them, it is not enough to justify translators in choosing a form of language that harks back to a dim past, but merely one that is determined to encourage the reader to rediscover the meanings of familiar terms that we may too readily take for granted. Translating it, therefore, it will not be defensible to

---

Translation', *Talisman,* 20 (Winter 1999–2000), 3–7; and Richard Sieburth, 'Ms Fr 270: Prelude to a Translation', *Esprit Créateur,* 40:3 (Fall, 2000), 97–107.

11   Mallarmé, *Œuvres complètes*, edited by Bertrand Marchal (Paris: Gallimard, 1998), I, 36. The second volume of this new edition has not yet appeared, hence the need to refer to the prose writings in the 1945 edition.

use the kind of lexicon or syntax that struggles for effect through deploying archaisms or rare words.[12] The sentence order in this poem is not especially unusual either: it has about it much of the rhythm of educated speech. Whereas Mallarmé frequently alters habitual syntactical structures, demanding translations that generate constructions capable of creating an equivalent sense of surprise in the reader, this poem neither needs nor justifies such an approach.

That so beautiful a sonnet has inspired many translations is not surprising, but what may be less expected is the startling differences those translations reveal not just in technique and choice, but in their initial premises about the function of translation. In contrasting them, and above all in trying to assess them, I am deeply aware of the difficulties with which the translators have to contend, of the compromises that certain choices impose, and of the rank ingratitude of the mere act of comparison, but in doing so I hope to indicate something of the nature both of translation and of Mallarmé.

A translation driven above all by pedagogical concerns offers a suitable starting point in that it makes its initial premises so clear. Charles Chadwick's 1996 prose version runs as follows:

Will this be the day, dawning lively and lovely, when my creative talent will at last soar upwards, like a bird breaking free, with one wild blow of its wing, from the frozen waters of a lonely lake, beneath whose frosty surface lies a transparent glacier made up of successive days of failure.
A former day remembers that it too was once like a magnificent swan, but that, not having sung in time of its true home, the sky, before the numbing onset of sterile winter inactivity, it was only with a feeling of hopelessness that it finally dragged itself away across the ice.[13]

---

12   The archaising translation has, in fact, been inflicted on Baudelaire more than on Mallarmé (see my *Baudelaire's World* (Ithaca, NY: Cornell University Press, 2002)) Since fewer of Mallarmé's poems address a 'tu', he has usually escaped the clumsiness of those who choose to translate *tu* as 'thou' with all the archaic verb forms such a choice imposes.

13   Charles Chadwick, *The Meaning of Mallarmé: a bilingual edition of his 'Poésies' and 'Un coup de dés'* (Aberdeen, Scotland: Scottish Cultural Press, 1996), p.37.

As the title of his collection, *The Meaning of Mallarmé*, suggests, this is a translator who is also and perhaps primarily a commentator, using his English versions to explain what he believes the poem 'means': the swan, therefore, appears not as a bird so much as 'my creative talent', the flights that have never taken place are glossed as 'successive days of failure', the swan of the past (which I interpret to mean that the swan, having lost what made it a swan, its purity and its power to fly, can think of itself only in the past) ceases to be a swan at all and becomes 'a former day'. But even leaving aside differences of surface interpretation, is this what Mallarmé 'means'? Does he intend to limit the swan to a one-for-one allegory in which the bird stands for poetic talent? Doesn't he mean to suggest something through the sharp 'i' sound of the rhymes, through the possible pun in 'coup d'aile ivre' (a blow of the wing) which also sounds like 'coup des livres' (a blow of the books)? And isn't there a significant difference in effect between the English version's simile (the day was like a swan) and the French poet's metaphor, which leaves to the reader the task and pleasure of discovering the point of comparison? Does prose, to go back to even more fundamental questions, mean what poetry means? What does rhythm, the ordered rhythm of verse rather than that of prose, add to meaning? Chadwick's translation is a useful point of departure in that it so clearly articulates its purposes and in doing so points so plainly to both the possibilities and the limitations of such an approach.

Contrasting various verse translations projects a different light on the question, revealing additional facets of the process by which Mallarmé's object is made to 'bathe in its new atmosphere'. Thus David Paul's version, with its valiant attempt to capture something of the sound values in Mallarmé's rhymes, offers the following quatrains:

> Today...
> This had lake forgot, haunted beneath its frost
> —Will today in its beauty, vigour, virginity
> With one wild wing-beat break the ice, set free
> The translucent glacier of flights never released!

A swan of another era recalls how it is he
Who must resign himself, magnificent yet captive,
For never having sung that region where to live
When sterile winter dazzles with its inanity.[14]

David Paul's translation does more than strive to create an English equivalent for the rhyme scheme and images of the original. It also draws, although not always advantageously, on a knowledge of the broader context of Mallarmé's poetry. 'Inanity,' for instance, is instantly recognisable as a word that has crept in from one of the poet's most famous formulations: 'l'aboli bibelot d'inanité sonore.'[15] Mallarméan though it may be, 'inanity' does not feature in the swan poem, which speaks rather of *ennui*, the profound boredom seen as the *mal du siècle*, the century's besetting illness. *Ennui* may make the sufferer feel that everything is inane, but it is not in itself inanity. The main problem with this translation, however, concerns its structure and syntax: Mallarmé makes us wait for the subject of the verb, 'aujourd'hui', a word that, through surprising the reader by appearing as a noun, helps shatter the ice deposited by habitual modes of reading. Mallarmé accumulates his adjectives, building up to the subject, delaying the setting of scene or the depiction of the protagonist. Paul, however, begins with the original sonnet's third line, using a formula that is not only archaic – 'this had lake forgot' – but that also makes the lake the subject, not the object of forgetting (it is forgotten in winter because it no longer has the watery quality that designates lake, just as later the swan will be described as a former swan because it has lost that capacity to fly that designates bird). Changing the subject results in this case in a weakening of the focus, which Mallarmé's sonnet maintains unshakeably on the swan. Worse still is that unidiomatic translation of 'la région où vivre' as 'that region where to live'. As a result, it is Mallarmé's complex, multiple meanings that are held 'magnificent yet captive' in Paul's version.

The Irish poet Ciaran Carson offers a very different vision of the swan in his translation, one more sensitive to the poem's metaphorical

14   David Paul, *Poison and Vision: Poems and Prose of Baudelaire, Mallarmé and Rimbaud* (Salzburg: Salzburg University, 1996), pp.177–9.
15   Mallarmé (1998), I, 37.

values and its semantic density. That sensitivity is already evident in the somewhat contrived title conferred on the untitled sonnet in an attempt to signal, however desperately, that in French the word for 'swan' is also a pun on sign:

> At the Sign of the Swan
> The beautiful today, untouched by human hand,
> Swings towards us with a stagger of its drunken wing
> To crash the frozen lake as cold as anything,
> Ghosted by the glacial distances it never spanned!
>
> A fabled swan the image of an ampersand
> Is mute, for all his freed necessity to sing
> His icy habitat of winter's fosterling,
> Where dim suns yawned their tedium across the land.[16]

The rhyme scheme is maintained (although at the cost of the banal filler 'as cold as anything'), the rhythms are good, and even if we are unkind enough to wonder if the dim suns in the last line are some kind of Chinese dish, we can still hear in that line a kind of Yeatsian monster dragging itself toward Bethlehem to be born. But this is not translation so much as re-creation, in which accuracy is often sacrificed: the 'region où vivre', for instance, is that of the warm lands with open water to which wild swans migrate in the European fall. It was of these lands that the swan should have sung, not this version's 'icy habitat' and 'dim suns'. In addition, 'ghosted by the glacial distances' is conjured more out of the need for sound play than any compunction to convey Mallarmé's image of the flight from winter's threat to summer's promise. Whatever its value as a poem in its own right, Carson's revisions result in Mallarmé's poem being more profoundly metamorphosed than the Syrinx of Ovid's tale, the maiden transformed into a reed.

Kate Flores provides a quite different version for the 1962 Doubleday bilingual anthology:

---

16   Ciaran Carson, *The Alexandrine Plan* (Loughcrew, Ireland: The Gallery Press, 1998), p.51.

The pristine, the perennial, the beauteous today
May it crack for us with lunge of drunken wing
This hard, forsaken lake haunted beneath the crust
By the crystalline ice of flights not ever flown!

–A quondam swan recalls that it is he,
Magnificent but in despair of extricating himself,
Having left unsung the region where to be
When winter glistened sterile with ennui.[17]

This starts well, and remains fairly faithful, although 'crystalline ice' carries different connotations from the frozen movement of 'transparent glacier'. Above all, there is a considerable difference in meaning between Mallarmé's question 'will it tear?' and the translator's plea 'may it crack'. In the translation, the narrative voice longs for a particular solution, one moreover that will merely crack the ice, while in the original, that voice reveals intellectual curiosity and perhaps resignation rather than emotion, and the voice is profoundly aware that if the swan's freedom is to be obtained it will be so only at considerable cost: for freedom to be gained, something has to be destroyed, and to convey that suggestion Mallarmé uses a far from banal verb, 'déchirer', implying rend apart rather than just crack. The violence inherent in the situation is intensified by the implication that the swan may also be rent apart, an implication conveyed in the French sentence structure, where the indirect object 'us' comes before the direct object 'the lake', with a flickering suggestion that we (swan, watcher, poet, reader) will not just witness but also share whatever fate befalls the lake. The second quatrain in Flores's version collapses under the strain, with the introduction of 'quondam', a word described by the Oxford English Dictionary as rare and thus no parallel for the everyday word 'autrefois', the weak rhythm of the second line and the clumsy, unidiomatic expression 'the region where to be', although its final line regains some ground with that forceful and cogent 'When winter glistened sterile with ennui'.

17 In Angel Flores, *An Anthology of French Poetry from Nerval to Valéry in English Translation with French Originals* (Garden City, New York: Doubleday, 1962), p.159.

Three further examples reveal how much variation there can be, even in translators who seek close equivalences of the text. In a Proust-haunted version published in 1957, C. F. MacIntyre suggests:

> The lively, lovely and virginal today
> will its drunken wings tear for us with a blow
> this lake hard and forgotten, haunted below
> the frost by the clear glacier of flights not made?
>
> A swan of past times remembers he's the one
> magnificent but striving without hope
> for not having sung a land where he could stop
> when the ennui of sterile winter has shone.[18]

Ten years later, G. S. Fraser would propose the following, crisper translation, suggestive of American modernist poets:

> The virgin, bright and beautiful to-day
> Dare it now shatter with a drunken wing
> This hard, forgotten lake, this ice where cling
> These flights of mine that never flew away...
> Once was a swan, remembers it is he,
> Magnificent but hopeless in his strife,
> For never having sung the realms of life
> When winter shone in bleak sterility.[19]

And the productive team of Patricia Terry and Maurice Z. Shroder provide this:

> Will never and alive the beautiful today
> Shatter with a blow of drunken wing
> This hard lake, forgotten, haunted under rime,
> By the transparent glacier, flights unflown!

18   Mallarmé, *Selected Poems*, trans C. F. MacIntyre (Berkeley, CA: University of California Press, 1957), p.83.
19   William Jay Smith, *Poems from France* (New York: Thomas Y. Crowell, 1967), p.109.

> A swan of long ago remembers now that he,
> Magnificent but lost to hope, is doomed
> For having failed to sing the realms of life
> When the ennui of sterile winter gleamed.[20]

In offering 'never and alive' as a translation of 'le vierge, le vivace', Terry and Shroder seem to have adopted something similar to the parallel sound structures that Clive Scott would later propose. The repeated 'v' is captured neatly in their version, where the word 'never' is justified by the suggestion of the virgin never having accepted desire. While they have abandoned rhyme, they leave its ghostly image in their version through the translation of 'givre' as 'rime'. And 'the realms of life' for 'la région où vivre' has the merit of being both idiomatic and acceptably accurate.

Most satisfying among those I have read is Henry Weinfield's 1994 translation, which combines accuracy with a good poetic and aesthetic sense:

> The virginal, vibrant, and beautiful dawn,
> Will a beat of its drunken wing not suffice
> To rend this hard lake haunted beneath the ice
> By the transparent glacier of flights never flown?
>
> A swan of former times remembers it's the one
> Magnificent but hopelessly struggling to resist
> For never having sung of a land in which to exist
> When the boredom of the sterile winter has shone.[21]

And then perhaps a personal attempt:

> The pure, perennial and beautiful today,
> Will it rip us apart with a wild wing's blow
> This hard forgotten lake that's haunted below
> By the transparent glacier of flights never made?

---

20   In *Stéphane Mallarmé, Selected Poetry and Prose*, ed. Mary Ann Caws (New York: New Directions, 1982), pp.45–7.

21   Henry Weinfield, *Stéphane Mallarmé: Collected Poems*. Translated and with a Commentary by Henry Weinfield (Berkeley, CA: University of California Press, 1994), p.67.

A swan of the past remembers that it's he
Magnificent but with no hope breaking away
For failing to sing of the regions far away
When winter's sterility glittered its ennui.

Translators, understandably, tend to stand on one another's shoulders, drawing on the work of their predecessors for both positive and negative inspiration. To turn from the icy realms of 'Le Cygne' to the various translations of the opening lines of Mallarmé's paean to summer and desire, 'L'Après-midi d'un faune', and especially to set them down in chronological order, is to see something of how the baton is handed over from one translator to another, but it is also to sense the translator's essential isolation, faced with a text which in many ways is irreducible to any language other than its own.

In her collection of translations published in 1928, Dorothy Martin is among the first to grapple with the difficulties of conveying that deceptively simple opening:

Ces nymphes, je les veux perpétuer.
                Si clair,
Leur incarnat léger, qu'il voltige dans l'air
Assoupi de sommeils touffus.
                Aimai-je un rêve?[22]

Martin's version preserves the quiet tone, even if it struggles, as all later translators struggle, to seize the density of the opening line:

I would those nymphs perpetuate.
                So fair,
Their tender rose, it hovers in the air
Tufted with sleep.
                This love a dream? And gone?[23]

Those questions arise with what seems perfect simplicity, the kind of simplicity achieved only after much thought. In 1945 Wilfrid Thorley

---

22   Mallarmé, 1998, p.22.
23   Dorothy Martin, *Sextette: Translations from the French Symbolists* (London: The Scholaris Press, 1928), p.43.

would work harder, to less effect, using a layout that moreover fails to preserve the hesitations, pauses, and movement of the original:

> I would perpetuate these nymphs. How frail
> Their sunlit incarnation like a trail
> Of drowsy down upwafted! Is it true
> My love was all a dream?[24]

'Sunlit incarnation' moreover appears to be a misreading of 'incarnat' which evokes less the concept of an idea made form than the colour of flesh.

In 1951 Eugene Delroi offered a version that draws even sharper attention to what is particularly problematic in these opening lines, where the faun, returning slowly to consciousness after sleep, grapples with the impossibility of determining what is memory and what illusion, what happened and what his senses and desires urge him to believe happened:

> I would have these nymphs live on.
>   So pure
> Their delicate incarnation drifts in air
> Drowsy with cramming sleep.
>   Do I love but a dream?[25]

'Would have' in the opening line is not only too formal but insufficiently urgent for 'je veux' in which we hear the imperious, childish expression of a demand that cannot be met. The present tense of 'Do I love' falls to seize the implications in the faun's sudden realisation that whatever happened, whether it was lived or dreamed, is now past. And 'drowsy with cramming sleep' suggests a despairing lunge at the network of suggestions, implications, and echoes in Mallarmé's 'assoupi de sommeils touffus'.

C. F. McIntyre builds on previous attempts to create this 1957 version, which nicely captures the pauses and rhythms, but risks in the last line a reading that is at once both too definite and too dismissive:

24   Wilfrid Thorley, *The French Muse* (London: Frederick Muller, 1945), p.61.
25   Stéphane Mallarmé, *Afternoon of a Faun*, trans. Eugene Delroi (Chicago: Taurus Press, 1951), n. p.

> I would perpetuate these nymphs.
> So clear,
> their light carnation, that it drifts on the air
> drowsy with tufted slumbers.
> So I loved a dream?[26]

In comparison with this airy and mobile translation, Frederick Morgan's strikes the ear as pedestrian, attaining a certain level of textual accuracy without conveying those elements embedded in rhythm and image:

> These nymphs, I would make them endure.
> Their delicate flesh-tint so clear,
> It hovers yet upon the air
> heavy with foliage of sleep.
> Was it a dream I loved?[27]

It would seem that knowing that aspects of a poem have eluded the best efforts of previous translators can sometimes provoke desperate measures. Thus, the difficulty all these translators face in finding a satisfactory version appears to have goaded Hayden Carruth in his 1981 publication into an offering freighted with too much baggage to succeed:

> These nymphs whom I itch to perpetuate–
> so clear
> Their lightness, yet incarnate, flesh of this air
> Rosy with woodland slumber.
>
> Was loving a dream?[28]

It is not just the physicality of that itch that proves embarrassingly problematic if not parodic, but also the reading of 'Leur incarnat

26   Mallarmé, *Selected Poems*, trans C. F. MacIntyre (Berkeley, CA: University of California Press, 1957), pp.45–7.
27   In Angel Flores, *An Anthology of French Poetry from Nerval to Valéry in English Translation with French Originals* (Garden City, New York: Doubleday, 1962), pp.152–6.
28   Stéphane Mallarmé, *L'Après-midi d'un faune*, trans. Hayden Carruth (Tucson, AZ: Ironwood Press, 1981), n. p.

léger' as a pun folding together the colour (Carruth's 'rosy') with the idea of their being incarnate, truly there in flesh and blood, not just in the imagination, a point Mallarmé – vitally – leaves unresolved. Just as the pleonasm of incarnate flesh is troubling, so also is the translation of 'Assoupi de sommeils touffus' as 'woodland slumber' which jettisons the implication that sleep itself is like a thickly wooded forest, replacing it with the much more banal idea that sleep merely took place in the woods.

Patricia Terry and Maurice Z. Shroder are more successful in facing those challenges in their contribution to Mary Ann Caws's 1982 anthology of selections from Mallarmé:

> I would perpetuate these nymphs.
> So clear,
> The glow of them, so nimble in the air
> Drowsiness encumbers–
> Did I dream that love?[29]

Building on all these, one might try something like this, something that leaves aside the rhymes in the hopes of coming a little closer to an English equivalent, something that tries to seize the tone of the faun as well as the density of the images:

> I want those nymphs to last forever.
> So bright
> Their floating rosy glow, it quivers in the air
> Drowsy with branching sleep.
> Was it just a dream I loved?

Several inferences might be drawn from comparing these translations in a parallel reading with the original. First, that seeking rhymes frequently, although not inevitably, leads to distortions, and given the considerable dialectal range in the pronunciation of English vowels, often risks in any case failing to satisfy at least part of the audience (the rhyme of 'one' with 'shone' above is a case in point). The search for similarity of sound, especially consonantal, may prove

29   In *Stéphane Mallarmé, Selected Poetry and Prose*, ed. Mary Ann Caws (New York: New Directions, 1982), pp.63–9.

more successful. Archaisms, whether of syntax or semantics, fail to
convey Mallarmé's language, which is more the product of familiar
words in an unfamiliar context (*ptyx* is a playful exception) and a
sentence structure placed under extreme stress through compression,
ellipticism, and inversion. The semantic density of Mallarmé's language, its suggestions of word play and its echoes of similar terms,
challenge the translator to find words equally rich and dense, but not
to the extent of producing misreadings: as the problem of the word
'incarnat' in 'L'Après-midi d'un faune' indicates, it may be better to
chose the dominant implication rather than distort the poet's meaning
by over-punning. Rhythm seems to be the area in which the translator
is most likely to come close to Mallarmé, or as close as it is possible
for an inflected language to approximate one that is not. But since
rhythm is not just perceived by the ear but also appreciated by the eye,
the airy patterns of Mallarmé's opening to 'L'Après-midi d'un faune'
and the white space between the quatrains of the French sonnet form
need to be maintained. Translators who impose the structures of the
English sonnet on 'Le vierge, le vivace et le bel aujourd'hui', as for
instance G. S. Fraser does in the extract quoted above, introduce a
further misrepresentation for readers who cannot enjoy Mallarmé in
the original.

Nothing gets you so rapidly under the skin of a text as an attempt
at translating it; nothing makes you so aware of its idiosyncrasies, its
wordplay, its sounds, and its rhythms. Few things make students talk
more about poetry than criticising a group of translations of a poem
they have read: all of them can see elements that fall short, and they
feel free to tell you what they think, where they feel less free to
criticise the poem itself. And nothing perhaps is quite so humbling as
trying to do such translation for yourself, and realising how hard it is
to reach those inaccessible parts translators try to reach.

PAUL GIFFORD

Translating the spirituality of Absence: Valéry's 'Station sur la terrasse'

The sense of spirituality has often, in French writing of the last hundred and fifty years, abandoned received and orthodox religious forms and taken refuge instead in art, particularly in poetry. In the century just closed, it has been mainstream, almost neo-orthodox, for poets to follow Mallarme's orphic design to 'reprendre à la religion notre bien'.[1]

Following Nietzsche, the much rationalised Western soul has, more generally, eliminated its Platonic *arrière-monde*. Amputated in self-understanding from the homeland of its belonging, increasingly reflexive, criticist, deconstructionist, twentieth-century Eros remains nonetheless – by reason of these very choices – haunted by an essential Absence which it claims and cherishes as a last clue to its own 'transcendence' of the mundane and the material. With the ontological homeland disappears the possibility of any conceptual word, any philosophic or theological naming of the signs of being.

Poetry here recovers as its province the spiritual stirrings of which philosophy has lost its competence to speak and which religious faith has, for the larger number, ceased to be able to address cogently. The counsel given by Paul Valéry's psalm 'Onomastique' is, in this sense, a charter of the twentieth-century poet: 'Ecoute le son de la Voix, Vierge ou Veuve de mots'(*C*, XXI, 870–1).

---

1   See Paul Valéry, *Cahiers*, 29 t. *in facsimile* (Paris: CNRS, 1957–1961), XVI, 326 (abbreviation: *C*). A youthful letter to Pierre Louys, written at the time of Mallarmé's intensest influence, already proclaims that 'la Beauté a été depuis le christianisme mordue au cœur par la chimère' and that the modern artist must reclaim his own; see H. Mondor, *Précocité de Valéry* (Paris: Gallimard, 1957), p.223.

This 'poetic spirituality' is finely and quintessentially epitomised in a prose poem of 1942 by the same writer, which is to be found in one of the last *Cahiers*. This text, usually designated by its semi-official title 'Station sur la terrasse', represents a formidable challenge to the translator: in respect of its cultural intertext, its shifts of tonal register, its abstract musicality, its diamantine suggestiveness, and the sheer athletic precision of its rendering of things at the limit of the sayable, unseen and yet profoundly known. We may take the French original as starting point for a discussion of the challenges it poses to the translator and of appropriate strategies of response. The outcome will, it is hoped, be a minimally leaky and maximally effective English rendering:

θθ ou Mémoires de Moi

Question et Discours
Que pourrait, que devrait aujourd'hui faire un 'poète'? Etat des choses de l'âme, de l'esprit et de cet art.

(1) Station sur la terrasse −

Je suis monté sur la terrasse, au plus haut de la demeure de mon esprit − Là, conduisent l'âge, les réflexions, les prévisions − les justifiées, les démenties, les coups excellents, les échecs, l'oubli des personnes, des noms propres, des articles de critique, etc.
Et scintillent dans le ciel de nuit poétique les constellations, seulement soumises aux lois de l'Univers du langage, qui se lèvent, se couchent, reparaîtront…
Là, *Hérodiade*, l'*Après-Midi*, le *Tombeau de Gautier* − etc., mais il n'y a plus de noms d'auteurs. Les personnes *n'importent plus*.
Et comme j'étais à considérer ces 'signes', la question ci-dessus *se posa* −
Se posa comme un temps d'arrêt et de muette puissance, comme un grand oiseau tout à coup tombé sur mes épaules et chargé tout à coup en un poids. Mais ce poids d'un grand oiseau se faisait sentir capable de m'enlever. Et il me ravit, moi et mes 70 ans, moi et mes souvenirs, mes observations, mes préférences, et mon injustice essentielle.
Et surtout je connus toute la valeur et la beauté, toute l'excellence de *tout ce que je n'ai pas fait*.
Voilà ton œuvre − me dit une voix.
Et je vis tout ce que je n'avais pas fait.

Et je connus de mieux en mieux que je n'étais pas celui qui avait fait ce que j'ai fait – et que j'étais celui qui n'avait pas fait ce que je n'avais pas fait. – Ce que je n'avais pas fait était donc parfaitement beau, parfaitement conforme à l'impossibilité de le faire, et cela (ce que ne savent pas les autres) – je le voyais, je le concevais, et je dirais même que je le tenais et le touchais avec une extraordinaire et extrême Précision.

Si tu veux, ma Raison, je dirai --, (tu me laisseras dire) – que mon Ame, qui est la tienne aussi, se sentait comme la forme *creuse* d'un écrin, ou le creux d'un moule et ce vide *s'éprouvait* attendre un objet admirable – une sorte d'épouse matérielle qui ne pouvait exister – car cette forme divine, cette absence complète, cet Etre qui n'était que Non-Etre, et comme l'Etre de ce qui ne peut Etre – exigeait justement une *matière* impossible, et le creux vivant de cette forme *savait* que cette substance manquait et manquerait à jamais au monde des corps – et des actes…Ainsi doit le mortel convaincu de son Dieu dont il conçoit les attributs qu'il forme par négations successives des défauts et des maux qu'il trouve dans le monde ressentir la présence et l'absence essentielles de Celui qui lui est aussi nécessaire que le centre l'est à une sphère impénétrable, que l'on finit reconnaître *sphère* à force d'en explorer la surface et de raisonner sur les liaisons de ses points…

Mon œuvre était *cela*.

Labeur, souffrances, événements, douceurs ou glaives d'une vie, espoirs surtout, mais désespoirs aussi, nuits sans sommeil, amis charmants, femmes réelles, heures, jours, -- siècles soudains, sottises faites, mauvais moments – – tout cela, et tant d'années – il fallait, il fallut tout cela pour que se creuse dans la masse d'existence et d'expériences confondues et fondues – *ce* noyau, merveille, à coups de *négations* finalement chef-d'œuvre – insupportable et le triomphe de l'impossible pur !…

Ici (2) – La question intiale – Analyse de cette volonté poétique – et d'abord d'un terrible *Pourquoi* ? Ce pourquoi demande : d'où tirer l'énergie de vouloir ce qui s'adresserait à ce qu'il y a aujourd'hui *en fait d'hommes* ? Les meilleurs mêmes ne songent qu'à l'*instant* – Ils sont incapables de cette pensée : *Faire c'est se faire* (*C*, XXV, 618–19).

Let us suppose that our translation is designed for an anthology of poetic texts addressed to the cultivated English-speaking reader. We are then able to imagine a short introduction offering contextual information, and some limited recourse to explanatory notes (which the translator must not take as crutches but should certainly not shun either, since they justify strategic translation decisions and enhance reader response).

Our introduction will explain the moment of writing and the textual environment; it should also offer some pointers to the literary specificity of the translated passage, particularly in its relation to Mallarmé. This text was written in 1942, a moment overcast with the tragedy of French defeat and occupation; it is fraught with the 70-year-old poet-analyst's awareness of his own impending end, and also with his foreboding sense of the ending of a rational, humanely ordered Europe. Both the strategic self-communing of this text and its characteristic Valéryan discouragement about the possibility of being heard in the utterance of high or intimate poetic truths by an all-too-human humanity are resonant in this context.

The passage is one of the myriad heterogeneous fragments composed in Valéry's private laboratory of thought, the *Cahiers*; the problem of whom to speak to – of how 'discourse' becomes 'address' – is indeed intrinsic to his entire adventure of self-enfoldment in perpetual lucidity. Ordinary in one sense, this entry is extraordinary in others: the manuscript version shows it to have been improvised very rapidly, developing to unwonted length among other notes in response to a sure and compelling inspiration, and obeying the gravitation of the poetic by virtue of the emergence of a deeper sensibility that is stirred into awakening by the strategic and initiatory Question of existential weight: 'What could, what should a 'poet' do today?'

The two classifying rubric signs added by Valéry at the head of this unusually extended note require explanation. The double theta refers to the perpetually theorised (since 1921) project of a Socratic Dialogue 'Of things divine': deconstructing all ideas inherited from the European past and attempting to re-invent transcendence and divinity.[2] 'Memoirs of Myself' evokes Valéry's longstanding concern, parodically represented in *Mon Faust,* for an 'autobiography of the mind'. Literature and spirituality are thus designated, at the threshold to the text as organising principles of the poetic meditation to follow; they are also pointers to tone and register.

Mallarmé is omnipresent in this circuit of self-communing: explicitly so in the titles quoted; more implicitly in the image of the constellations of human achievement projected into in an ideal night

2   See my *Paul Valéry: le dialogue des choses divines* (Paris: Corti, 1989).

sky (Valéry of course knew the sonnet 'Quand l'ombre menaça'; and, as disciple elect and confidant of the 'suprême et paternel ami', he was the first to set eyes on the manuscript of 'Un coup de dés'.[3] Genetically, this text is an offshoot of the seventh and last (still unpublished) of a brilliant series of essays on Mallarmé, which Valéry was composing in 1942 under the title 'Traité des choses hautes et passions de l'esprit'.

Implicitly, both the writing and the model of a spirituality of Absence refer to Mallarmé in a dialogic psychodrama, in which the son both endorses and refutes the model of the father. For Valéry, the will to poetry in this algebrist of language, this creator of an intrinsic, non-representational world, is sacrificially consecrated to 'le but le plus élevé, le plus pur, qu'on eût jamais songé à assigner à l'Etre'.[4] It embodies an ethic, even a mystique: 'Tout en lui s'ordonnait à quelque fin secrète si haute qu'elle transformait, évaluait, abolissait ou transfigurait les choses comme une certitude ou une lumière de l'ordre mystique le peut faire'.[5] 'Mystique singulière et dévorante', Valéry insists in his final unpublished essay, 'qui dut se préciser dans une conception du langage, pour un peu je dirais du Verbe' (Ibid., p.70).

Yet the son repudiates the father's quasi-theological estimate of the efficacy and dignity of poetic language. The attempt to represent the mystery of everything by the mystery of language divinises 'la chose écrite'; and the Mallarmean conception of 'le Livre' consecrates the ultimate idolatry of a 'solitaire ébloui de sa foi'. Here, in the last resort, is the most sublime of 'littérateurs'; and while setting himself to desire and aspire with the intransigent intensity of Mallarmé – 'j'ai de ton pur esprit bu le feu le plus beau'[6] – Valéry will insist that the consummation of the human spirit is not to be found in any form of language-object, however profound or magical, but in the work of self-fashioning expended on the poetic subject himself.

3   See '"Le Coup de dés", Lettre au Directeur des *Marges*', in *Œuvres*, t. I, pp.622–30.
4   Dossier 'Mallarmé III', Bibliothèque nationale de France, f. 96.
5   Paul Valéry, ed. Hytier, *Œuvres* (Paris : Gallimard, (Pléaide), 1957), I, 680.
6   'SM mélodieusement', Dossier 'Vers anciens II', f. 146, BNF.

This subterranean dialogue gives the translator some of his trickiest problems. True, the Mallarmean dislocations of syntax ('Et scintillent dans le ciel...seulement soumises...') are residual only, and easy enough to imitate in English. More challenging are the modulations of imagery: the Mallarmean swan has to become a vigorous Valéryan bird of prey, capable of alighting on the shoulder of the poetic subject and 'catching him up' or 'snatching him up' into a visionary ecstasy that soars to the highest places of the mind. For the translator, the perils of obscurity and bathos attend the introduction of this fantastic bird, which, replacing the received signs written in the night sky of the father, ushers in the original Valéryan variation on the Mallarmean theme. There is a dynamic of metaphoric realisation to be observed here: the bird is anticipated in the first '*se* posa', referring to the poet's galvanising Question, which is then immediately realised as metaphor in the pivotal *reprise* of the same expression. The question therefore has to 'land' or 'alight', rather than merely 'be raised', 'occur' or 'crop up'. – 'Landed like a pause of silent potency, fallen on my shoulders and abruptly weighing down upon me.' (The metaphoric transformation of question into bird is complete and comprehensible in this rendering; so that we can dispense with the literalness of 'abruptly transformed into a weight', which is awkwardly over-explicit in English.)

The displacement towards the subject of the poet's justifying finality provides another key point of difficulty. The text's last word in answer to Mallarmé ('*Faire, c'est se faire*') is quintessentially Valéryan: not only in its refusal of the properly literary impulse to communicate one's substance in order to please a reading public, or in its radical re-investment of Mallarmé's 'finest fire', but also in the deceptive simplicity of the quasi-algebraic formula struck. Here, the temptation is to translate exegetically ('Poetry too is, in the end, a matter of *auto-poiesis* or self-fashioning'); but this would be to lose the gnomic bite and resonance of the original. The simplest version will be the best: '*Making is self-making*'.

Apart from these nodal points in the subterranean communing of son with spiritual father-in-poetry, the text is not lexically or syntactically obscure. It has, on the contrary, an achieved transparency characteristic of ultimate self-intimacy and self-understanding. This is to be preserved at all costs by the translator, most particularly in the childlike simplicity of the address to the poet's own rational soul, pleading for the pre-rational and trans-rational dynamic of desire and expectancy experienced 'auprès d'un cœur, aux sources du poème' (or as a fascinating variant of this same expression from 'Le Cimetière marin' already has it: 'auprès d'un cœur <u>dont *je suis*</u> le poeme').[7] ' If you will, my Reason, I will say – (you will let me say) that my soul which is yours also...' This same intimacy of self-communing demands, I would suggest, that the title expression 'Question et discours' be rendered by the particularising translation 'Question and address', since the English word 'discourse' lacks the easy generality of reference claimed by its French counterpart: it is, on the one hand, too technical and academic; on the other, it entirely misses the speaker's enunciatory positioning in relation to the explicit and implicit 'Others' of the text, hence also the whole function and character of the particular 'speech act' constituted by the text. (Alternatives: 'utterance' is altogether too imprecise; while 'speech' courts involuntary echoes of declarations at election time or of retirement parties).

We here enter the crucial domain of tonal register, mediating the poetic timbre and the spiritual tenor of the speaking voice. For the mature Valéry, 'l'obtention de la voix [...] définit la poésie pure'(*C*, VI, 176). It indeed encompasses the entire range of other considerations to which the poet – and his translator in turn – have to be attentive: musicality; metaphoric and symbolic suggestiveness; generic affiliation and resonance; cultural embeddedness and allusion.

The expression 'Station sur la terrasse' with its aspirational symbolism and its thematics of the elevated 'point de vue' dominated by the ideal night sky, but in turn dominating and recapitulating the mundane world of everyday experience epitomises a number of these features. The 'terrasse' is not so much a city-dweller's balcony (as in Baudelaire's 'Recueillement'); rather, it is an (unspecified) vantage point belonging to Mediterranean myth or nature: the towers of Semiramis' Babylon, the wine-grower's sun-drenched mountain slope, the open roof-terraces of Greece; or (of course) the elevated natural

---

7   Variant quoted by J.Hytier, *Œuvres*, I, 1684. My italics.

platform offered by the graveyard of the Mont St Clair at Sète. There is not much to be done with it in the translator's target text, except perhaps by way of appending a specifying footnote to the English word 'terrace'. The French word 'station', on the other hand, is well-nigh impossible to transpose directly into English; firstly because of the overwhelming cultural connotation 'Liverpool St'; secondly because Valéry's strongly realised second sense – a moment of poised and contemplative intensity – is retained in English only in the expression 'stations of the Cross', a sense which in most of the English-speaking world is now largely archaic and lost, save to practising Catholics and Anglo-Catholics. This might be pointed out in the same footnote. The target text could retain something of the reference and resonance of the source text, and even an echo of its alliterative form, if we were to use the expression 'Stasis on the terrace'; this at least brings together the suggestions of physical immobility, inner poise and enlarged, contemplative vision in an elevated site. (Bathos, if not involuntary comedy, is courted by attempts to translate the French noun by standard English verbal forms: 'standing', 'dwelling', 'remaining motionless', 'pausing', 'lingering', 'tarrying', 'loitering', etc). 'Stasis' (cognate with 'ecstasy') is exactly right; but if this term is still felt to be culturally obscure, then 'Moment of poise' would be an accessible – if more prosaic, and less musical – alternative.

The generic belonging of the text is crucial in exactly the manner pointed to by the classifying *sigles*. It shows a counterpoint between *autobiography* (with its reflective musing, its memories inflected by desire, reverie and self-judgment, its intimate self-questioning and sometimes brutal self-summaries) and the *songs of spiritual experience*: psalm, prophetic epiphany, the searching simplicity of the gospels, and also mystical writings (those borrowed from the 'negative' or apophatic way, particularly the 'colloque dans le fond et le nu de l'âme' of St John of the Cross) – the whole leavened by a touch of the fantastic and of symbolist esoterism.

The musical aspect of this challenge is certainly primary. The text is, for the most part, written in Psalm-like verses, full of the cadences of rhetorical symmetry, repetition and restatement. It is linked by 'naïve' narrative and logical connectors, allowing it to espouse freely the movements of self-address and to expand with the flow of emotional intensity. Its cadences are enhanced phonically and mnemonically by assonance and alliteration:

> There is your work – a voice said unto me.
> And I saw everything I had not done.
> And I knew ever more clearly that I was not he who had done what I had done – that I was he who had not done what I had not done... So that what I had not done was perfectly beautiful, perfectly like unto the impossibility of doing it.
> And this, all unbeknown to other people, I saw, I conceived, I would say that I held and touched it with extreme and extraordinary Precison.

The rhythmic and alliterative patterns here are largely transposable. But, as ever in this text, the translator is walking a tightrope between exalted and moving spiritual fervour and an ever-possible effect of bathos, incurring the promptly prosaic judgment in all of us that declares all paradox mumbo-jumbo, all solemnity pretention and all religious fervour absurd. The danger here for the English translator is certainly greater than for the French poet, since cultural unfamiliarity with the mystical tradition, with the scholastic vocabulary of Being and Non-Being, and in general with a high liturgical tradition on which French Symbolism is nourished are not available resources of linguistic memory on which the translator can count in the reader.

The same is true more broadly of the latter's culture-specific memory as such. Before it finds explicit expression in the comparison with the believer's waiting upon his God, the secret homophony of spiritual experience is adumbrated in a series of allusions which the English-speaking reader is likely to miss entirely (and which are therefore worth footnoting): to Pascal's conception of knowledge as a sphere encompassing the knower, in which the centre is everywhere and the circumference nowhere;[8] or to Augustine's conception of a divine presence antecedent within the self, *interior intimo meo* – 'closer than I am to myself'.[9] Valéry's liturgical imagination, well-nourished by the 'spiritual exercises' he had assiduously practised in 1891–1892 under the pseudonym of 'Le Jeune Prêtre', is evident in

8   Definition adapted by Valéry in 'L'Idée fixe', *Œuvres,* II, 251.
9   *Confessions,* III, vi, 11; cf. *C,* XXVIII, 3: 'Qui crois-tu qui puisse s'être logé au centre de toutes choses TOI, si ce n'est celui que je suis?'.

the key image of the soul as a jewel-casket. This recalls, in an-
thropocentric transposition, a ciborium, this image no doubt inter-
resonating with that of Mallarmé's 'dernière cassette spirituelle'. We
have seen that the title expression itself, 'Station sur la terrasse' falls
into this same pattern of traditional religious memory and re-imagined
liturgical allusion.

This homophonic echo, with its analogical shadow of religious
reference, has to be perceptibly translated. Firstly and at least, the risk
of bathos must be held at bay by careful rendering of potentially
disruptive expressions: ' la forme creuse d'un écrin', for instance, is
better translated as 'the hollow form of a jewel-casket' than as 'the
hollow form of a casket' (which, in American English at least, implies
a coffin – and sends us back, with Evelyn Waugh, to 'Whispering
Glades' and the Californian way of death!). More than this: the text
requires, at least in its 'plateau' moments, to be distanced from prosaic
usage and appropriately equivalent associations activated: dignified,
transparent, fervent, tinged with a high and venerable archaism. The
easiest way of achieving the homophonic echo, is of course to introduce, at least by way of discreet impressionism, the language and
cadences of the King James Bible and of the Anglican Prayer Book
('We have followed too much the devices and desires of our own
hearts. We have done those things which we ought not to have done
and we have left undone those things which we ought to have done;
and there is no health in us'). 'Like unto' is, on this basis, preferable
to 'resembling'; 'upon' to 'on'; 'even so' to 'thus'; 'whence' to
'where... from'.

This procedure must of course be sparing and well judged if the
speaking voice is not to be traduced rather than translated. It is
symptomatic of the tiny and shrinking space left to the inner voice by
our 'up-front', 'bottom-line' utilitarianism, terrified of any interiority
not patterned by the agreed values of the consumer society, that the
expression 'I say unto you' has become unusable, the property of
satirists. Excessive zeal by the translator in this subtle and crucial area
will be, therefore, a major blunder; additionally so since the 'parallel'
spirituality adumbrated is precisely *not* Christian. Of all things, what
the negative soul most conspicuously rejects or discounts or fails to

conceive is the Incarnation.[10] Instead, this spiritual form represents –
formidably purged and reduced by all the devices of the 'era of
Suspicion' directed against the premature and mythical complements
of human desiring – a reflexive and criticist variant on the theme of
negative and aspiring Eros. Plato or Plotinus might have recognised
his own in this quasi-religious fervour of ascesis and ascent directed
towards a supreme Good which is experienced as Absence, since it
must forever be lacking from the world of bodies and their acts.
Lacan, too, with his inverted psychoanalytical re-mapping of Plato, is
anticipated in the subject's perpetually allusive flight beyond
imaginary and language-bound nameables towards the 'lost Object of
desire'. Even Derrida, we might think, is foreshadowed in the negative
soul's deferral of closure and her ever-renewed expectancy (yet we
observe also the tenacious *centredness* of the self-uttering psychic
subject and her unblushing avowal of experienced and rationally
mysterious ontological *depth*). A further, more obvious limit to this
translating solution is that it must accommodate the tonal shifts that
result from the movement between visionary insight and the confrontation with an entirely prosaic and discouraging historical present.

The challenge of this text overall is to render Valéry's 'écriture
de précison', which proceeds with accomplished transparency from a
hyper-acute hearing of the psychic stirrings and tensions at the sources
of the prose poem that is written here, but also of the lifelong poem
that has been lived out existentially – and which, in some sense, we all
ultimately share. To the extent that the translator succeeds, he will
make the reader prophetically aware that, beyond the now settling dust
of twentieth-century deconstructionism and the dying pretensions of
Romantic–Symbolist orphism – there is, if we can hear it, a nearly-
sayable truth of being, allusively written in the psychic flesh of our
desiring, not to be reduced or replaced or eluded; and to the ap-

10 The Voice is, self-situatedly, *no longer* Christian; yet conceivably also *not yet*
    Christian. The 'living hollow' suggests the moulding Object; and the form of
    absence written in the desiring flesh has no sense except as presupposing an
    antecedent Presence somehow withdrawn and imperceptible. The dilemma of
    this tension haunts Valéry, and is perhaps, indeed, resolved in favour of the
    latter alternative by the last scribbled entry of the *Cahiers* (see my *Paul Valéry:
    le dialogue des choses divines*, pp.400–17).

prehending of which, poetry can sometimes be a not unworthy mediation.

If the question was 'What can, what should a poet do today?', this answer of Valéry's, in English as in French, will be worth hearing:

θθ or Memoirs of Myself

Question and Address
What could, what should a 'poet' do today? State of the things of the soul, of the mind, of this art of poetry. But before I had laid out before my expectancy the elements of my thinking...an idea came to mind and made room for itself.

(1) Stasis on the terrace

I ascended to the terrace, unto the most high places of the dwelling of my mind – Thither lead age, and reflections and foreseeings – those that came true, those that came to naught, the excellent moves made, the failures, the forgetting of people, of names, of critics and their articles, etc.
And there in the night sky of poetry, subject only to the laws of the universe of language, there shimmer the constellations that rise and disappear below the horizon only to re-appear...
There Herodiade, the Après-Midi, the Tombeau de Gautier – etc, but no longer are there any authors' names. Individuals no longer count.
And while I was thus contemplating these 'signs', the above question landed.
It landed like a pause of silent potency, like a great bird suddenly alighting upon my shoulders, abruptly weighing down upon me. But the great bird was, as I sensed from its weight, capable of lifting me away. And catch me up it did, me and my 70 years of age, me and my memories, my observations, my preferences and my essential injustice.
Then most of all was borne in upon me the worth and the beauty, the entire excellence of everything I have not done.
There is your work – a voice said unto me.
And I saw everything I had not done.
And I knew ever more clearly that I was not he who had done what I had done – that I was he who had not done what I had not done...So that what I had not done was perfectly beautiful, perfectly like unto the impossibility of doing it.
And this, all unbeknown to other people, I saw, I conceived, I would say that I held and touched it with extreme and extraordinary Precision.
If you will, oh my Reason, I will say --, (you will allow me to say) – that my soul which is yours also, felt itself to be the empty form of a jewel-casket or the

hollow of a mould and this void in me experienced itself as awaiting an admirable object – a sort of material spouse such as could not exist – for this divine form, this utter absence, this Being that was but non-Being and, as it were, the Being of what cannot Be – required precisely an impossible substance of matter, and the living hollow of this form knew that such substantial materiality was lacking and would forever be lacking from the world of bodies -- and of acts... Even so must the mortal convinced of his God, whose attributes he conceives, fashioning them by successive negations of the defects and ills he discovers in the world, experience the essential presence and absence of Him who is as necessary as its center to a sphere, a sphere impenetrable that is finally recognised to be a sphere by dint of exploring the surface and reasoning on the interconnections of its points...

That was my work.

Toil, sufferings, events, sweet things or sword thrusts of one's life, hopes most of all, but also occasions of despair, sleepless nights, charming friends, women actually known, hours, days – sudden centuries, foolish mistakes, bad times – that, all that and so many years – all that was necessary and it took all that and the disgust or the disdain or the remorse of all that, and the mingling and the refusal of all that for there to be hollowed out in the mass of existence, of experiences run together and melted down into each other – this kernel space, this marvel become at length by dint of negations a masterpiece – intolerably exquisite, and the triumph of a purity here below impossible!...

Here (2) – The initial question. Analysis of this will to poetry and firstly of a terrible Why? This why asks: whence can one draw the energy of will required for anything that might be addressed to the type of humanity existing today? Even the best think only of the moment. – They are incapable of the thought: Making is self-making.

MICHAEL BISHOP

Seven contemporary poets and the *sujet poétique*

Il allait, où n'est plus
Rien que l'on sache, mais
Eprise de son chant, dansante, illuminée,
L'accompagnant l'abeille

Yves Bonnefoy
Les Planches courbes[1]

What follows cannot constitute an *état présent* of contemporary French poetry, but it can afford a concise, textually sensitive discussion of a freely chosen and loosely representative range of very recent work by seven major contemporary voices: Robert Marteau, Esther Tellermann, Eugène Guillevic, Louise Herlin, Gérard Titus-Carmel, Marie-Claire Bancquart and Jean-Paul Michel, to all of whom I owe much, not only for their personal generosities, but, of course, principally, for the gift of their respective *œuvres*. What follows, then: seven translations, followed by compact analysis of individual poetic manners – formal, aesthetic and tonal modes and tactics –, very briefly situated in relation to current French debate over the status and characteristics of the *sujet poétique*, the whole topped off by a short epilogue offering some reflections on the status of translation and translator in this optic.

I. Robert Marteau

The grass and trees became wet overnight,
Which means a new silence reigns about us,
Intense, hanging in the stillness of the greenery
Raised in its cascade like a rock face towards
The sky spread with an inverse and variable

1   Yves Bonnefoy, *Les Planches courbes* (Paris: Mercure de France, 2001), p.20.

Light traversing the grey of clouds seemingly
Static but yet journeying, since at times
We see them uncovering the sun,
For a moment like the jellyfish, swimming,
Offered to the incoming tide and then the beach.
A bough stirs, a gift to the immenseness
That drops of water briefly lace with sound
When a quick breath of air tells their beads upon
A dried lamina, cast prematurely to the ground.
                    (Attichy, Tuesday, 26 August 1997)

This sonnet from *Rites et offrandes* (p.110),[2] one of some five hundred and thirty-seven of this 2002 collection, should be read not only in the context of Robert Marteau's recent persistent, less obsessive than serenely elected, attachment to an old and honourable structure, but equally in arguable association with similar practices adopted by poets as yet tonally diverse as Jacques Réda or Yves Leclair. That this reveals modal nostalgia and a contentment with the daily challenge of fusing immediacy of experience and a certain conservative aesthetic agenda, hardly needs emphasising. Yet there is much that is free here, even if the alexandrine constraint remains: only occasionally rhymed verse; a discreet but sure lyrical expression, at once close to observation (and its implicit celebration of what is) and offering both rational meditation ('an inverse and variable light') and spiritual emotiveness ('a gift to the immenseness'); a seeming disregard, despite the three metaphors deployed, for the finery of over elaborate figuration and language's possible special effects (punctuation, arcaneness, fragmentation, etc.). The sonnet thus remains very grounded, conceiving itself not as an act and place of manner, linguistic prestige or play, intellectual shimmer, but rather as another, lightly framed though ontologically caressed and caressing entry in a journal begun some fifteen years ago and continuing still today, a journal allowing for the working through of self-world relationships without either those overt sentimentalisings or heavy abstractions the hyper-self-conscious self may often impose. Intensity and nuance thus quietly meld; theorisation of the space of the written is not yielded to;

2   Robert Marteau, *Rites et offrandes* (Seyssel: Champ Vallon, 2002).

nor, implicitly, does this mode suggest the prevalence of its interiority (whether deemed important or transcendent) in relation to its mission of what Reverdy called poetry's 'consubstantiation'.[3] The full rhythmic breathing of Marteau's sonnet, with its two long sentences, tends to imply a poietic capacity to gather and unify, rather than explode and rupture, and yet no pretension seems to hover about this piece or others. This does not preclude, elsewhere, moments of doubt or anxious moral frustratedness, but it does suggest a global confidence in the pertinence, and the simplicity, of a poetic gesture seeking to eschew the dysphoric without indulging in any aggressive exhilaration, which, perhaps, the poetic climate in France – with some rare exceptions – might deem lacking in lucidness and that dourest of yet favoured modes, realism, realisticalness.

II. Esther Tellermann

Anxiety of July 5th
(fragments)

She is falling without the shadow of signs.

And what if the sky has not shared
columns
where can the calling be decentred?

---

3   See Pierre Reverdy, *En vrac* (Monaco: Editions du Rocher, 1956), pp.190–1, the point here being that self-world relationships achieve a degree of ontological harmony and equilibrium which, via the text, language, counters any sense of alienation or existential problem, yet without, curiously, anchoring such achievement in some strict textual interiority. What Reverdy will call 'cette émotion appelée poésie', as the prefatory text of *Flaques de verre* argues, 'n'est plus pour moi, elle n'a jamais été pour moi dans les livres [...] Elle plane magistralement sur la vie' (Paris: Flammarion, 1984, préface de Daniel Leuwers, p.24). If, then, we can regard the lyrical as rooted in the literal, the aesthetic, Reverdy catapults it back, away from the text, towards not just the cerebral, the mental, nor even Georges Perros' notion of visceral, circulatory lyricism (cf. Jean-Claude Pinson, *Habiter en poète* (Seyssel: Champ Vallon, 1995), p.240), but towards some immaterial, cosmic space of being.

Uneasiness.
Cornered faces.
Emergency.
Heat.
Time to bury them

Circumscribed journey
green spelled out
an island unknots her
follows her
a wake left between the grasses
a silver line disfigures the postcards.

To the rhythm of grey seas
moorings
snap fragileness.

Sleep at the branching of the day
you might say the proportions of the river mouths
the approach of voices
at water level.
To calm concern.

Waiting like shards.
– To pray all I had was the swaying to and fro.
She deferred her pain.

What this suite from Esther Tellermann's 1993 *Distance de fuite*
(pp.63–8)[4] would seem to accomplish is a catapulting of poetic text,
of, too, the self's relation to text and self-world relations as lived
through text, into a radical other space of functioning and conception
– certainly when compared with Robert Marteau's sonnet. Elliptical
both syntactically and semantically, compacted, dense, seemingly
discontinuous despite both the willed gathering of the individual com-
ponents of each 'fragment' of the suite and, of course, the assembly
that creates the suite itself, here is a poietic discourse – and a *poiein* as
gesture and process[5] – that, yet, for all its obscurities, remains

4   Esther Tellermann, *Distance de fuite* (Paris: Flammarion, 1993).
5   Jean-Marie Gleize speaks, in his *A noir* (Paris: Seuil, 1992), in connection with
     Lamartine's *Raphaël* of 'une *autre* poésie (« la poésie sans lyre »), qui oscille

manifestly felt and intense. Certainly, much depersonalises, blurs the drawn lines of the body of the self and shatters any narrative flagrancy. But none of this can cast the text out of its lyrical orbit, nor strip it of its emotional, psychological aura. These remain the *microrécits* of an anxiety lived, anchored in time, though spatially indeterminate. No manifest aesthetic agenda would seem to vie for precedence over the ontological, even if it is clear there is a hyperalertness to form: the latter plays itself out as intimately stemming from the pursuit of being, meaning, value, and any 'beauty' available one could assume to be as deferred as they themselves, folded into the complex and perhaps complexed disruption of their sought wholeness. It is not surprising, then, to find that the tonality of this *poiein* is shifting, moving – I have argued this elsewhere[6] –; less elusive than simply unfinished, incompletely articulated – an incompleteness central to the ongoing quest for the meaning of the self's narrative journey: a meaning, of course, that poetry, despite any sense we may have of its incapacity, is constantly creating-making-affirming, negatively or otherwise.

III. Eugène Guillevic

> Years ago,
> When I was a lad,
> I felt I was a stranger to the world,
> It was
> As if I wasn't a part of it –
>
> And I applied myself
> So as to incorporate myself within its entirety.
>
> Now my end is drawing near,
> And I know it is, I am living it,

entre le pôle du silence et celui d'une surexpressivité transgressive' (p.51), a remark that could be thought through with a perhaps surprising pertinence in the context of Tellermann's manner.

6   See Michael Bishop, *Contemporary French Women Poets, vol.I, From Chedid and Dohollau to Tellermann and Bancquart* (Amsterdam/New York: Rodopi, Coll. CHIASMA, 1995).

Now
I need make no effort
To feel the world fully
Each and every second.

It is there, I am in it,
I belong to it.
Within it I find pleasure.
                                    12 May 1995

This poem, from the posthumous *Quotidiennes* (p.63)[7], is to be read –
and we know this, the poem implicitly tells us this – in the light of the
entire evolutive sweep of Guillevic's oeuvre. *Quotidiennes* is beyond
the *quanta* of the later years; assembled, it yet remains unassembled
by the poet himself;[8] its texts are thus at once unfinished and fatally
definitive, diary entries that have become a farewell legacy. The poem
translated offers a simple, uncluttered narration of the major achievement poetry has, perhaps, helped Guillevic bring about: a re-creation,
a re-poeticising or remaking, of self-world relationship. The text is
matter-of-fact, unpretentious, seemingly serene (even though anxieties
are at times visible elsewhere in this collection): a recognition of the
fact that what Guillevic often terms *conscience* can efficaciously act
upon *choses*, 'apply' itself (as the true centre of self) to a remodelling
of being, feeling and doing, an empowered appropriation and integration where alienation had once ruled. We should not see this as
implying, essentially, an embrace of a Pongian aesthetics of *l'objoie/
l'objeu*, such an aesthetics being founded upon a compensatory,
analogico-differential mechanics with, at its centre, a poetics of
minimality and near ontological failure. The pleasure Guillevic manages is neither simply textual nor even necessarily connected to poetic
process: the reconciliation and belonging evoked here carry no such
explicit reference, poet though Guillevic may be. The poem's coherence and continuity, its rhythmic flow certainly establish a space of
transparent *poieis*, but there is, here, no sense of a folding back upon
this space as refuge, either mildly derisory or vaguely transcendent:

7   Eugène Guillevic, *Quotidiennes* (Paris: Gallimard, 2002).
8   The volume is edited by Lucie Guillevic-Albertini and Bernard-Joseph Samain.

the poem, for Guillevic, has long shed both its alienatedness and the quasi-prestige of its half-redemptive, somewhat noble textual interiority. Its purpose and the tonal modes that accompany this purpose are allied rather to a 'beauty' of self-interrogation hopefully, as here, synonymous with self-affirmation and plenitude *ici et maintenant.*[9]

IV. Louise Herlin

(Phoenix)

The thousands and thousands of angles for grasping things,
landscapes – the climate bathing
nature objects humans
– angles of attack – are far from being exhausted

The visible, still full of surprises, treasures
for cherishing, mysteries, renews itself

The thousand-facetted world keeps us company,
peopled storied changing adventurous,
within reach,
on our screens,
flush with where we are: the veranda leads to it,
doors, windows give out onto it,
it comes in when we want air,
it invades place – ever ready to settle in and spread out

Grabbing hold of it, standing up to it,
bluntly addressing it, nothing is more salutary

Full of sources and resources, the world never stops
spurting forth, remaking itself, rising like a phoenix from its ashes

9   As Yves Bonnefoy has variously argued – I am thinking here of his *Le quatre cent et unième livre*, in *Entretiens sur la poésie (1972–1990)* (Paris: Mercure de France, 1990) – textual, aethetic closure always may be deemed a temptation, even an inevitable reality of sorts, yet 'c'est aussi l'occasion qui nous est donnée de nous débattre contre sa griffe [et d'y maintenir] le sentiment du mystère d'être' (p.369).

Imprisoned, it breaks free
starts its teeming once more, reality
immediately regaining body and life and volume

'(Phoenix)', from Louise Herlin's 2002 *Chemins de traverse* (p.47),[10] is the poem of feasibility – and thus the poem of the poem of feasibility, and, in that, not unlike Guillevic's daily self-meditation above. Its tone is buoyant, elevating (without the weight that can drag down Baudelairian poetics, and without, of course, the latter's symbolist agenda); its optativeness floated, felt to be ever resurgent, is by no means simply aesthetic, if, by that, we mean centred on formal, textual, 'plastic' transcendence. If form strikes us here, it is in its freedom, its self-allowing fluidity, a cumulative and iterative gathering of language in order to speak, beyond itself, beyond any self-satisfaction it might be tempted to settle for, of existence, of the endlessly available meanings, conceptions – and, of course, therefore, conceivable *mises en langage* – of the earth.[11] The latter, far from being rooted in those dominant collectively espoused equations that may proliferate at a given moment or epoch, ceaselessly liberates itself, reaffirms that 'openness' poets as different as Hölderlin or Du Bouchet have dwelt upon, cutting through the platitudes of the observable, alert to the mystery, the surprise, the becomingness of being and its ever renewed presence, self-(re)presentation. The poem's kaleidoscopic, yet cohering spirals of interrogation and affirmation repeatedly seek to bring home the reality and deep pertinence of this openness, its 'salutariness', its 'readiness', its inexhaustibleness, the fact, too, that, at bottom, 'reality' is an individual's process of energetically and psychically engaging with the physicality of ever evolving utterly malleable incarnation.

10   Louise Herlin, *Chemins de traverse* (Paris: La Différence, 2002).
11   In his *Théorie des tables* (Paris: P.O.L, 1992) Emmanuel Hocquard sketches out a poetics of the simultaneity of 'poème autobiographique' and 'poème grammatical': thus does the poem become what Deguy would call 'poème du poème', a 'theory' (: *theoria*, procession, discourse, etc.) of what it is, 'en rapport avec la représentation, l'identité et la fiction' (Hocquard, n.p.).

IV. Gérard Titus-Carmel

> And all memory shattered head on at the edge of day I drew from the presence
> of shadow some bitter pleasure not understanding why I confessed the price of
> my shame without the other offering me in return something similar yet I was
> inclined to the commerce of words and ready to discuss anything I was so
> young and transparent oh how weighty was the silence how wildly it lulled me
> into dizziness approaching the well into which I could so easily tip over and
> lose myself in the cyclopean gaze of the earth its black extinguished iris at the
> bottom of the long vertical bowel dug deep like a sounding device and hot upon
> the periphery of its stone lips when the dull heavy kiss of the bucket rang out
> still today I keep the burning memory of its kiss like a band around my
> forehead iron and sun upon my temple.

If Robert Marteau's sonnet opts for continuity and discursiveness held
coherent by its punctuation, and if Louise Herlin's poem chooses a
spontaneously self-forming series of short linked articulations, Gérard
Titus-Carmel, in this poem from his 2000 *Travaux de fouille et d'oubli*
(p.50),[12] elects to offer a form-sensitive text (one of many in a highly
mathematicised oeuvre, a square of fused, compressed language, a
kind of monolith or stela, a Mallarmean *tombeau* wherein the
dysphoric and the melancholic yet may raise some 'minute monument
of the soul' whose achievement, and, more importantly perhaps for
Titus-Carmel, the very process of whose assembly, may operate that
spectral transmutation of loss, even death, into some *form* and *mode* of
rebirth, despite, no doubt, any aura of failure that may be felt to linger
– via the haunting logic of *Un coup de dés* – at the very apogee of
poietic construction. Of course, this Mallarmean parallel is far from
telling all, as we might expect. Titus-Carmel's textual space deploys
the tensions of shatteredness and persistent, burning memory, the
tensions, too, of pleasure and bitterness.[13] It offers, equally, a subtext

12   Gérard Titus-Carmel, *Travaux de fouille et d'oubli* (Seyssel: Champ Vallon,
      2000).
13   When Jean-Michel Maulpoix writes, in *Du lyrisme* (Paris: Corti, 2000), that 'le
      lyrisme exprime l'*enlèvement* du sujet dans le langage, à condition d'entendre
      ce terme dans toute la richesse de ses sens: « enlever » signifie aussi bien retirer
      et faire disparaître, qu'emporter avec soi, prendre par force ou par ruse,
      soulever, et, au figuré, exalter et transporter d'enthousiasme, ravir, gagner,
      exécuter brillamment' (p.24), such a wealth of pertinence assists us in

of great emotional power, of drama at once enigmatic, barely fathomed, and half-revealed via language's grappling with the obscure, the shadowy, the unconfessed, the vertiginously perhaps unconfessable of any *sujet poétique*, faced as it may be with the nightmarish, the 'cyclopean', the experience of the earth's – the other's, being's – half-blinding intensity ever stigmatising the self, marking, branding the place of a psyche coming to deem itself fatally torn, half love, desire, passionate continuity, half trauma, awed disturbance.

VI. Marie-Claire Bancquart

But at Night

Well, my heart, so you're brushing against
creaming off
the millenium's paucity of news?

You're snaring
a mere bit of sky in the midst of the bombs?

You're exorcising
your blood placed end to end
more than twice as long as the Earth's circumference?

You're gathering about yourself
surveyable pains

But at night
you open that slightly stained gate, unbolted
found at the bottom of old gardens, leading to the tenderness
of an ageless tree. You become a bud. You consent.

understanding the complex nature of the relationship in Titus-Carmel between language and subject, form and feeling, aesthetics and ontology. If there is 'dream', transcendence, pure poetic alterity, 'la poésie', as Bonnefoy argues in *Il reste à faire le négatif*, 'est autant la critique du rêve que sa forme la plus extrême. Et en cette ambiguïté elle garde ouverte cette question du négatif et du positif qu'elle ne peut, à elle seule, résoudre' (*Entretiens sur la poésie*, loc. cit, p.252).

'But at Night', from Marie-Claire Bancquart's 1994 *Dans le feuil-letage de la terre* (p.100),[14] is a poem of intimacy and gentleness 'before' the self, a monological (as Bakhtin might, somewhat oddly, say) discourse that yet immediately confirms the layered complexities of the self – less its ambivalences than its spaciousness, its capacity to sense its own depths, its shifting alterity beyond the socio-political, even the ethical, its instinctive gesturing towards the salvaging, at least, of some azured minimum in the midst of apparent contradiction, radical contrast. The 'exorcism' sought confirms this desire to explore, both poetically and via pure mentation, such otherness as the self deems livable; just as the gathering and measuring would seem to take stock of the physical challenges confronting any movement beyond the strictly physiological; just as, too, the heart is turned to, not as a site of transcendence, but as the seat of a guidance, a knowing that penetrates into what is, feeling what is joyous and what is not, what corresponds to desire and what does not. 'But' – that Reverdyan *seme par excellence*, pivotal, plunging into dire negative vision or recuperative, transformative, as here –, the nocturnal realm, of dream, pure psychicalness, vision and liberation or expansion of self, softly exits the equations of temporality and materiality, pushes open the door of a purer metaphoricalness, perceives as available a meta-physical and original growth and potentiality, and, no doubt most importantly, reaches for an allowance, that consent to what is which Bonnefoy, at his peak, can sense to be of prime pertinence to the self's adventure and the narration we offer it. If, formally, the poem proceeds via textual spurts, and these, clearly, gather to a climax entailing the shift in perspective just outlined, such structuring mani-festly corresponds to the intensity of the self-articulation of a *sujet poétique* not faintly surrendering to any tinselled aesthetic shimmer.[15]

---

14   Marie-Claire Bancquart, *Dans le feuilletage de la terre* (Paris: Belfond, 1994).
15   To the question as to whether, nevertheless, Bancquart's poetics might rea-sonably correspond to Jacques Roubaud's view that poetry 'est en nous le monde qui parle, le monde privé de sens, qui nous parle par et dans la langue, directement dans la langue' (quoted by Jean-Claude Pinson in his excellent *Sentimentale et naïve* (Seyssel: Champ Vallon, 2002), I should be inclined to refuse this implicit reduction of the poietic to pure *signifiance*, arguing, more or less with Pinson, that referentiality and 'existential' meaning (language's

'But at Night' opens up a space wherein a wrestling with a deeper creativeness may occur. No banal 'self-story', as Michel Deguy might say; no overtly lyrical manner, either, dependent upon flagrant rhetorical means. Rather a self-exploratory allegoricalness that eschews sheer literality, textual play and interiority and, both via its questioning and its assertiveness, implies a confidence in language's conveyance, its fundamental if rough *adéquation* to the reality of feeling, thought and dream.

VII. Jean-Paul Michel

> We sail upon a superb vessel Light shoots out from
> beneath its stem Day and night the Earth like
> a lamp such a vessel calls for a crew of Kings
> The guy ropes shine forth the decks shine forth Bright
> the ship's bows bright
> the masts
>
> A hundred times we have opened dazzled eyes given
> thanks Paris terraces in May or
> at night the surprise of the June sky a hundred
> times we have blinked before the splendour &
> thanked Habit offends
> such flashing brilliance – one step away beauty
> is ablaze
>
> Perhaps we ought not to teach beyond &
> then, only, we would give thanks at the right
> level
> Light shoots out from its stem within without s
> plashed all over we
> rub our eyes in disbelief n
> ot knowing this vessel of glory bears
> us up – What only is possible is
> opening our eyes in the light

orientation in the direction of [self's perceived] being), would prise Bancquart's poetics away from such a tight association with Roubaud's.

even if it led us to our
ruin dazzled fatal
opening our eyes we
offer thanks

We are the children of light
– It alone teaches us, guides us, takes our hand in
the dark flashing brilliant within us
without

Will ever be given to us speech on the level
we should await it – infinite mirror
of the infinity of lights &
shadow In unique modulation oh let it
reveal and enlighten, testify and raise up whoever speaks
with things revealed.

A single just speaking,
just once. Poetry would not
have failed.

We sail upon a superb vessel &
we weep
                          Ascoli Piceno
                          I VIII 97

A poem of embrace of a ubiquitous energy already uplifting us, a
poem that sings the praises of what renders possible all that is possible
– it is clear that the dominant tonality of Jean-Paul Michel's characteristic poem (taken from the 2001 *« Défends-toi, Beauté violente! »*)[16]
is not just laudatory, celebratory, but one of confidence and commitment, open, bright-eyed receptivity and exuberant self-aband-
onment. None of this implies a blindness to the earth's contrasts, but it
requires a radical shaking up of the self in order to release fully that
dimmed and dulled sense of the intrinsic extraordinariness of all
existence, its lights and 'lamps' (as Salah Stétié, too, might have said),
its motion, its becoming, its livable astonishments and its implicit
emblematicity, in order to let go, too, of that melancholia that is in
profound disharmony with the energy and 'regalness' of all being.

16   Jean-Paul Michel, *« Défends-toi, Beauté violente! »* (Paris: Flammarion, 2001).

Beauty, in this perspective, penetrates to the heart of all phenomena, all states, all modes of being, all happenings; it is synonymous with the freely deployed and deployable energy of being; it is a kind of 'violence', a leaping into being at all moments of all that is, beyond ethics, beyond the ethical concerns we harbour, for inherent to the very irreducible mystery of incarnation. Certainly, for Michel, the poem has its role in the conveyance and exploration of this Beauty, but it is not a mimetically functioning role, innovatively magnificent at formal, textual levels. Michel's form exists to permit and, in turn, urge passionate meditation; its oddities (s/plashed, n/ot, etc.) do not arise so as to draw to themselves idle prestige, but rather to emphasise and practise jubilation and liberty. The 'aesthetic' agenda, in brief, is cosmic, ontological, merely traversing the poem, but focussed upon a 'defence and illustration' the text can only hint at.[17] All of this, to be sure, requires a bold, felt and powerfully desired assumption of poietic space as one in which the subject may – indeed, must – both open up itself/himself to a buoyant fullness of exchange with the world, and accept the urgency of its/his relationship with the other-as-reader. Poetry, in this way, risks moving beyond its locked-in subjectivity to a mode of co-creativity, less persuasive – and in no way coercive – than contagiously exuberant.

To translate the above seven poems, and then to plunge into those further 'translations' implied by critical commentary, is to give oneself to a strongly self-engaging and 'intersubjective' (as Jean-Pierre Richard might say) pluralising, self-multiplying experience. If a marrying of sorts occurs, it is of necessity imperfect, for the 'contract' is conceived of on and in my terms and is arguably unidirectional; it appropriates, refigures, its mimesis moves away from the other whilst paradoxically seeking to draw close. Of course, the translator-cum-

---

17   Speaking of the *sujet lyrique*, Jean-Michel Maulpoix writes of its constant self-diffraction, the adventure of its self-deployment: 'Il n'est pas un, mais multiple, aléatoire, tel un nœud inextricable de contradictions, ou tel un lieu optique dans l'œil duquel le monde entier se constelle' (*Du lyrisme,* loc. cit, p.375), and it seems to me that this diffraction and teemingness, whilst somewhat suggested by form, cannot finally be spoken by a language, by a textuality, which, if not impoverishing, can only catch a fraction, a glimmer, of that inexhaustible light flooding the subject's traversal of what is.

critic can afford no anguish in such processes of transferral. He or she may be wise to deem the final translated text arrived at as carrying no closure, as remaining, in a sense, as unfinished and as relative as, on the one hand, the poet may deem his or her poem as a new text reopens its inquiry, or, on the other hand, the critic may hold to be unfinishable a life-long meditation of any given text or oeuvre. Finally, after whatever appropriation comes about, translation and critical analysis are best perceived as gifts: exchange resumes, return is made in relative fullness, a promise of some further play of affinity and difference may be explicitly or implicitly offered. The translator's experience of selfhood, expanded, perhaps, as here, significantly multiplied as one moves from poet to poet, is integrated within that center of his or her inner being, just as, after weighing that odd skirmishing with his or her translated or analysed *étrangeté* or 'otherness', the poet may recover an identity perhaps slightly widened at the margins. Seven small gifts, doubled, here, for, too, a colleague and friend who has given much to many.

Louise Herlin

Next to nothing, minimal, machines switched off, people without a sound
The void around
Make room, let come — the air, a breath —
wind in the grass
An eddy over the pool of memory in glints :
A stroke of pen to tease it out
as words spread on the page
And creeping time comes to a halt

(translated by Peter Broome)

Très peu, presque rien, machines tues, gens silencieux
Le vide alentour
Laisser venir, advenir — un souffle, l'air —
le vent sur l'herbe
Un remous moirant l'eau de la mémoire :
Qu'un trait de plume l'allonge
en mots couchés sur la page
Et l'heure lente ne passe plus

So many plans, entreaties, wishes, prayers
One would love to have been better loved
— with more inventiveness, with more élan,
more ardently no less the other way around,
with tender, fervent love love life
… has slipped away, slips on

And happenings go their own sweet way
We've precious little hold on them
and precious little strength to nudge them
left or right a touch

with cast lines of desire
with oars of love, its leads,
its long extension leads

(translated by Peter Broome)

Tant de projets, vœux, appels, prières
On eût aimé être aimé mieux
— avec plus d'invention, de fougue,
plus ardemment et vice versa,
aimer d'amour tendre et fervent la vie
… a passé passe encore

Les événements suivent leur voie
À peine si l'on a barre sur eux
À peine peut-on les infléchir
à gauche, à droite, un peu

avec les perches du désir
avec les rames de l'amour, ses longes,
ses rallonges

WALLACE KIRSOP

Baudelaire's readers, commentators and translators in Australia around 1900

In an essay on Baudelaire first published in the short-lived Melbourne journal *The Heart of the Rose*, in 1907, Archibald T. Strong referred to 'that handful of Anglo-Saxons who love and understand French literature, and have watched with sympathetic delight the gallant and successful efforts of a long line of great craftsmen and men of genius to evolve the highest poetic form out of the unpromising stuff of the French language'.[1] The 'handful' included other persons born and resident in Australia, not all of whom would necessarily have endorsed Strong's view of the French language. Be that as it may, Strong, whose secondary and tertiary education was received in England, was a witness to and a participant in the Francophilia that was one of the significant strands in Australian intellectual and cultural life in the late nineteenth and early twentieth centuries.

One suspects that Europeans were, and are, disconcerted by the notion that people living at a tremendous distance from London, Paris, New York, Berlin and Vienna could somehow – and at times without even travelling to the centres of civilisation – be informed about the literature and thought of the Northern Hemisphere. When Beatrice Webb visited Australia in 1898 she remarked that Isaac Isaacs, a future Chief Justice and Governor-General, was:

---

1   Volume 1, no 1, 9 December 'in the year of the Commonwealth SEVEN', p.24. The essay was republished under the same title 'Charles Baudelaire' in Strong's *Peradventure: a Book of Essays in Literary Criticism* (London: Simpkin, Marshall, Hamilton, Kent and Co. Ltd, [1912] (issued a year earlier by Lothian in Melbourne)), pp.23–7.

the only man we have met in the colonies who has an international mind
determined to make use of international experience. And this, in spite of the
fact that he has never left Australia.[2]

Although the caustic comments she and Sidney made about most of
the politicians and dignitaries they met and interrogated were doubtless deserved, there were inevitably private spheres – like the practice
of poetry – that they could not and did not observe. Sidney's im-
pressions, given in an interview on his return, of the Australian press
are a clue to what made certain sorts of awareness possible:

> The principal Australian newspapers are as good as anything we have in
> England; they are far superior to all but one or two of our provincial dailies. I
> am not sure that they are not even better in some respects – in comparative
> freedom from party control for instance – than any English journal (Ibid.,
> p.144).

The virtues of conscientious reporting extended to cultural matters, so
that bibliographies of nineteenth-century French authors that ignore
the Southern Hemisphere – hence South America as well as the
various British colonies and dependencies – can be curiously defi-
cient.[3]

Educational traditions derived from the British Isles are enough
to explain the pre-eminent position of French among the modern
languages taught in the secondary schools of the Australian colonies
before and after Federation in 1901. A small minority was affected by
this, of course, just as an even more elite group encountered French
language and literature in the universities established in the colonial
capitals at intervals after 1850. What is more surprising for those of us
used to seeing most of our graduates leave their French studies behind
as a seemingly banal rite of passage is that in those generations there
were people who, whatever their daily work, made an effort to keep
up their reading of the authors who were fashionable in Paris. The
discreet multi-culturalism of nineteenth-century Australia, a state of

---

2   See A. G. Austin, ed., *The Webbs' Australian Diary 1898* (Melbourne: Sir Isaac
      Pitman & Sons Ltd, 1965), p.68.
3   See Wallace Kirsop, 'Foreword' to the 'Zola: Modern Perspectives' special
      number of the *Australian Journal of French Studies*, XXXVIII, 2001, 301–4.

affairs that was effectively hidden or suppressed between the two World Wars, needs to be invoked to help us grasp a cultural ambience much wider than the classroom.[4] The presence of a recognisable and well-integrated French or Francophone community, proportionately more numerous than after 1945, was also a factor in keeping Australians aware of the breadth of the traditions they had inherited. Redmond Barry, the most influential of Victoria's 'cultural evangelists' in the nineteenth century, had a clear understanding, realised in his grand design for the Melbourne Public Library, of the need for an unapologetically catholic approach to collecting and documenting the human past:

> We may now have visibly before us the noble acts of patriotism, heroism, piety, and virtue, not of the narrow area of our own Britain – fertile as it is in great names – but those which adorn the history of all lands represented amongst us. [...]
> And where can the testimony of these virtues be preserved more suitably than in Public Libraries, free of access to all who esteem such recollections, who desire that their minds may be refreshed and their principles confirmed by intercourse with the great exemplars [...][5]

The taste of many Melbourne and Sydney readers of French in the late 1890s did not run, let it be admitted, to such lofty sentiments. Among the 'New Books added to the Book Lovers' Library, 215 Collins St' advertised by Henry Hyde Champion in his *Book Lover* in May 1899 were a number of French novels, including titles by Paul Bourget, Pierre Louÿs and Hugues Rebell (p.8). In his *Worshipful Masters*, A. B. Piddington, successively University of Sydney lecturer, politician and judge, alludes to Sir George Innes's habit of buying French novels a dozen at a time from Angus and Robertson in

4   For a more detailed, but none the less summary treatment of these questions see Wallace Kirsop, 'Classrooms, Connoisseurs and Canons: Nineteenth-Century French Literature in Australia', *Australian Journal of French Studies*, XXX, 1993, 145–53.

5   *Address on the Opening of the Free Public Library of Ballarat East, by Sir Redmond Barry, on Friday, 1st January 1869* (Ballarat: printed at The Star office; Melbourne: H. T. Dwight, 1869), pp.18–19.

Sydney.[6] Innes died in 1896, having gone from politics to the Supreme Court bench. Ten years later his widow married Georges Biard d'Aunet (1844–1934), son of Léonie d'Aunet, Victor Hugo's mistress, and Consul then Consul General in Sydney between 1893 and 1905.[7]

Some other Sydney lawyers, for example Sir Frederick Jordan, H. S. Nicholas and Frank Leverrier, great-nephew of the astronomer, ranged more widely in their reading of French literature. However, few people can have matched the seriousness with which Alfred Deakin, the second Prime Minister of Australia, tackled a programme of self-instruction in a language he had not studied formally since his early schooldays. From his shipboard labours at French on his way to and from the Colonial Conference in London in 1887 right through to his long stint as party leader in Federal Parliament between 1903 and 1913 the subject bulked large in his reading. It is – in these times – more than a little quaint to see letters from the Prime Ministerial office to an academic teacher of modern literature on the philosophy of Hamelin and Renouvier and to discover that the writer was regularly reading the *Revue des deux mondes*, the *Revue latine* and the *Annales politiques et littéraires*.[8]

Meanwhile in Sydney, a long way away from the provisional Federal Capital in the South, there was a small group of devotees of French poetry from Baudelaire through to the Symbolists. Although we do not know how closely David Scott Mitchell (1836–1907) studied the *Œuvres complètes* in the Michel Lévy edition of 1868–1869 or the *Epaves* of 1874 – this latter title bought from Angus and Robertson in Sydney – there is no doubt that these volumes sit in the Mitchell Library of the State Library of New South Wales alongside their owner's incomparable Australiana collection. Similarly we can only guess at his familiarity with the several Stendhal works in his

---

6   Sydney: Angus & Robertson, 1929, pp.261–2.

7   See Ivan Barko, 'Georges Biard d'Aunet: the Life and Career of a Consul General', *Australian Journal of French Studies*, XXXIX, 2002, 271–91.

8   See J. A. La Nauze and Elizabeth Nurser, eds, *Walter Murdoch and Alfred Deakin on Books and Men: Letters and Comments 1900–1918* (Carlton: Melbourne University Press, 1974), passim.

collection,[9] but there is incontrovertible evidence that the reclusive bibliophile, who spent his whole life in his native New South Wales, was a diligent, acute and retentive reader in more than one field.[10] By a happy accident the poet and scholar Chris Brennan was set to work in 1900 on the cataloguing of the substantial non-Australian part of Mitchell's library.[11] Thus we encounter the key figure in the Australian vogue of French poetry of the second half of the nineteenth century.

Brennan's interest in Baudelaire has been analysed more than once,[12] so it is not necessary to chronicle an influence that lasted from the beginning of the 1890s till his death in 1932. Indeed the starting-point was the loan of Piddington's copy of *Les Fleurs du Mal* in October 1891. Later, in Brennan's 1892–1894 sojourn in Berlin, Mallarmé was to take over as the principal source of poetic inspiration, but the old allegiance was never forgotten. Similarly it is obvious that Brennan approached Baudelaire with the same philological rigour as he did the author of *Vers et prose*. Collecting texts as a prelude to *recensio* is almost as systematic in the one case as in the other. As he told a literary survey: 'no reading of poetry can be fruitful [...] without close and exhaustive study of at least one small portion of the work of each poet'.[13] This was private work, pen or pencil in hand. In contradistinction one finds the public proselytising, less often in the classroom, perhaps, than in more informal gatherings over food, and especially drink, where Brennan was a famous talker

9   See Wallace Kirsop, 'A Note on Stendhal's Early Australian Readers', *Australian Journal of French Studies*, XX, 1983, 252–6.

10   See Mungo William MacCallum's address at the opening of the Mitchell Library on 8 March 1910 in F. M. Bladen, *Public Library of New South Wales: Historical Notes* (2nd edition; Sydney: William Applegate Gullick, Government Printer, 1911), pp.82–6.

11   See David J. Jones, *A Source of Inspiration & Delight: the Buildings of the State Library of New South Wales since 1826* (Sydney: Library Council of New South Wales, 1988), p.38.

12   See, in particular, Axel Clark, *Christopher Brennan: a Critical Biography* (Carlton: Melbourne University Press, 1980), and, on Baudelaire volumes annotated by the Australian, Wallace Kirsop, 'Notes on Brennan's Reading of Baudelaire', *Australian Journal of French Studies*, VI, 1969, 337–47.

13   *The Lone Hand*, 1 November 1912, p.82b.

and reciter. The official record suggests that an average of thirty people attended the poet-librarian's six lectures on 'Symbolism in Nineteenth-Century Literature' between 15 June and 18 July 1904 for the University Extension Board of the University of Sydney.[14] A complete class list does not seem to be available, but the series was promoted by his friends Piddington and Jordan, a future Chief Justice of the Supreme Court of New South Wales.[15] Far fewer people attended a series two years later on 'Homer and the Homeric Question' despite the fact that Hellenism was the most formidable of all Brennan's talents.[16] Yet the Symbolism lectures were pitched at a high level reflecting their author's closer acquaintance and clearer grasp of the subject than anyone writing elsewhere in the English-speaking world at the beginning of the twentieth century. Brennan has, therefore, to have some credit for putting the Symbolist school on the Australian agenda, and not just in French studies.

Specialists do not need to be told about the critical and exegetical school that grew from this Sydney beginning. Brennan's pupils Randolph Hughes and A. R. Chisholm continued in another generation a tradition that led eventually to the work of Gardner Davies and Lloyd Austin. Bertrand Marchal's obituary of the former designates Australia generously as the 'deuxième patrie de Mallarmé' and calls Chisholm's two pupils 'les deux plus éminents mallarméens de notre temps'.[17] Unlike Davies, Austin was very much concerned with

14   *Calendar of the University of Sydney for the Year 1905* (Sydney: Angus & Robertson, 1905), p.401. See the text reproduced in *The Prose of Christopher Brennan*, ed. A. R. Chisholm & J. J. Quinn (Sydney: Angus and Robertson, 1962), pp.48–173.
15   See Axel Clark, op. cit., p.189.
16   The manuscript has remained unpublished. The printed report of the Extension Board (Acc. no.405, agency G.12, series 25), kindly made available by the University of Sydney Archives, admits (p.5) that a 'course […] intended especially for students and amateurs of Greek Literature […] had no popular appeal' and that its 'attendance was, therefore, small'. However, the Board was unrepentant about 'assistance to the limited number whose aim is exact scholarship or finer literary appreciation of the classics'.
17   See *French Studies*, XLVI, 1992, 118–19.

Baudelaire as well, as his publication list indicates.[18] The earlier poet
has not been neglected by younger members of what must now be
called very loosely the 'Melbourne School', even if Mallarmé continues to enjoy greater favour.[19]

Brennan's enthusiasm and curiosity were transmitted to a wider
circle of friends and literary contemporaries. He was not loath to lend
books and to participate in debate about his favourite poets. They thus
came into the public arena as well as into the libraries of his
acquaintances. The extent of the osmosis between Brennan's collection and that of his future editor J. J. Quinn is a telling instance of
the latter.[20] More important, at least for the exposure of Baudelaire
and Mallarmé to Sydney and Australian readers, was the dialogue
with A. G. Stephens, the most influential critic of that generation.[21]
Through the 'Red Page' (the literary section) of *The Bulletin* of J. F.
Archibald (reinvented as Jules-François rather than John Feltham,
such was his Francophilia) and through his own *Bookfellow*, Stephens
brought to bear his quite considerable knowledge of Parisian writing
trends and provided a forum for Brennan and others. It is this outward
face of the taste for recent French poetry that needs to be sketched
both in Sydney and in its rival, Melbourne.

It is not being unfair to Melbourne to say that, before 1914,
critical writing about Baudelaire and his successors did not venture
beyond the essayistic. Given that the only effective outlets were
magazines – not all of them shortlived, as the career of *The Bulletin*
since 1880 demonstrates – or newspapers, commentators had to use

18   See, in particular, *L'Univers poétique de Baudelaire: symbolisme et symbolique*
      (Paris: Mercure de France, 1956).
19   See, for example, Jill Anderson, ed., *Australian Divagations: Mallarmé & the
      20th Century* (New York: Peter Lang, 2002).
20   See Wallace Kirsop and Robin Marsden, 'C. J. Brennan, J. J. Quinn and the
      Library of St Patrick's College, Manly', *Bibliographical Society of Australia
      and New Zealand Bulletin*, 18, 1994, 173–8.
21   The cosmopolitan dimension of Stephens's work is brought out in Leon
      Cantrell, 'A. G. Stephens, *The Bulletin*, and the 1890s', in Leon Cantrell, ed.,
      Bards, Bohemians, and Bookmen: Essays in Australian Literature (St Lucia:
      University of Queensland Press, 1976), pp.98–113, and *A. G. Stephens:
      Selected Writings*, ed. Leon Cantrell (Sydney: Angus & Robertson Publishers,
      1977). There is scope for a more systematic examination of the topic.

those media or the lecture platform. Some academic journalists like A. T. Strong and Walter Murdoch did not hesitate to collect their occasional pieces later in volumes for which there appears to have been a steady Australasian market. Strong's *Peradventure* includes a piece on 'Poe and Baudelaire' that, like most of the rest of the volume, was originally printed in the Melbourne *Herald.*[22] The greatest impact was probably achieved through two journals financed by the firm of Lothian[23] in 1907–1909: *The Heart of the Rose* and *The Trident.* The latter was originally trilingual (English, French and German), directed monthly in a run of 3000 to the educational sector. In its second year it reverted to English and a broader cultural audience, without giving up its interest in European literature in general. Strong contributed some of the verse translations that he eventually brought out in *The Ballades of Théodore de Banville.*[24] He had a penchant for exercises in fixed form, having included in his first book, *Sonnets and Songs:*[25]

> Rondeau of Baudelaire
>
> IN Baudelaire the stern white ray
> Beats sheer upon the graven way,
>   Metallic glints affront the eye,
>   The shades are ink: the tense hot sky
> Holds earth in cruel rapier-play.
>
> Nor dappled dusk of frond and spray,
> Nor veiling grace of cloudlet gray,
>   Can stem the naked noonday high,
>   In Baudelaire.

22   Op. cit., pp.16–22.
23   An overview of the fortunes of the firm can be found in Stuart Sayers, *The Company of Books: a Short History of the Lothian Book Companies 1888–1988* (Melbourne: Lothian Publishing Company Pty Ltd, 1988). Cecily Close's 'The Publishing Activities of Thomas C. Lothian, 1905–1945', Monash University Ph.D. thesis, 1988, and some associated papers provide the most detailed account of the growth of a firm whose archives are deposited in the State Library of Victoria.
24   London, Macmillan, 1913.
25   Edinburgh & London, William Blackwood and Sons, 1905, p.12.

Yet here doth Beauty often stray,
And, though mid mists of waning day
  There flits no shadowy Naiad sky,
  Yet fierce Delight is ever nigh,
And Passion's self hath endless sway
  In Baudelaire.

One of the more surprising consequences of this early twentieth-century flurry about French poetry was that it brought precious inspiration to Shaw Neilson, an altogether more important and accomplished practitioner of the art than Strong. Neilson, who knew no French, read and owned the first number of *The Heart of the Rose* with Nettie Palmer's translation of Verlaine's *Art poétique* and obviously cherished it.[26] However much he may have owed to the tutelage of A. G. Stephens – essentially by letter – during the first three decades of the twentieth century, it is worth noting that this itinerant country labourer was almost forty before he first visited Melbourne in 1911. The triumph of print over distance...

On the whole our tradition, unlike the Japanese, has not valued translation as a fundamental critical activity, a supreme expression of communion with a foreign text. However, there is ample evidence not only that Brennan conceived of producing literal and polished versions as one of the tasks of the exegete,[27] but also that many readers and would-be writers a century ago were ready to accept the challenge of competitions in translating French poetry.

In no.3 of *The Bookfellow* on 25 March 1899 Stephens announced a forthcoming article by Brennan on Baudelaire and a prize: [...] by way of encouraging translators a prize of 10s.6d. is offered for a good English version of this poem by Baudelaire to accompany that article–

26 See Helen Hewson, *John Shaw Neilson: a Life in Letters* (Carlton South: The Miegunyah Press, 2001), pp.13–16.
27 See Wallace Kirsop, 'Brennan as Exegete: some documents from the Mallarmé corpus', *Australian Journal of French Studies*, XVI, 1979, 233–243, and the translations embedded in the series of articles on Baudelaire and others that Brennan wrote for Stephens in *The Bookfellow* and then *The Bulletin* in 1899 (*The Prose of Christopher Brennan*, pp.286–322).

Harmonie Du Soir
[...][28]

The result, as reported in no.4 of 29 April 1899, was disappointing:

> I regret that Baudelaire's 'Harmonie du Soir' has proved too difficult for the
> corps of translators attempting it. Versions which are not good have been
> received from J. W. R.; G. G. McC.; Scotty (who says with some truth that
> 'there is a jar of mechanical structure in the original,' effective though it be);
> Acolyte; D.; K. B.; P. T. F.; Byrne Kay; Novice; and F. T. H.; and versions
> which are not good enough from W. L. F. M.; N. B.; H. S.; D. B.; D. C.;
> A. V. G. (two); W. W. H.; J. L. K.; and Hanam. None is up to print-standard.
> Yet Baudelaire's poem is beautiful and technically interesting; and was worth
> the attempt. I defer till next number a more detailed commentary; and in the
> meantime translators may try this easier sonnet by Verlaine. (It should not be,
> but is, necessary to say that the rhyme-scheme must be preserved; *and* the
> meaning; and as far as possible the atmosphere and melody.)

Mon Reve Familier
[...][29]

In the event Stephens did not return to Baudelaire, but, in what was to
be the last number of the first series of *The Bookfellow*, no.5 of 31
May 1899, he awarded the prize to one Verlaine translation, which
was 'only tolerably good', and reproduced a few others.[30]

It is tempting to guess the identity of the quite numerous
competitors (with some new initials the second time), but the task is
generally too difficult. 'G. G. McC.' suggests almost irresistibly
George Gordon McCrae (1833–1927), who was involved in the
literary world of Melbourne during most of a long life. A collection of
his verses published in 1915 claims that he 'has a particular

28   Page 12.
29   Page 3.
30   Pages 22–5.

admiration for the literature and people of France'.[31] His minor talent has been overshadowed for modern Australians by the story of his mother Georgiana, illegitimate but acknowledged daughter of the last Duke of Gordon,[32] and imbued with the French culture she absorbed at *émigré* schools in London in the early nineteenth century. Her world and her son's in Melbourne was that of society before and after the 1850s gold rush and of literary and Bohemian circles comprising people like R. H. Horne, Adam Lindsay Gordon and Marcus Clarke. It is not clear whether it ever intersected with a somewhat raffish French community represented amongst others by the Consul Lionel de Chabrillan, his wife, the notorious Céleste Mogador, and the photographer Antoine Fauchery.[33] None the less it was the last-named who had a genuine connection with advanced groups in Paris. Indeed his *Lettres d'un mineur en Australie*, with a long preface by Théodore de Banville, were issued by Baudelaire's publisher Poulet-Malassis in the same year as *Les Fleurs du Mal*. Later immigrants and temporary residents over the following decades had less modern tastes, so that the discoveries of Piddington, Brennan, Stephens and their friends have to be regarded – paradoxically no doubt – as native achievements. *The Bookfellow*'s competitions are in some ways a debased form of this obsession, but it is salutary to recall that there were – at the same time in the 1890s – Australian parallels to the effort Stefan George was putting into his 'Umdichtungen' of *Die Blumen des Bösen*.[34] In the end it was a good deal more than a trivial episode.

31 *The Fleet and Convoy and other verses* (Melbourne & Sydney: Lothian Book Publishing Co. Pty Ltd, 1915), p.6.

32 See Brenda Niall, *Georgiana: a Biography of Georgiana McCrae, Painter, Diarist, Pioneer* (Carlton: Melbourne University Press at the Miegunyah Press, 1994).

33 See Dianne Reilly & Jennifer Carew, *Sun Pictures of Victoria: the Fauchery–Daintree Collection 1858* (Melbourne: Currey O'Neil Ross Pty Ltd on behalf of the Library Council of Victoria, 1983).

34 See Stefan George, *Sämtliche Werke in 18 Bänden*, Band XIII/XIV: *Baudelaire. Die Blumen des Bösen. Umdichtungen* (Stuttgart: Klett-Cotta, 1983).

Terence McMullan

Trading places: crazy years of cultural exchange in Paris and Madrid

During the 1920s and 1930s, while Adrienne Monnier and Sylvia Beach were making their discreet but invaluable contributions to literary Paris, León Sánchez Cuesta was performing a similar function in Madrid.[1] Although he was, for more than a decade, a familiar figure on the lively literary scene which flourished in pre-Civil War Spain, the exact nature and importance of his involvement in the creative effervescence of the period has never been closely examined. Detailed analysis of this self-effacing yet remarkable bookseller's activities and influence reveals a fascinating picture of cultural enrichment fostered by a network of relationships and contacts whose ramifications deserve to be better known.

León Sánchez Cuesta became a bookseller by accident. He was originally destined for an administrative or academic legal career.

1   Accounts of the contemporary situation in Paris are available from Adrienne Monnier, *Rue de l'Odéon* (Paris: Albin Michel, 1960) and Sylvia Beach, *Shakespeare and Company* (London: Faber and Faber, 1960). As for Madrid, nearly all the factual information used in this discussion comes from León Sánchez Cuesta's private papers which include the following four categories of written documents: (1) *Cartas* or Letters received by León Sánchez. All references to this source will be identified thus: (C.day-month-year). (2) The *Registro de Pedidos* or Bookshop Register. All references to this source will be identified thus: (R.day-month-year). (3) *Facturas* or Book-bills. All references to this source will be identified thus: (F.day-month-year). (4) Letters to others written by (or on behalf of) León Sánchez Cuesta. All references to this source will be identified thus: (LSC.day-month-year). The León Sánchez Cuesta archive documents listed above have all been consulted on several occasions in the original. Where appropriate, this material was elucidated or supplemented by many private conversations with Sánchez Cuesta. All translations from the Spanish are mine.

Born in 1892, he came from Oviedo where his father owned a toyshop. There were ten children in the family (nine boys and one girl), but whereas his brothers emigrated to Mexico, he stayed in Spain and gained a law degree from Oviedo University. At the age of twenty-one he began postgraduate work in Toulouse under the supervision of Maurice Hauriou, an international authority on administrative law. However, at the end of his first year the Great War broke out and he had to return home. By 1915 he was in Madrid intending to complete his doctoral thesis and planning to sit official entrance examinations for the Attorney General's office and Crown Prosecution service. To facilitate this process he was admitted to the Residencia de Estudiantes, an event which would transform his life and determine its future course.[2]

Gradually, as he was integrated more and more into the Residencia environment, the young Asturian encountered and grew friendly with a number of people who already were or would soon become significant figures in pre-Civil War Spanish culture. Among the most notable was Juan Ramón Jiménez who lived at the institution from 1913 until 1916. León remained on good terms with this eventual Nobel prizewinner who was arguably the most distinguished and influential poet of his day, and their relationship subsequently had an important effect on Sánchez Cuesta's professional development. In the meantime, he undertook various duties to support himself financially. He was asked to give classes on literature, history and logic at the Residencia de Niños by its director Luis Santullano. There he met the recently-arrived sixteen year-old Emilio Prados with whom he would also maintain a close personal friendship and professional connection through the future activities of the Imprenta Sur. In addition, the Residencia de Estudiantes employed León Sánchez as a law tutor. He also contributed to the summer course for foreigners, and acted occasionally as administrative assistant to the director, Alberto Jiménez Fraud. It was probably at this period, too, that he first made the acquaintance of Pedro Salinas, his future brother-in-law,

2   See John Crispin, *Oxford y Cambridge en Madrid: La Residencia de Es-tudiantes (1910–1936) y su entorno cultural* (Santander: La Isla de los Ratones, 1981).

whose involvement with the cultural activities of the Residencia went back as far as its 'Fiesta de Aranjuez en honor de Azorín' in which Salinas had participated on 23 November 1913. Even after Sánchez Cuesta's five-year period as a *residente* had ended, he continued to feel part of that milieu, and regularly helped out there. An issue of the magazine *Residencia* includes a group photograph dated March 1925 where he appears sitting on the front row between Salvador Dalí and Federico García Lorca.[3] His affable relationship with Luis Buñuel, who lived at the institution from 1917 to 1925, dates from then as well. It would be no exaggeration to say that León Sánchez Cuesta's Residencia years were a defining phase whose formative effect on him would prove to be crucial.

By 1920 circumstances forced León Sánchez to confront the problem of how to earn a living in the outside world. On Alberto Jiménez's recommendation, Manuel Aguilar, head of the Sociedad Española de Librería y Publicaciones (a branch of the Hachette company), the biggest exporter of Spanish books, sent him to do a survey of the Mexican market. He made two trips of six or seven months each in 1921–1922, dealing directly with booksellers, making contact with people in the import-export business, and generally getting to know the trade through experience. When, at the end of 1922, the Sociedad Española de Librería ran into serious economic difficulties, he returned to Madrid where salvation awaited in the shape of Domingo Barnés, director of the La Lectura publishing house. Premises were provided in the company building at number 25, Paseo de Recoletos, almost opposite the Biblioteca Nacional, for Sánchez Cuesta to set up his first bookshop, the Librería de Arte y Extranjera de La Lectura, which opened at the start of January 1923.

With its sofa and armchairs, it seemed more like a reading-room than a bookshop. The tidiness of its catalogues and card-index reminded certain customers of an American bookstore. In some ways it

---

3   *Residencia*, I, núm.1 (Enero-Abril 1926), 88. The photograph is identified as: 'Un grupo de Residentes en el "transatlántico"' (a wooden balcony that ran the full length of one pavilion's façade made it resemble an ocean liner). Lorca stayed at the Resi on and off between 1919 and 1928, whereas Dalí lived there from 1922 to 1926.

must have resembled an annexe of the Residencia given that Alberto Jiménez Fraud, Juan Ramón Jiménez, José Ortega y Gasset and Alfonso Reyes were regular visitors. Now and again Antonio Machado would drop in to ask after 'Juanito' (Juan Ramón Jiménez). Despite starting out under the umbrella of La Lectura, by early November 1924 the bookshop was financially autonomous though still occupying the same accommodation in Recoletos. A new phase of absolute independance commenced, however, in April 1925 when the business moved to its definitive pre-Civil War location at number 4, calle Mayor, whereupon it took a new name, the one by which it established itself as the most famous Spanish bookshop of its day: the Librería León Sánchez Cuesta.

Rather than being a bookshop in the conventional sense, the calle Mayor premises consisted essentially of an office in a first-floor flat. The building could hardly have been more centrally situated, standing as it did a few steps from the Puerta del Sol. But, it had no shop-window, there was no plaque or commercial sign at street-level. Customers had to find their way up the stairs, open a door, and enter through the service area where piles of book-orders were being parcelled for dispatch. Having asked for the proprietor they then found themselves ushered into a spartan room about 15 feet by 20 at the back (the balcony overlooked the calle Arenal). A couple of tables, some chairs, shelves and catalogues made up the rather basic furniture of what Rafael Alberti later called, perhaps with poetic licence, 'una pequeña librería íntima'.[4] With little or no scope for passing trade or casual clients, the bookshop functioned and survived commercially, to a large extent, by mail-order. Those who did turn up in person tended either to know León Sánchez already or to have some link with the Residencia de Estudiantes. An informal *tertulia*, or regular get-to-

---

4   'I had just come from a small intimate bookshop, whose proprietor, a great friend of all of us, had managed to find me a rare copy of Rimbaud's poems', Rafael Alberti, *La arboleda perdida* (Buenos Aires: Fabril, 1959), p.278. Although Sánchez Cuesta is not mentioned here by name (no doubt to spare him official disapproval from the Franco régime of the time) his bookshop-records for the 1920s show that Alberti was supplied with a copy of Rimbaud's *Poésies*, not in Autumn 1928 as the Spanish poet's memoirs recalled but three years earlier (F.5–10–1925).

gether, grew up around Juan Ramón Jiménez and those eager to meet the great writer usually saddled Sánchez Cuesta with the delicate task of introducing them.

Although the Librería León Sánchez Cuesta was a self-sufficient business, two factors reinforced its ties with the Residencia de Estudiantes of which it became, in effect, the designated bookshop. Most of the operation involved supplying technical works on law, science, medicine or economics either to the big Mexican importers such as Pedro Robredo and Porrúa Hermanos, or, more significantly, to seats of learning on both sides of the Atlantic, often at the behest of Hispanists who had been León Sánchez's contemporaries at the Residencia. Nevertheless, what enhanced the bookshop's reputation was the, quantitatively much smaller, literary side of things.

As Sánchez Cuesta worked to strengthen and consolidate his position, he was greatly helped by the fact that he acted as agent for various publications all of which, directly or indirectly, were associated with the Residencia de Estudiantes. These fell into four main categories. First there were the twenty-eight titles actually produced by the Residencia, which ranged from literary texts by contemporary authors like Azorín, Jiménez, Machado and Unamuno to scholarly studies on science, law, economics, music, history and philosophy. Then came about forty items, issued under the imprimatur of Juan Ramón Jiménez, which encompassed seven of his own collections, twenty Rabindranath Tagore translations done with Zenobia Camprubí; the couple's joint Spanish version of Synge's *Riders to the Sea*; the complete set of the magazine *Indice* (1–4) plus the six volumes that made up the Biblioteca de Indice; and various pamphlets such as *Sí, Unidad, Diario poético*, and *Ley*. Next came the publications of Alberto Jiménez Fraud, the director of the Residencia, who had also been a freelance publisher since 1914. His total of around sixty works included the Colección Granada, the Colección Infantil Granada, and Clásicos Granada; the Jardinillos, the Colección Abeja, and Senderos de Arte; and the Lecturas de Una Hora. Finally, in Léon Sánchez's 1926 catalogue, eight Obras Varias featured the magazine *Litoral*, destined to become another jewel in the bookshop's crown.

Sánchez Cuesta's accumulation of this prestigious list of titles partly explains how his bookshop came to act as a literary focus and a cohesive factor in a Spanish cultural scene remarkable for its compactness. He was identified with the Residencia de Estudiantes because he not only administered their publications, he also supplied the libraries of the Residencia and its affiliated institutions, and the core of his clientele were present or former *residentes* who recommended his services. Through the Residencia connection he ended up distributing Juan Ramón's works which attracted the sort of customers who were themselves active or budding writers. Jiménez's *cuadernos*, or poetry pamphlets, then provided a model for the productions of the Imprenta Sur. This in turn encouraged other members of the younger generation to send samples of their magazines and books to the calle Mayor in search of an elite readership. Nevertheless, high-profile though all these developments were culturally, in practical terms they smacked of a cottage industry rather than a commercially viable enterprise. Sales even of such publications as those by Jiménez and *Litoral* rarely reached three figures. Yet what they lacked in financial potential was compensated for by their aesthetic appeal. If most of these authors could only speak to a minority audience, at the end of the day, Sánchez Cuesta's willingness to bring them to the attention of, if not a wider, at least a more discriminating public was very much a labour of love.

As *concesionario*, or exclusive distributor, of these publications, the Madrid operation developed a distinctive character, its reputation spread and business prospered. Soon it was time to expand. French literature had always played an important part in León Sanchez's activities. For example, by 1926 he was providing two hundred of his private customers with copies of *Les Livres du Mois*, a list of the latest book-titles produced by Bibliographie de la France (LSC.25–1–1927). But problems with French suppliers persuaded him to set up a wholesale book-purchasing facility in Paris.[5] So he spent three and a half months in the French capital, from late February until early June

5   He also produced his own list of recent Spanish publications along the lines of
     Les Livres du Mois. By 1930 he informed F. Rodríguez Marín that each month
     individual clients were receiving, between his Madrid bookshop and the branch
     in Paris, 1000 catalogues listing new titles of Spanish and French books
     (LSC.4–7–1930).

1927, making the necessary arrangements.[6] Later he informed Antonio Solalinde that his original plan now included a retail outlet to meet the Parisian demand for competitively priced Spanish publications. (LSC.11–11–1927).[7] This showcase for recent Spanish literature was significant in itself. But by creating a rapid and efficient system of importing into Spain the most up-to-date French titles, León Sánchez found himself in the unique and privileged position of directly connecting Paris with Madrid.

His new bookshop was located at 10, rue Gay-Lussac. Further down, on the opposite side of the street, at number 31, stood Paris university's Institut d'Etudes Hispaniques, which augured well. A short walk away was the rue de l'Odéon where Sylvia Beach's *Shakespeare and Company* and Adrienne Monnier's *La Maison des Amis des Livres* were situated. Meanwhile Luis Sánchez Cuesta (a brother back from Mexico) and Juan Vicens were looking after things in the calle Mayor. León wrote to tell them that the new premises were in a good street that opened onto the Boulevard St Michel opposite the Luxembourg Gardens. It was easily accessible and very close to all the publishers and booksellers. Much larger than he would have liked (with a floor area of about 5 metres by 5 metres), it had a back room, and a basement as big as the shop. The entrance door in the middle had a shop window on either side. It also had display cases on the street. (C.3–3–1927). At the bookshop's opening, one window displayed photographs and works of Juan Ramón Jiménez and his contemporaries, while the other presented young writers, with emphasis on *Litoral*.[8] A sketch by Pancho Cossío later served as an advertising logo on business cards.

6　In 1927 Sánchez Cuesta had entered into a business agreement with Juan Vicens (another ex-*residente*!). Though well off, Vicens' money was tied up in a flour mill at Cifuentes (Guadalajara) whose disposal occupied him for the next few years. Their partnership seemed to trigger the search for a firmer foothold in the French market.

7　Alfonso Reyes had told him of this gap in the market adding that in Paris there was no bookseller familiar with the important new writers in Spain (C.11–2–1925).

8　León Sánchez reporting to Emilio Prados on his new Paris venture, said that, of the Spanish books he had taken there, the publications of *Litoral* had attracted

The rue Gay-Lussac became a port of call for Spaniards domiciled in Paris or just passing through such as Jorge Guillén, his friend Jules Supervielle, Fernando de los Ríos and the painter Ramón Gaya. Luis Buñuel was a regular. During León Sánchez's stay in the French capital to set up the business they had seen a good deal of each other socially, attending films and concerts together. After Sánchez Cuesta returned to Madrid, Buñuel wrote from Paris: 'Dear León:

> [...] Do whatever you can to come in October. Remember that you promised me a night out when we could let our hair down, and I'm still waiting. As, by then, I shall be very friendly with Josephine Baker, we'll go and spend a night at her "petite boîte" in Montmartre. You also left without seeing or spending a day at a film-studio' (C.28–7–1927).[9]

As sales flourished in the rue Gay-Lussac, the manager, Gabriel Escribano, eventually needed help.[10] Buñuel suggested his girlfriend

particular attention and people were surprised that such beautiful things were produced in Spain. He also mentioned that the publishers of *Transition* (an English-language literary magazine based in Paris) were so impressed that they devoted part of their most recent issue to some of this material translated into English: a prose text by Salinas, poetry by Alberti, Espina, and 'Con guitarra negra', by Giménez Caballero. An accompanying note stated: 'Most of the (Spanish) poets in the present issue belong to *Litoral*, a group whose headquarters is in Malaga' (LSC.23–6–1927). The bookshop's distinctive façade subsequently featured in a scene from Buñuel's film *L'Âge d'or* (1930).

9   Buñuel worked on the set of the Josephine Baker movie *La Sirène des tropiques*. But, exasperated by the star's capricious behaviour, he eventually left the film before its completion. Luis Buñuel, *Mon dernier soupir* (Paris: Robert Laffont, 1982), pp.109–10. Six of his letters to León Sánchez Cuesta (including the one quoted here) are reproduced in Agustín Sánchez Vidal, *Buñuel, Lorca, Dalí: El enigma sin fin* (Barcelona: Planeta, 1988), pp.139, 140, 145–7, 149.

10   By June 1927 contact had been established with Spanish teachers from the lycées, and Professor Martinenche of the Sorbonne had also promised to recommend the bookshop to his pupils (C.2–6–1927). After the summer Escribano was urgently requesting that textbooks be sent from Madrid to meet the demand (C.9–11–1927).

(and future wife) Jeanne Rucar for the job. Her presence there meant that he remained an assiduous visitor to the Paris bookshop.[11]

Attempts were made to establish contacts with French colleagues. Escribano told León Sánchez that José Bergamín had called in and that together they had gone to Mlle Monnier's as Bergamín wanted information about Valéry. Escribano had hoped to take the opportunity to talk to her about the Spanish bookshop but she was away on summer holiday and it wasn't possible (C.3–9–1927). When Juan Vicens took over in Paris,[12] this process continued. He informed Sánchez Cuesta by letter that he had recently been in *Shakespeare and Co.*, had spoken with 'Juanita's friend' and with Miss Beach who had both been extremely nice, promising to come to the Spanish bookshop and to recommend them to everyone. While he was there Joyce had come in. Vicens also said he would pay a visit soon to 'Mme [sic] Monnier' (C.3–6–1928).[13]

11 Escribano explained to León Sánchez that they could only afford to pay her 350 francs a month so Buñuel insisted on making up the difference to 500 francs without Jeanne's knowledge (C.20–11–1927). Her own version of this subterfuge is somewhat inaccurate, namely, that Luis was not subsidising put paying her entire monthly 300-franc salary, to which she put a stop when she found out. Vicens employed her sister Georgette as secretarial help when Escribano left in the summer of 1928. Six years later Georgette took over the now renamed *Librería Española de París*. See Jeanne Rucar de Buñuel, *Memorias de una mujer sin piano* (Madrid: Alianza, 1991), pp.38–9.

12 A legal contract (16–4–1928) gave Vicens ownership of the Gay-Lussac premises while Sánchez Cuesta kept the Madrid bookshop. But they continued to trade under the same name and co-operated for their mutual import-export benefit. They even did temporary exchanges, with León Sánchez replacing Vicens in Paris and vice versa.

13 The 'Juanita' mentioned here was, of course, Jeanne Rucar. In her memoirs she speaks of her friendship with Myrsine Moschos who worked for Sylvia Beach, and also recalls meeting James Joyce in *Shakespeare and Company* on more than one occasion (op.cit., 39). Joyce, whose *Ulysses* had been published by Sylvia Beach in 1922, was the familiar spirit of *Shakespeare and Company*, just as Paul Valéry was of Adrienne Monnier's *La Maison des Amis des Livres*, while Juan Ramón Jiménez had a similar relationship with León Sánchez Cuesta's Madrid bookshop. Later Vicens wanted to publish a Spanish version of *Ulysses* (C.5–2–1929; C.7–2–1929) to be done by Dámaso Alonso (who had

Buñuel's links with the Gay-Lussac bookshop were further reinforced by the fact that Juan Vicens was now its proprietor. They had
been close for several years. Juan Vicens belonged to an Aragonese
clique at the Residencia which included Pepín Bello and Luis Buñuel.
Even more significantly, Vicens, his wife María Luisa González,
Buñuel and Salvador Dalí had all been members of the mock 'Order
of Toledo' and appear in photographs taken at the Venta de los Aires
in 1924.[14] When Buñuel first reached Paris in 1925 he and Vicens
would go drinking together and even dreamed of opening a cabaret
(Sánchez Vidal, op. cit, p.132). Vicens was mentioned as one of the
dedicatees of a book Buñuel was working on (Ibid., pp.146, 158). The
would-be film director even tried unsuccessfully to persuade his friend
to fund his frustrated cinema projects (quoted in Sánchez Vidal,
p.318). All of which puts into perspective a letter which Vicens sent
León Sánchez from Paris together with two copies of Breton's *La
peinture surréaliste,* one for the Madrid bookshop and one for Buñuel.
Vicens praises the book, for which he thinks there will be a demand,
as he has read it and liked it. As a result of this and of attending a
recent Miró exhibition, he states that he is becoming seriously in-
terested in the Surrealists and that Breton's theories represent the most
viable way forward (C.20–5–1928). This enthusiasm led him to take
the initiative at times in spontaneously sending to Madrid recent
avant-garde publications, such as an issue of *Le Grand Jeu*, which he
describes as a more or less orthodox Surrealist magazine (C.1–8–
1928). In these circumstances, when he had lunch with Hinojosa three
days later, it is hard to imagine that Surrealism was not discussed.

In the second half of January 1929 an event occurred which
brought this issue into sharper focus. From Figueras, where they were
preparing the script of *Un chien andalou*, Buñuel and Dalí wrote an
insulting and gratuitous letter to Juan Ramón Jiménez as a calculated

translated Joyce's *Portrait of the Artist* in 1926 under the pseudonym Alfonso
Donado) but Vicens soon lost interest (C.18–2–1929).

14   Illustrations of this can be found in Sánchez Vidal, op.cit., p.77, and in Rafael
Santos Torroella, *Dalí residente* (Madrid: Consejo Superior de Investigaciones
Científicas y la Asociación Amigos de la Residencia de Estudiantes, 1992),
p.21.

act of Surrealistic iconoclasm. Despite the scandalousness of their unprovoked assault, Vicens felt able to report the pair's subsequent Surrealist progress in a tone which was cautious rather than disapproving. According to his account, Buñuel was finishing the interior shots of the film and seemed happy with the result though there was some doubt as to where it could be screened because of its strong and shocking images of priests dragged along the ground, naked women and so on. Dalí, he added, had made a real impression. Three or four dealers were competing for his work and the Surrealists were lionising him (C.15–4–1929). On 15 May 1929, an article in *La Gaceta Literaria* by Ernesto Giménez Caballero, one of the Spaniards who kept up with the Gay-Lussac bookshop on his way through Paris, contained an extraordinarily worded allusion to 'Surrealism. (I don't like calling it that, dear Dalí, dear Buñuel, dear Vicens)'.[15] By connecting these three individuals he gives a clear impression of Vicens as someone immersed in a Surrealist atmosphere. Vicens' favourable reaction, within a month, to the first screening of *Un chien andalou* therefore seems all the more predictable. He reports that it is a shame that it is so short and fast-moving (the result of financial constraints) but that it has turned out better than everybody hoped. The Surrealists (Miró, Max Ernst, Tzara, etc.) have responded enthusiastically as have avant-garde film-makers. Everyone is saying that it is what was needed, that nothing like it has been done before, that it is ground-breaking and full of ideas. Buñuel has received various offers from film companies. The problem is one of censorship but if this could be addressed it is sure to be a success. It has been extravagantly praised in the *Intransigeant* and others have promised to publicise it in the press. Vicens applauds the honesty and sincerity of its approach, its total lack of literary or aesthetic priorities. The avoidance of clever or pretty effects, he says, has also been much admired since even Man Ray's attempt at Surrealist cinema did not avoid this trap (C.8–6–1929). It is extremely instructive to compare the impression of unqualified appreciation conveyed in these comments with the dry and caustic assessment by Emilio Gómez Orbaneja who about the same period observed to Sánchez Cuesta that

15   Quoted in Sánchez Vidal, op.cit., 318.

he had called at the bookshop in Paris where at that time, Vicens, Dalí and Buñuel were indulging in their 'Aragonese aesthetic excesses' (C.26–6–1929). Thus Vicens emerges clearly as, at the very least, a Surrealist by association.

When León Sánchez founded a branch in the rue Gay-Lussac, he eased and accelerated the flow of French books into Spain. Another dimension was added to the already distinctive character of his Madrid bookshop. Hitherto considered the essential source of publications from the Residencia, Juan Ramón, and the Imprenta Sur, as well as the ideal place to find books or magazines issued by the younger generation of Spanish writers, after 1927 the calle Mayor premises also came to be regarded as the most efficient and best informed supplier of the latest titles from Paris. Moreover, at the helm in the French capital was his partner and collaborator Juan Vicens, a front-line representative, someone on the spot, as it were, whose sympathetic relationship with Buñuel and Dalí made him a virtual eye-witness to avant-garde innovations emanating from Surrealist circles, which thus became instantly available to a Spanish public. By fostering access to and awareness of these radical developments, Sánchez Cuesta and Vicens therefore acted as cultural enablers who brought a progressive and contemporary Paris closer to Madrid.

Mortified by the unwarranted epistolary attack from Buñuel and Dalí, Juan Ramón Jiménez had adopted a more reclusive lifestyle which meant curtailing his visits to the Madrid bookshop and distancing himself from a younger generation some of whom he had previously thought of as his disciples. If this withdrawal in January 1929 can be seen as somehow emblematic of a wider shift in aesthetic sensibilities at this time, the same might be said of Luis Cernuda's arrival to work for León Sánchez. All that can be stated with certainty from documents of the period about Cernuda's tenure at the Madrid bookshop is that he was definitely employed there from late March 1930 until mid November 1931.[16] Nothing directly linked Jiménez's

---

16   This conclusion is based on the fact that Cernuda's highly individual hand-writing appears for the first time in a Registro de *Pedidos* entry for 31 March 1930 and the last example of it occurs on 10 November 1931. Between these dates it is by far the dominant hand occupying no less than 122 out of the 128

departure and the younger poet's appointment which, after all, happened over a year later. Nevertheless, an accidental yet complementary symmetry endows these two events retrospectively with symbolic significance. The fact that Cernuda (who had been teaching in France from November 1928 until June 1929) was still in the throes of his Surrealist phase, made his presence in the calle Mayor a symptom of broader and more subversive changes of emphasis then transforming Spanish culture.

In any attempt to understand the nature of the service that Sánchez Cuesta delivered to his customers, several factors make Vicente Aleixandre a particularly suitable subject for study. Since the picture available derives almost entirely from information stored in the bookshop archives, any client chosen for detailed examination has to be adequately represented in those documents. Aleixandre's intermittently delicate health and convalescent regime gave him a greater than average tendency to order by post from a single supplier thus leaving a paper trail of his reading habits. His consistent enthusiasm for books, and the fact that he could afford, within reason, to buy more or less what he liked, satisfy other essential criteria as well: his dealings with the calle Mayor were both quantitatively substantial and spread over a fairly protracted span of time, which makes them potentially more reliable and significant as a source of evidence. Nor should it be forgotten that the period covered by these data (roughly speaking the decade prior to the Spanish Civil War) was of exceptional importance in Aleixandre's evolution as a writer. His talent

relevant pages. This period of employment is consistent with references in letters that Cernuda sent Higinio Capote on 16 June and 21 August 1930, reproduced in José María Capote Benot, *El surrealismo en la poesía de Luis Cernuda* (Sevilla: Publicaciones de la Universidad de Sevilla, 1976), 277 and 279. Cernuda got the job (like his lectorship in Toulouse and later Misiones Pedagógicas post) on the recommendation of Pedro Salinas. At the calle Mayor he replaced José María Quiroga Plà, a writer and translator as well as being Miguel de Unamuno's son-in-law. León Sánchez wrote to Bruno del Amo (LSC.12–11–1930) seeking for Cernuda paid translation work such as Quiroga Plà had been given. By November 1931 Cernuda had left the calle Mayor for a post at the *Patronato de Misiones Pedagógicas* and was ordering books for them (C.17–11–1931).

was then at its early formative stage. Artistically, he was, perhaps, at his most susceptible to external stimulus because his own distinctive poetic voice was still in the process of defining itself. After all, these were the very years when this future Nobel prizewinner laid the foundations of his life's work in five volumes of verse, emerging from the total obscurity of 1925 (when his name initially enters the bookshop records), to produce his first collection *Ámbito* (published by the Imprenta Sur in 1928), and eventually to win the 1934 Premio Nacional de Literatura with *La destrucción o el amor* (1935). Aleixandre's total of 303 items requested can be reduced to 275 orders successfully completed. Of these more than half (166) were in French, which confirms the importance of the calle Mayor bookshop as an importer of books from Paris.

About a fifth of the French items were translations from German and English, stressing Aleixandre's preferential recourse to that language for works unobtainable in Spanish. Carlos Bousoño cites a letter from the poet where he admits discovering Freud in 1928.[17] This fits the facts recorded independently in the bookshop archive. Aleixandre asked León Sánchez to send him details of Freud's works available in the Spanish versions (C.18–8–1928) when he ordered *The Interpretation of Dreams* of which volumes one and two were subsequently delivered. But he had to accept some Freud titles in French. While on the topic of reading certain books in French translation, the case of James Joyce deserves comment. As early as February 1926 Aleixandre had requested two copies of *Ulysses* since the work was advertised as published in France, but he cancelled the order a week later in the belief that the whole work was written in some terrible Irish dialect (C.24–2–1926). The author of *Pasión de la tierra* always acknowledged Joyce's impact on him, so he must have waited at least three more years to read *Ulysses* which was not issued in French translation until February 1929.[18]

17   Carlos Bousoño, *La poesía de Vicente Aleixandre* (Madrid: Gredos, 1968), p.16.
18   Richard Ellmann, *James Joyce* (Oxford, New York, Toronto, Melbourne: Oxford U.Press, 1983), p.615.

Another master of the European literary non-rational who dominated that artistic period and whose influence on Aleixandre coincided with that of Joyce was Rimbaud.[19] There is no trace in the documents of the author of *Les Illuminations*, an absence which serves as a reminder that this list of book-orders does not purport to furnish a comprehensive account of either the Spaniard's purchases or his reading habits. Nevertheless, ample documentation does exist of Aleixandre's enthusiasm for a whole range of important French writers, particularly those active in the contemporary avant-garde. So the extent of his familiarity with such literature, which has long been a critical bone of contention, can now be confirmed once and for all.

Even by 1993, the best circumstantial evidence of French Surrealist influence on Vicente Aleixandre was an objectively undocumented statement made by the poet to José Luis Cano nearly twenty years before:

> First: That in 1929 [he, Aleixandre] began to write *Pasión de la tierra* [he actually started it in 1928], under the influence of the precursors of Surrealism: Lautréamont, Rimbaud – specifically *Les Illuminations* –, Joyce, Freud. Second: That when the book was already quite well advanced he began to read the French Surrealists – Breton, Aragon, Eluard and others –, whose books he ordered from the bookseller León Sánchez Cuesta [...].[20]

The wealth of relevant data preserved in León Sánchez's archive thus fills a long-standing vacuum, and puts the debate about Surrealism and Spain on a firmer footing.

Surrealists occupy a special place in the broad spectrum of French writers from every literary genre who feature among Aleixandre's bookshop orders. The first to do so was Eluard whose *Capitale de la douleur* (C.12–3–1929/R.14–3–1929/C.26–3–1929/F.30–4–1929) appears on the same book-bill as Lautréamont's *Œuvres*

19 Bousoño, op.cit., 15. Bousoño quotes from a letter Aleixandre wrote him on 8 July 1949, which makes this one of the Spanish poet's earliest comments on the subject.

20 Vicente Aleixandre, *Pasión de la tierra*, ed. de Gabriele Morelli (Madrid: Cátedra, 1993), p.32. The quote is from J.L.Cano, *Los cuadernos de Velintonia. Conversaciones con Vicente Aleixandre* (Barcelona: Seix Barral, 1986), 16 de mayo de 1974, p.210.

complètes. Once contact had been established, Aleixandre read very extensively, acquiring titles by members of the movement's inner circle such as Breton, Aragon, Eluard, Crevel and Desnos, as well as items by the less prominent Ribemont-Dessaignes, Baron, Bousquet, Char, Michaux, Tzara and Artaud. His purchases also encompassed Surrealist pamphlets, and issues of the magazines *La Révolution surréaliste, Le Surréalisme au service de la révolution,* and *Minotaure.* Nor is Lautréamont the only Surrealist precursor on a book-list which includes Sade, Freud and Vaché too. Nevertheless, what astonishes here is not just the variety of the entries but their chronological distribution. Two-thirds of all the Surrealist and affiliated publications ordered by Aleixandre appear grouped in a preliminary cluster between April 1929 and December 1930. Thereafter his commitment flags rather. Apart from magazines, and titles by minor figures, from January 1931 onwards the Surrealist book-orders become sparser, as though he were barely maintaining an interest whose earlier intensity had now been thoroughly absorbed.

Although Vicente Aleixandre's letters to Sánchez Cuesta were essentially examples of commercial correspondence, they contain occasional asides or passing remarks, fascinating hints or insights, which contextualise and shed light on the Spanish poet's early development. A recurring motif from 1925 to 1928 is the 'Boletín de publicaciones francesas' distributed by León Sánchez to clients on a monthly basis. Aleixandre directly refers to this catalogue as very useful for any orders he may want to place (C.10–12–1925). If an issue fails to arrive he asks for it anxiously, and often seeks items by explicitly linking them to this list. As a bibliographical guide it proved an invaluable lifeline for an emerging writer eager to find his way.

Additional help came from León Sánchez Cuesta himself. A good illustration is the Spanish poet's request for 'a book by Pierre Revérdy [sic]. Pierre Revérdy is a French poet with whom I am unfamiliar. I do not know the titles of his books. As you have a branch in Paris I think you should be able to find me a book of poems in verse. Which? One of his most recent' (C.10–7–1927). When unsure of an author's name or a title he observes 'You will know better than me' (C.6–10–1928). Deferring to León's professional expertise he virtually invites him to choose books on his behalf, particularly those by French Surrealists with whose work it is clear that he was still fairly unfamiliar.[21] For instance, he orders something by Aragon: 'a book of poetry published after 1925. I am leaving it up to you to send me the one you prefer if there are several as I imagine there are but don't know. If there is nothing available, send me instead one by Paul Eluard. Even if it's in prose (prose poems) it doesn't matter.' (C.12–3–1929). Some indications are approximate: 'René Crével [sic] (or Crever, or something like that)' and 'Jacques Vascher [sic] – (his latest published work)' (C.18–10–1929). He misremembers details or may have overheard them in casual conversation: 'Louis Aragon, *La grande joie'* [sic] (C.24–12–1929) for *La Grande Gaîté* (which he confuses, perhaps, with the same author's *Feu de joie*); and René Crével [sic], *L'Amour difficile* (C.2–1–1930) instead of *La Mort difficile*, an appropriately Freudian slip. Aleixandre had a standing order with the Madrid bookshop for 'in general all the new Surrealist titles as they come in' (C.2–1–1930), and Sánchez Cuesta supplied these at his own discretion, though Aleixandre could be impatient: 'Haven't you received any new Surrealist works?' (C.2–3–1930). So the bibliographical advice dispensed by a well-informed León Sánchez clearly had a helpful orientating effect.

After the expansive optimism of the 1920s or *années folles*, the Librería León Sánchez Cuesta had to confront a difficult period when the Republic came. Partly this was due to a change in León's domestic life. In December 1931 he married Andrea Bonmatí, the sister-in-law of Pedro Salinas, and their son Pablo was born in July 1933. New family responsibilities entailed working harder for longer. A serious illness necessitating two operations also left him incapacitated from September 1933 until September 1934. Economic recession constricted his activities throughout the early 1930s. The Depression proved catastrophic for the book trade. There was a dramatic rise in the

---

21 In conversation with me, León Sánchez recalled that once in the late 1920s when the Spanish poet was discussing his work in progress the bookseller remarked that it sounded like Surrealism, whereupon Aleixandre asked 'What is Surrealism?' One thing is clear, if these epistolary solecisms are used to chart his progressive absorption of Surrealism, the process appears to have been both leisurely and prolonged.

number of bad debts among foreign customers, some American university bookstores even went bankrupt and could not pay for stock supplied, while various kinds of currency restriction played havoc with the import-export market in books. It was, perhaps, a sign of the times that while in 1931 Sánchez Cuesta found himself servicing the needs of the Vatican Apostolic Library in Rome, he spent 1932–1936 dispatching Spanish periodicals and magazines to the Mezhduna-rodnaya Kniga in Moscow.[22] The calle Mayor and the rue Gay-Lussac drifted apart. Miguel Rodríguez Núñez succeeded Vicens, but was unable to cope and by January 1934 had transferred virtually all León Sánchez's orders for French titles to the Maison du Livre.

By some miracle, the bookshop records survived the Civil War largely intact. Otherwise the story of León Sánchez Cuesta, who never wrote a book or kept a diary, would have been consigned, unfairly, to oblivion. Yet, as Juan Guerrero Ruiz remarked: 'Your bookshop deserves its place as one of the most agreeable locations in literary Madrid' (C.5–8–1926). Words by Adrienne Monnier probably best sum up what made León Sánchez, according to Lorca, 'the great Spanish bookseller':

> si tout homme conscient peut s'exalter sur son métier et saisir les rapports admirables qui le lient à la Société, quels ne seront pas nos sentiments à nous, libraires, qui, avant toute pensée de gain et de travail basée sur les livres, les avons aimés avec transport et avons cru à la puissance infinie des plus beaux![23]

---

22 Founded in 1923, the Mezhdunarodnaya Kniga (International Book) corporation, owned by the Soviet government, arranged the export and import of printed materials.

23 Adrienne Monnier, op.cit., pp.232–3.

Vénus Khoury-Ghata

Within the mirror it was dark
the woman venturing in armed with her lamp tracked the sombre signs
swept over the steps of those whose transit took them from wall to wall

Sat in a corner she might watch those importunate travellers with their trailing
shadows
behind their backs
they tucked from sight things taken from the mantlepiece
hairpin
photo of newly weds
horseshoe
dried bouquet
tiresome petty larcenies whose payload of regrets they weighed

the flowers had not retained the name of their garden of origin
the horseshoe had forgotten the age of the door
only the photo harboured vague memories
and the hairpin the bride had used to incise her husband's heart

(translated by Peter Broome)

Il faisait sombre à l'intérieur du miroir
la femme qui s'y aventurait avec sa lampe traquait les taches d'obscurité
et balayait les pas de ceux qui le traversèrent pour se rendre d'un mur à l'autre

S'asseoir dans un angle lui permettait de guetter les passants indélicats suivis
de leur ombre
derrière leur dos
ils dissimulaient des objets pris sur la cheminée
épingle à cheveux
photo de mariés
fer à cheval
bouquet desséché
larcins fastidieux dont ils évaluaient la teneur en regrets

les fleurs n'avaient pas retenu le nom de leur jardin
le fer à cheval avait oublié l'âge de la porte
seule la photo avait des réminiscences
c'est avec l'épingle à cheveux que la mariée avait incisé le cœur de son époux

There was a country here
fire drained from the women's fingers
bread left the furrows high and dry
and cold devoured the children all with jonquils round their necks

There was a wall here
which in times of plenty branched out on its own
became rectangular
turned square
but never circular so as not to slight the fountains guardians by appointment of
the roundness of the day
There was a huntsman here
who knocked down his house to get to the forest
and find that his rifle shots were bursting the ear-drums of the rock

There was a pebble here
which at the slightest glimpse of a dead man on the move turned tumulus

There was a night here infinitely white
a tree infinitely black
which pulled its bark up to its chin when midday made the shadows open-eyed

There was the echo of another echo here
and the horns of the mighty oxen melted as merely a wing brushed by

(translated by Peter Broome)

Ici il y avait un pays
le feu se retira des doigts des femmes
le pain déserta les sillons
et le froid mangea tous les enfants qui portaient une jonquille autour du cou

Ici il y avait un mur
qui se multipliait par lui-même en temps de prospérité
devenait rectangle
devenait carré
jamais cercle pour ne pas humilier les fontaines seules détentrices de la
rotondité du jour

Ici il y avait un chasseur
qui renversait sa maison pour se rendre dans la forêt
et constater que ses détonations perçaient le tympan du rocher

Ici il y avait un caillou
qui se transformait en tumulus à la seule vue d'un mort qui passait

Ici il y avait une nuit infiniment blanche
un arbre infiniment noir
qui remontait son écorce jusqu'au menton lorsque midi dilatait les ombres

Ici il y avait l'écho d'un autre écho
et les cornes des grands bovins fondaient au seul passage d'une aile

JOHN MCCANN

Mallarmé and the art of celebration

For many readers, Malcolm Bowie's title seems to say it all: *Mallarmé and the Art of Being Difficult.*[1] As he points out, there have been difficult poems before Mallarmé's and they have been seen as enjoyable. In Mallarmé, as in so many other modern poets, however, difficulty is no longer a tease, a come-on, behind which the essential meaning of the poem hides decorously. Rather, it is now the essence:

> For Mallarmé the best thought is that which most scrupulously acknowledges its own frailty; and the more scrupulous the thought becomes the thinner the partition which separates it from total vacuity. (Bowie, pp.17–18)

This is bleak and troubling. Yet Bowie, as he elsewhere makes clear, is concentrating on a particular type of poem, especially 'Prose pour des Esseintes' and 'Un coup de dés'. Here, difficulty is a virtue. It is a refusal to maintain 'a pleasant continuity of discourse' (Bowie, p.16). He is challenging the reader, causing him or her to feel 'upset and indignant at these studiously disjointed texts' (Bowie, p.17). This is the other aspect of 'being difficult'. Bowie's title has a suitable ambiguity in that 'the art of being difficult' can apply to the poem or to the poet. In the latter case it becomes a personality trait. It indicates someone who will not blithely follow conventions, who will not hesitate to rock the boat.

Such people are often of high integrity and Bowie's reference to scrupulousness places Mallarmé in that category. But they can also be anti-social and unlikeable. If anything, they may seek to be unpleasant and may be brutal in their honesty. Bowie remarks that: 'Mallarmé has the power to hurt' (Bowie, p.153). What he is rightly stressing is the intensity of Mallarmé's poetry. He is anxious that it not be tamed:

1   Cambridge University Press, 1978.

Something is going wrong when criticism conscientiously refuses to take heed of the singular disruptive energies which works of art possess, and quite as badly wrong when those energies are normalised by being made into a test of political acceptability. I am not suggesting that Mallarmé is an artist in terror, a manipulator of our fears, but that his poems do at moments make rapid thrusts against the reader's sense of his own coherence, and that in Mallarmé's account the negative in human experience can be complete and irremoveable (Bowie, p.154).

Bowie concludes by claiming that there is also an 'inveterately human power which seeks to check or replace [the classic human answers to death] – the power which enables Mallarmé in the face of terror, as in the face of joy, to pronounce his slender, strong "but yet"' (Ibid.). These concluding words in Bowie's argument – but not in the book which continues with an appendix and other critical paraphernalia – invite the reader to his or her own 'but yet'.

As this study will show, there is another side to Mallarmé, one which allows us to see him as anything but a difficult person, even though he does not flinch from writing difficult poetry. Mallarmé, as will be seen, is a delightful poet – one who delights in and celebrates the real. After all, thought must have an object. Whereas Baudelaire deals with imagined cityscapes – his poems almost inevitably begin with a leap towards the hypothetical – Mallarmé, on the other hand, seems to celebrate the concrete in many of his poems: a fan, a candelabra, a billowing curtain. Or else it is a specific situation – the toast. There is an engagement with the real. However, as Bertrand Marchal points out, this is not the same as realism. What Mallarmé gives the reader is an interpretation – the world made sense:

Pour autant, Mallarmé ne saurait ignorer qu'il y une antériorité des choses par rapport au langage, et que celui-ci n'a pas pour fonction d'avérer la réalité mais de lui donner un sens.[2]

Language cannot prove reality but it can make sense of it. Thus, there is more to the concrete than simple depiction. There is indeed a complexity of thought – Bowie's 'best thought' – but that complexity,

2   Bertrand Marchal, *La Religion de Stéphane Mallarmé: poésie, mythologie et religion* (Paris: J. Corti, 1988), p.85.

far from always being upsetting, can flatter and engage the attention of
the reader in a way that establishes a social bond. It is a sharing.

How this might work can be seen in a little poem like:

> Comme un délicieux effet
> Ou, je dirai plus, en échange
> Du soleil que votre cœur fait
> Considérez la fauve orange.[3]

This is one of the *vers de circonstance* that Mallarmé composed to
accompany gifts – in this case, candied fruit offered for New Year's
Day 1896. There is a whole section in the *Œuvres complètes* from
pages 117 to 130 entitled 'Dons de fruits glacés au nouvel an'. This
poem, like its companions, may not be classified with the major
poems but it is entirely in keeping with Mallarmé's poetic practice,
with its twisted syntax and bending of sentence structure as well as an
acute sensitivity to the weight of individual words. Yet such a poem
would hardly count as 'being difficult'. There is no doubt as to its
referent. However, the most interesting thing about the poem is perhaps the way in which it is read – and was read. Although it is now
published as part of Mallarmé's complete works, originally it would
have been accompanied by the candied fruit. The poem would have
been secondary to the gift. It would have been read by the dedicatee
alone, in the first instance, and then shared with people close to her if
she chose. It would not have been for the general public. Furthermore,
the 'vous' would be a direct address to one specific person and not an
'overheard' address as it now must be. There would be no need to reconstruct the gender by invoking the tradition of 'galanterie' within
which the poem is situated. In short, the poem is read differently now
and in a way that confronts difficulties which were not originally
there.

The poem is far from simplistic. It may deal with the trivial but it
does so with a high degree of artistry. The subject is less important
than the way the poet and reader(s) respond to it. What the poem is

---

3   Stéphane Mallarmé, *Œuvres complètes*, ed. by Henri Mondor and G. Jean-
     Aubry (Paris: Gallimard, 1945). All future references are to this edition and are
     given in the text.

about is not an issue – a paradox stemming from the fact that for the first reader at least, the subject was physically, i.e. really, present. What counts is the response. Presentation is all. Clarity and ambiguity are wittily combined. For example the 'Du' at the beginning of the third line juggles two meanings, depending on whether it is the complement of 'effet' or of 'échange'. The first meaning is that the woman's heart is like the sun which produced the ripe fruit and so it is being given to her as a just tribute. The second again proposes that her heart is like the sun but that the poet is offering the fruit, which is also like the sun, as an exchange. The poem flirtatiously offers and asks for love. The two compliments complement each other nicely. Indeed, it is interesting that even in talking about the poem, using unavoidable terms like 'complement' and 'compliment' (or their French equivalents), one discovers such linguistic felicities. It is as though language is ever producing sense. There is always more meaning.

Similarly, the word 'fauve' proves to be exceedingly rich in significance. To begin with, 'fauve' and 'orange' can be used as either a noun or an adjective and the reader must execute a quick and nimble interpretation. It is evident that Mallarmé is using 'fauve' in its old sense of 'reddish yellow'. This is appropriate for the noun 'orange' which it qualifies and, since this adjective is enhancing or emphasising an inherent characteristic of the word, it precedes its noun. Indeed, it would be hard to find any other adjective of colour that could be applied to the noun 'orange' without changing its essence. Mallarmé has used the only suitable adjective. There is a level of precision that runs counter to his reputation for ambiguity of the kind that we have just witnessed. It is possible to say that the word 'fauve' is right and no other word will do. Mallarmé's language is not capricious but unarguable. It has certainty.

The combination 'fauve orange' produces a vivid impression of very strong colour. It is a combination to be savoured, just like the fruit. Because the sense is old-fashioned, it also gives something of that quality to the quatrain as a whole. This is not something rooted in the fleeting present but has its roots in the venerable past. Thus the other meaning of 'fauve', which is 'wild (feline) beast' deriving from the application of 'fauve' to beasts having that colour of hair, is excluded. However, we are conscious of that exclusion. After all, the excluded meaning is more common now. Yet that exclusion works to complement the primary meaning. This is a galant compliment, part of the civilised communication between close friends. Such friendship is governed and made safe by artifice and convention, approved by tradition. It does not shun the light. There is no place for the unbridled desires of the faun (a 'fauve'). Yet, one might well ask if the wild passions are definitively excluded or is awareness of their exclusion an acknowledgement of their power?

This question is particularly apt here. There is another aspect of the word 'fauve' that is excluded but which clamours for attention. The term 'Fauve' exists in English as one of those foreign terms which have been adopted without translation. It refers to a school of painting that post-dates the poem under consideration by about a decade. Consequently, it is not a reference to those artists whose bright and vibrant colours have such a powerful effect on the viewer. Yet, despite this lack of validity but given the way the term is used, it would be hard for the reader not to have in his or her mind the Fauves, if only to exclude them from Mallarmé's intended meanings. It is chance but not insignificant chance in that it signifies. Thus, the word still appears to prophesy, creating a moment of uncanniness. As Jonathan Culler has remarked: 'The uncanny is not simply weird or bizarre but suggests deeper laws.'[4]

What, in this case, might those laws be? They govern the making of meaning. This is a poem that is part of a ritual marking a threshold – it celebrates a present friendship by marking it in the present but also indicates that it will continue in the year just started. The progress of time is an inherent part of the dynamic of the poem. This is a poem that is as aware that there is a future as much as a past and a present. If the word 'fauve' is seen as a prophesy of an art movement, then it is because that is an interpretation, or as Marchal says 'un sens', that the reader puts on it, in the light of what was to come. In short, the meaning of 'fauve' is not the truth of reality but an interpretation of it, the discerning of a significant pattern. The process of interpretation is a rich and collaborative one, involving both author and reader. Set up

---

4   *On Deconstruction: Theory and Criticism after Structuralism* (London, Melbourne and Henley: Routledge and Keegan Paul, 1983), p.24.

within parameters drawn by the former, it is like a recursive mathematical formula capable of producing results ad infinitum – after all the other meaning of 'sens' is 'direction', as though words were moving along a path (in space and/or in time) touching on various meanings. We might see the word 'fauve orange' as frozen in a moment of meaning, a 'cygne d'autrefois', straining to reach the glories that lie in the future.

This is not a fresh orange but a candied one, an 'orange d'autrefois'. It is not what might be considered a 'real' orange but one that has been preserved by artifice. However, in another sense it was not preserved, or rather, preserved so as not to be preserved. That is, it was intended to be eaten. Thus, although the poem accompanied a real object, it no longer does so. In fact, the poem that explains the significance of the gift, is now all that testifies to the fact that it was once real. Furthermore, and here we enter the realm of speculative interpretation not unlike the one that takes us along the path towards the 'fauve/Fauve' meaning, it is possible (and likely) that the poem was intended and indeed seen as being part of the gift. The recipient may even have seen the poem as more important to her than the object. The poem would then be the true gift – an interpretative pirouette copying that in my parsing above of 'fauve' and 'orange'. Thus it is possible to view the poem not as an accompanying comment but as a co-equal. It is an object in the real world just like the orange. Its language is not just a reflection of reality. It is now part of reality, treated by the recipient as an object.

Throughout all this, the constant is that the gift, whether sweetmeat or poem or both, is a celebration of friendship. The darker elements mentioned above are a foil to the sense of joy and the humour that pervade the poem. This is something that Bowie's 'art of being difficult' seems to exclude. Indeed the portrait of Mallarmé as a writer with 'the power to hurt' and whose readers may find themselves 'upset and indignant' seems to have little to do with the sort of person who would send a new year's offering along with witty poems designed to charm. There would be no galanterie, no sugaring of the pill – or of the orange. These two views of Mallarmé would not be contradictory in Bowie's view since, as we have seen, what the latter prizes are discontinuities, the 'singular disruptive energies that works of art possess'. Thus it would be perfectly possible for the poet to write, apart from his serious works, the squibs that are the *vers de circonstance*. Mallarmé would be the discontinuous author of discontinuous poetic discourses. It may be argued that the poem in question is a minor one and does not achieve the depth of thought that the major poems do. However, the image of the 'fauve orange' is very vivid, full of energy and with intimations of untamed wildness and disruptive forces. It takes place in a context of tradition, of preserving and nurturing certain kinds of female/male friendships, of preserving fruit. It celebrates the ending of the old year and the start of the new. Furthermore, as we have seen, it shares features with the major poems. It is perhaps more helpful to look not for discontinuities and disruptions but rather to accept that the common features delineate a 'sens', a direction or path along which his works are travelling. Mallarmé's poems can be situated along a spectrum, as can be seen clearly in the case of his poems for fans, some of which appear among the occasional verse while others are classified as major.

It is perhaps more accurate to see Mallarmé as a poet whose technique, whether he is dealing with profound or trivial matters, is always bent on engaging the reader, on amusing, on inviting him or her to participate. Mallarmé is a social poet. He writes for an audience that he understands. Consequently, he is able to cajole and titillate. He seeks to charm the reader, a verb that derives from 'carmen' – poem in Latin –, a usage picked up in Valéry's *Charmes*. It is not the intention to put readers off but rather to be convivial and welcoming. If Bowie sees Mallarmé as 'a manipulator of our fears', I would prefer to see him as someone adept at playing with our feelings on different levels. He is the sort of person who can be frivolous and witty, good company, but also when the occasion arises, can deal with more profound issues in just the same way.

It is in keeping with this that the first poem in his collection of *Poésies* is 'Salut'. He is greeting the reader as a host greets guests at a celebration. The welcome is to the volume as a whole but also applies to the particular circumstances of the poem under consideration. As the title indicates, the poem is an invitation to the reader to participate in the celebration of friendship:

Rien, cette écume, vierge vers
A ne désigner que la coupe;
Telle loin se noie une troupe
De sirènes mainte à l'envers.

Nous naviguons, ô mes divers
Amis, moi déjà sur la poupe
Vous l'avant fastueux qui coupe
Le flot de foudres et d'hivers;

Une ivresse belle m'engage
Sans craindre même son tangage
De porter haut ce salut

Solitude, récif, étoile
A n'importe ce qui valut
Le blanc souci de notre toile
                    (*Œuvres complètes*, p.27).

Just as the orange accompanied the earlier poem, so this one has a close relationship with reality. It was written to be recited at a literary banquet on 15 February 1893 organised by *La Plume* and at which Mallarmé presided. Mondor and Jean-Aubry quote the description of the event from *La Plume*:

Un fin sourire sur les lèvres, l'œil tant soit peu extatique, ému, tremblant ainsi qu'une jeune vierge sur qui pèsent les regards de toute une assemblée, le président du septième banquet, ce pur poëte, cet homme délicieux, Stéphane Mallarmé, se lève, prend sa coupe et d'une voix sonore, quoique mal assurée, dit l'exquis poëme qui s'inscrit au fronton de cette revue. Aussitôt les mains des convives font retentir la salle de bravos retentissants: trois ovations successives, soulignent d'affection sincère la gloire du maître, étonné lui, l'intransigeant esthéticien, de cette unanimité dans l'enthousiasme...
(*Œuvres complètes*, pp.1406–7).

The poem, then, is very much an occasional piece. The situation of the poet, surrounded by friends and proposing a toast, acts as a foundation on which are built rich and elaborate structures of meaning. The reference to 'cette écume', with the use of the demonstrative article, can only refer to the froth of the champagne in Mallarmé's glass. It points to it as surely as 'fauve orange' points to the candied fruit in the poem discussed above. There is a stability in this reference, lying beneath the dizzying flights of fancy of the imagery. This is summed up by the later use of 'tangage'. Mallarmé is standing on the solid floor which remains stable beneath him but in his imagination, made dizzy by the wine, he feels the floor move just as a sailor out at sea would feel dizzy standing on deck as it moves beneath him. In one case the dizziness produces the effect of the floor moving while in the other the movement causes the dizziness. Thus drunkenness turns the world topsy-turvy as cause and effect are swopped. Inebriation is a translation into the opposite – 'A l'envers', as the poem puts it earlier.

This is the key to understanding the image of the sirens in the last two lines of the first quatrain. Graham Robb rightly points to the difficulty of the image. He also sees the link between the bubbles of champagne and the drunkenness of the poet, producing what he calls an 'hallucination'. He points out:

> But the details of the hallucination are hard to explain. Jacques Gengoux's stunningly precise diagnosis is that some of the sirens are upside down because their busts are heavier than their tails, though this would surely have had the opposite effect.[5]

Robb goes on to make a number of interesting and productive suggestions of his own but ultimately his interpretation is prosodic, not thematic, in that the 'sirens are biological enjambments or the sonnet's structure in half-human form' (Robb, p.191). The interpretations of this image are perhaps complicated by the focus on the sirens. It is unnecessary to the success of the image to attempt to see sirens in the glass. Indeed to focus on this surreal image is to get lost in obscurity. Instead we should trust to Mallarmé's precision in translating what he sees into words. The reality is clear. Mallarmé is merely providing a precise description or interpretation of the glass of champagne that the newspaper article tells us he was holding. The 'écume' is made up of bubbles that rise up in quantity (hence 'mainte') and gather on the surface of the wine. They pass upwards from the realm of liquid to that of air where they burst and in this

5   Graham Robb, *Unlocking Mallarmé* (New Haven and London: Yale University Press, 1996), p.190.

manner die. Consequently, the bubbles are an apt illustration of the
'total vacuity' that for Bowie threatens frail thought. More importantly, what happens to them is the equivalent of drowning. Drowning
is when a human being (or animal) throws himself or herself down-
wards (or merely falls) into water (or indeed it could be any liquid)
and dies. Thus the way the bubbles move upwards and burst on
reaching the surface reminds Mallarmé of the process of drowning but
topsy-turvy, 'A l'envers'. The bubbles are like sirens because they rise
up from the depths of the sea into the air where, being bubbles, they
burst and meet their end. This is a very exact visual description of the
glass of champagne. It focuses on what is happening.

On this Mallarmé constructs further meanings. The sirens were
known for their song and this may evoke the sound that Mallarmé can
hear as the bubbles burst with a fizz. Furthermore, that song caused
sailors to take leave of their senses so they hurled themselves over the
side of the ship in an effort to reach the sirens – and were drowned as
a result. This fits with the intoxicating effects of the wine that Mallarmé describes later. However, in this topsy-turvy world, it is the
sirens not the intoxicated sailors who drown. All these meanings
remain subordinate to the image of the glass of champagne raised aloft
as a toast to the assembly. This does not prevent new patterns of
meaning being suggested but all are related back to the situation. Thus
'rien' which is initially a self-deprecatory introduction to the toast – it
is a mere trifle – joins with 'écume', 'vierge', 'ne [...] que' and
'coupe' to create a pattern of absence, dissolving, paring away. This is
an evocation of the insubstantial. At the same time, 'rien', which
comes from the Latin word 'rem', meaning 'thing', also sets up a
counter-pattern, suggesting a possibility of real substance beyond the
insubstantial. Furthermore, 'coupe' suggests the shape and form a
thing may take, the essential contours that make it what it is.

However, the primary meaning of 'coupe' remains paramount.
The event is not effaced. Other possible interpretations are an embellishment, enriching the sense. This can be seen by the treatment of
'vers' and 'coupe'. The former sounds like 'verre' but there is no
reason to suppose that Mallarmé wishes us to accept the reading
'glass' as though it were to give access to some secret, ultimate
meaning. Indeed the rules of prosody encourage in the listener a

preference for the masculine rhyme that 'vers' would give. Thus 'verre' is glimpsed as a possibility, no more. The world is not an illusion, behind which lies a truth available only to the initiated. Rather the whole world is imbued with multiple meanings, echoing each other in different ways. Consequently, 'verre' is echoed phonologically in 'vers' and semantically in 'coupe'. A further enrichment stems from the fact that 'coupe' can also refer to a caesura or point of rest in a line of verse. This is echoed by the placing of 'vers' and 'coupe' at the end of their respective lines so that form can reinforce idea. This multiplicity is like the profusion of fizzing bubbles in champagne, delighting and intoxicating the senses in a spirit of celebration.

This indeed is the point of departure for the poem. The poem is about a real event – as the newspaper report indicates. However, the relationship between event and text is, as we might expect from the poem accompanying the candied orange, quite complex. It is not a simple description. It is not a translation into words of an event that took place. That is true of the newspaper report but not of Mallarmé's poem. If Mallarmé picks up the glass, it is partly because that is what the conventions associated with a toast dictate. But he also picks it up because it is pre-written that he will do so. The poem is a prophecy because written before the event it appears to describe. The phrase 'cette écume' – which shows that Mallarmé has picked up his glass – also requires that he do so. The vacuity of the bubbles turns out to be creative. What Mallarmé does is determined by what he has written. If he were to have clutched his notes and read from them, the poem would have lost its point and been reduced to a nonsense. Thus the poem is in its turn dependent on the event. At once a creator of the event and a reflection of it and on it, it is delicately balanced – like the drunken man on his feet, proposing a toast.

RICHARD BALES

Proust's theories of translation

The only theory of translation which Proust formulates is an un-
orthodox one; on the other hand, it is very famous:

> Je m'apercevais que ce livre essentiel, le seul livre vrai, un grand écrivain n'a
> pas, dans le sens courant, à l'inventer, puisqu'il existe déjà en chacun de nous,
> mais à le traduire. Le devoir et la tâche d'un écrivain sont ceux d'un tra-
> ducteur.[1]

The context is the grand review of literary theory and practice which
Proust's Narrator undertakes in the wake of his determination that he
must finally realise his vocation and produce a work of art. Casting
aside dogmatism, the Narrator looks into himself and opts for a
personal line, both in subject-matter and in approach. So, 'je compris
que tous ces matériaux de l'œuvre littéraire, c'était ma vie passée' (IV,
478); and, within that life, objects present 'sous [leurs] signes quelque
chose de tout autre que je devais tâcher de découvrir, une pensée
qu'ils traduisaient à la façon de ces caractères hiéroglyphiques qu'on
croirait représenter seulement des objets matériels' (IV, 457). The
Narrator's conception of translation is, then, not only a broad one, but
a deep one as well – the allusion to Egyptian hieroglyphs provides a
dimension of historical and cultural profundity which confers a
clinching air of authority and, given the circumstances, an appropriately resonant artistic compass. The analysis is the Narrator's; but
we are in the presence of such incisive wisdom that one can only
assume that Proust the author intimately shared the sentiments expressed by his *alter ego*.

1   Marcel Proust, *A la recherche du temps perdu* (4 vols, Paris: Gallimard
    (Pléiade), 1987–1989), IV, 469. In subsequent references to Proust's novel,
    only volume and page numbers are given.

The Proustian conception of translation seems always to have been a broad one, concentrating on the implications of the word's etymology ('moving across') in a manner which goes far beyond the quasi-mechanical provision of a version in another language. Proust had, of course, engaged in such activity in the period 1900–1906, when he published translations of two books by Ruskin: *La Bible d'Amiens* (1904) and *Sésame et les lys* (1906). But we now know, from recent access to the manuscripts and allusions in the correspodence, that the 'donkey-work' was done by Proust's mother and friends such as Marie Nordlinger; he embellished their translations, not just stylistically,[2] but also in providing innumerable footnotes which clarify, expand, contradict, and generally interpret Ruskin's text.[3] Some of them are so huge that they swamp what is being glossed. Add to this the lengthy prefaces, which are tantamount to aesthetic manifestos structured as personal narratives, and we are in a situation where the translator is moving his subject-matter across into vastly expanded realms; not for nothing have commentators looked on the 'mere' translations of Ruskin – especially the preface to *Sésame et les lys* – as trial runs for *A la recherche du temps perdu*.[4]

With hindsight it is possible to perceive an analogous disposition at many points of Proust's writing career, and it is an attitude which instinctively adopts a visual field of reference, less powerfully than the hieroglyph metaphor, it is true, but with an impressive consistency. Back in the days of *Les Plaisirs et les jours* (1896) a multiple interpretation of 'translation' is already in play. In the set of poems entitled 'Portraits de peintres'[5] Proust claimed, in a letter to Robert de Montesquiou, to have been inspired to imitate the latter's *Les*

2   This is not to say Proust is cavalier with the sense: on the contrary, he 'cherche l'épithète juste, colle au sens, au rythme et à la musique de la phrase'. See Jean-Yves Tadié, *Marcel Proust* (2 vols, Paris: Gallimard (Folio), 1996), I, 731.

3   On these and other details concerning the activity of Proust as translator of Ruskin, see Cynthia J. Gamble, *Proust as Interpretor of Ruskin: the Seven Lamps of Translation* (Birmingham, AL: Summa Publications, 2002).

4   Tadié (op. cit., I, 773–7) provides a good summary of the anticipatory features.

5   See Marcel Proust, *Jean Santeuil précédé de Les Plaisirs et les Jours* (Paris: Gallimard (Pléiade), 1971), pp.80–2. Abbreviation: *JSPJ*.

Hortensias bleus,[6] but the real inspiration is clearly Baudelaire's 'Les Phares', that poem which addresses the nature of artistic vision and example. And the source automatically carries with itself a whole aesthetic package which would have become instinctive for a budding writer of the 1890s. If the artistic subject-matter is an appropriate demonstration of the possibility of moving images into words, it has to be said that Proust's execution is pedestrian: there is little beyond awed description (now synthetic, now specific) of his chosen painters (Cuyp, Potter, Watteau, Van Dyck), and although a certain amount of atmosphere is generated the accumulation of nouns linked by verbs in the present tense grows wearisome, and in fact militates against effective evocation.[7] Similar negative remarks could be made about the accompanying set of 'Portraits de musiciens' (Chopin, Gluck, Schumann, Mozart; see *JSPJ*, pp.82–4). What is instructive, though, is the mere existence of these poems – a fairly substantial gesture of artistic transposition early on in Proust's career.

After the years devoted to translating and annotating Ruskin, another similarly thought-through unit of transpositions appears: the *Pastiches* of various writers.[8] Based on an amusing extortion racket – a certain Lemoine claimed to be able to manufacture authentic dia-

6   The words he uses are 'non seulement l'admiration mais l'imitation'. See
     Marcel Proust, ed. P. Kolb, *Correspondance*, I (Paris: Plon, 1971), 393.
7   The following lines from 'Paulus Potter' are typical of these poems:
     Potter, mélancolique humeur des plaines sombres
     Qui s'étendent sans fin, sans joie et sans couleur,
     Les arbres, le hameau ne répandent pas d'ombres,
     Les maigres jardinets ne portent pas de fleur.
     Un laboureur tirant des seaux rentre, et, chétive,
     Sa jument résignée, inquiète et rêvant,
     Anxieuse, dressant sa cervelle pensive,
     Hume d'un souffle court le souffle fort du vent (*JSPJ*, pp.80–1).
8   See Marcel Proust, *Contre Sainte-Beuve précédé de Pastiches et mélanges et
     suivi de Essais et articles* (Paris: Gallimard (Pléiade), 1971), pp.7–59 and 195–
     207. Abbreviation: *CSB*. The authors pastiched in the first set (published in
     Proust's lifetime) are Balzac, Flaubert, Sainte-Beuve, Henri de Régnier, the
     Goncourts, Michelet, Emile Faguet, Renan and Saint-Simon. The second
     (posthumous) set is of Sainte-Beuve, Chateaubriand, Maeterlinck (twice) and
     Ruskin.

monds – these *tours de force* fit into the 'à la manière' tradition rendered popular by Paul Reboux and Charles Müller in 1908, but by common consent are far superior (see *CSB*, p.688). The frame of reference here is literary rather than pictorial; however, the procedures employed by Proust are directly germane to a study of the mechanics of transposition. Proust is not content with facile parody: on the contrary, each pastiche engages with the salient features of its chosen author's world in 'une exploitation systématique et parfaitement con-sciente d'une structure littéraire et stylistique'.[9] Far from being just an 'imitation' such as Proust (albeit self-deprecatingly) had claimed the 'Portraits de peintres' to be, these pastiches represent a direct im-plantation of one writer's mind within another's in an act which is simultaneously critical and creative: in revealing the *modus operandi* of each writer, and in giving it new, fictional, shape, Proust is in effect 'realising' an artefact which only had potential existence before he set to work. In other words, he is engaging in that sort of 'translation' which he was to advocate much later on, in that part of *Le Temps retrouvé* from which I quoted at the outset of this article.

Within the pages of *A la recherche du temps perdu*, the *locus classicus* of discussion amongst characters concerning this sort of translation is centred on the painter Elstir (II, 190–210). This fact alone is clear enough indication of how vital a visual field of reference is to discussion in this area. The episode of the encounter with Elstir is normally viewed as an artistic initiation in which the Narrator learns deeper values than he had hitherto suspected. But there is a sub-text of translation here as well, and it operates on multiple levels. Elstir is a creator, but he is an interpreter too; the Narrator is a pupil, and a potential creator; and there is an author who gives literary shape to all of these entities. The first thing the Narrator notices about Elstir's paintings is that they all put into practice a specific technique, one which consists 'en une sorte de métamorphose des choses repré-sentées, analogue à celle qu'en poésie on nomme métaphore' (II, 191), so that, for example, in 'Le Port de Carquethuit' the town seems to be transported into the sea and the boats inland (II, 192). And in another seascape, Elstir 'avait jusqu'à une telle profondeur goûté l'enchante-

9   Jean Milly quoted in *CSB*, pp.688–9.

ment [de la mer] qu'il avait su rapporter, fixer sur sa toile, l'imperceptible reflux de l'eau, la pulsation d'une minute heureuse' (II, 255). In other words, he practices pictorial translation, the better to release latent significance.

The preoccupation continues when Elstir switches to pedagogical vein, explaining to the Narrator what he should have appreciated on his first, disappointed inspection of the medieval church at Balbec. The whole of the iconography is geared towards giving a visual interpretation of biblical scenes and religious doctrine, for the moral enlightenment of the original, illiterate, viewers. Words were transposed by the sculptor into pictures; similarly, the modern commentator, in a new act of transposition, creates a fresh verbal formulation: 'l'époux qui aidant, à l'heure du Jugement dernier, sa jeune femme à sortir du tombeau lui appuie la main contre son propre cœur pour la rassurer et lui prouver qu'il bat vraiment, est-ce [...] assez chouette comme idée, assez trouvé?' (II, 197). Everything, for Elstir, is a question of formulating one means of artistic expression in terms of another, to such an extent that he uses the actual term 'translation' twice in the course of his disquisition on Balbec Church: the sculptor has displayed 'l'exactitude la plus minutieuse à traduire le texte saint' (II, 196), while in one particular scene 'il y a certaines paroles de l'office de l'Assomption qui ont été traduites avec une subtilité qu'un Redon n'a pas égalée' (II, 197). Elstir's words all add up to what is tantamount to a manifesto of interpretation.

The immediate effect which this attitude of Elstir's produces on the receptive Narrator is one of an authority from whom one can take away pedagogical lessons. And he applies them immediately, casting aside his purist view of nature, so that when once he would have tried to ignore bathers and boats when looking at the sea in an effort 'de me persuader que je contemplais le flot immémorial qui déroulait déjà sa même vie mystérieuse avant l'apparition de l'espèce humaine' (II, 255–6), now, moving Elstir's modernist ethos into his own life, he no longer sees the human presence in nature as a 'contamination', and grows enthusiastic about such frivolous items as women's hats and jockeys' caps (Ibid.). As readers, we can already tell that Elstir's advocacy of the fruitful cohabitation of the sublime and the banal will be heeded, because we have been witness to some dazzling pages of nature-painting on the part of the Narrator:

> Et dès ce premier matin le soleil me désignait au loin d'un doigt souriant ces cimes bleues de la mer qui n'ont de nom sur aucune carte géographique, jusqu'à ce qu'étourdi de sa sublime promenade à la surface retentissante et chaotique de leurs crêtes et de leurs avalanches, il vînt se mettre à l'abri du vent dans ma chambre, se prélassant sur le lit défait et égrenant ses richesses sur le lavabo mouillé, dans la malle ouverte, où, par sa splendeur même et son luxe déplacé, il ajoutait encore à l'impression du désordre (II, 34).

The verbal execution is of course Proust's as author. But there is an intradiegetic message too: within the fiction that asks us to believe that the text is written by a Narrator chronicling his younger *alter ego*'s saga, we can already glimpse a mastery of poetic prose which is the literary equivalent of Elstir's 'translations'.

This fertile interaction between the verbal and the pictorial for which Elstir stands as the emblematic figure is all the more powerful for being placed in contrast to a more dubious, if analogous, procedure. Charles Swann – in many ways the Narrator's role model – famously 'plaça sur sa table de travail, comme une photographie d'Odette, une reproduction de la fille de Jethro [de Botticelli]' (I, 221); 'adaptant ce qu'il trouvait beau [...] il le transformait en mérites physiques qu'il se félicitait de trouver réunis dans un être qu'il pourrait posséder' (Ibid.). Although promising key-words are there – 'adaptant', 'transformait' – the give-away word is 'se félicitait', with its overtones of selfishness. For what Swann has been doing is not engaging with art in a creative manner; on the contrary, he 'steals' Botticelli, whom he uses for his own private purposes of debatable aesthetic value. The same is true of the way in which he turns the 'petite phrase' of Vinteuil's violin sonata into 'l'air national de leur amour' (I, 215). And Swann's own experience subsequently proves to him that the exercise of 'translation' into the narrowly personal sphere was an untenable one: when he re-hears the 'petite phrase' after the end of his infatuation with Odette, 'il retrouva tout ce qui de ce bonheur perdu avait fixé à jamais la spécifique et volatile essence' (I, 340). The artistic appropriation rebounds on him, and this as a direct result of his distinctly unhappy translations of Botticelli and Vinteuil.

But, later on in the novel, it is Vinteuil who will turn out to be the key figure in the process of formulating the Narrator's theory of translation. In this respect, the episode where he listens to the first performance of that composer's septet works on even more levels than the Elstir episode had. To start with, the musician produces something from nothing: out of a 'vide infini', 'c'est dans un rose d'aurore que pour se construire progressivement devant moi, cet univers inconnu était tiré du silence et de la nuit' (III, 754). The creative component is there, then, right at the outset, and with the hint of colour it is expressed in a proto-painterly fashion. We are definitely in a world of Baudelairian *correspondances* here: it is joyfully that the composer 'choisissait la couleur de tel timbre' (III, 758), and each of these sounds 'se soulignait d'une couleur que toutes les règles du monde apprises par les musiciens les plus savants ne pourraient pas imiter' (Ibid.). One striking passage of the music reminds the Narrator of the sound of church-bells 'pareilles à celles qui incendiaient de chaleur la place de l'église à Combray, et que Vinteuil, qui avait dû souvent les entendre, avait peut-être trouvées à ce moment-là dans sa mémoire, comme une couleur qu'on a à portée de sa main sur une palette' (III, 755). The ultimate validation of Vinteuil's translations between the worlds of sound and vision comes with the most exalted of comparisons: as he 'peignait sa grande fresque musicale' Vinteuil is akin to 'Michel-Ange attaché à son échelle et lançant, la tête en bas, de tumultueux coups de brosse au plafond de la chapelle Sixtine' (III, 759). The historical dimension, with its inbuilt authority, is in all ways comparable to Elstir's *explication* of Balbec Church.

In analysing these areas in which Proust systematically investigates the possibilities of moving back and forth through different means of artistic expression, I have sometimes cautiously surrounded the word 'translation' with inverted commas; but there was really no need, as Proust's Narrator eventually comes to use the verb *traduire* in the Vinteuil septet episode. It is a natural outcome and inevitable development:

Quand la vision de l'univers se modific, s'épure, devient plus adéquate au
souvenir de la patrie intérieure, il est bien naturel que cela se traduise par une
altération générale des sonorités chez le musicien comme de la couleur chez le
peintre. (III, 761)

In joining the battery of vocabulary relative to the inter-artistic domain, the term *traduire* nicely moves from the lips of a practicing
artist/character (Elstir) to become part of the Narrator's rhetoric in
building his own *ars poetica*.

But this final link could not have been made were it not for a
quirk of fate. We learn – in a passage strategically placed after the
emotional revelation of the septet performance – that the work was
saved from oblivion by an unexpected agent:

[On disait que quand Vinteuil] était mort il n'avait laissé que sa Sonate, que le
reste demeurait inexistant en d'indéchiffrables notations. Indéchiffrables, mais
qui pourtant avaient fini à force de patience, d'intelligence et de respect, par
être déchiffrées par la seule personne qui avait assez vécu auprès de Vinteuil
pour bien connaître sa manière de travailler, pour deviner ses indications
d'orchestre: l'amie de Mlle Vinteuil (III, 765).

For Vinteuil's manuscript had been a veritable 'grimoire'; and it was
thanks to his daughter's friend alone that 'la lecture certaine de ces
hiéroglyphes inconnus' had been established (III, 766).[10] Now, with
mention of hieroglyphs, the final element is in place to enable the
Narrator to deploy a wide-ranging critical analytical approach when
the decisive moment comes for embarking on his own work of art.
And it is an approach which takes it as read that boundaries between
different means of artistic expression are easily moved across, indeed

10   The image is varied a little later on, with a comparison to a chemist's manu-
      scripts which are 'plus illisibles que des papyrus ponctués d'écriture
      cunéiforme'; deciperment permits 'la formule éternellement vraie' to emerge
      (III, 766–7). There is an important sub-text here: hitherto 'l'amie de Mlle
      Vinteuil' (she is always ominously called just that) has been portrayed as a
      thoroughly nasty person, responsible for leading Mlle Vinteuil down the path of
      lesbianism and hence breaking her father's heart. She is an excellent example of
      how, in Proust's analysis, human beings can display contradictory charac-
      teristics. There is nothing to prevent an immoral person from being a good
      translator.

that such 'translation' is of the essence when it comes to acts of creation.

In arriving at the conclusion that 'le devoir et la tâche de l'écrivain sont ceux d'un traducteur', Proust's Narrator is not only providing the constructive formulation of a lifetime's preoccupation with the notion of translation in all its variety. He is also adopting a standpoint which is quite as didactic as any tutorial of Elstir's. The declaration occurs in a context where the Narrator is reviewing pre-vailing means of literary expression which he might have adopted: popular or patriotic art, cinematographic technique, 'la littérature de notations' (IV, 473) – all of these are brushed aside as being inade-quate. What is common to them all (this is unstated by the Narrator, but it is easy to read his mind here) is that they are all unidimensional, concentrating on the one expressive or componential feature. Not for nothing does Proust, through his Narrator, say the writer has a 'duty' to be a translator: translation for Proust entails multidimensionality, a state of affairs which was present as far back as the 'imitations' of the 'Portraits de peintres'. So, in interpreting life, the artist needs to 'chercher à apercevoir sous de la matière, sous de l'expérience, sous des mots quelque chose de différent' (IV, 474). Moreover, adopting the translational mode guarantees a genuine engagement with life in its plenitude:

> En somme, cet art si compliqué est justement le seul art vivant. Seul il exprime pour les autres et nous fait voir à nous-même notre propre vie, cette vie qui ne peut pas s'«observer», dont les apparences qu'on observe ont besoin d'être traduites et souvent lues à rebours et péniblement déchiffrées (IV, 475).

Translation, for Proust, lies at the heart of the artistic venture. Far from being just one amongst available techniques, it is a mandatory procedure whose difficulty must not be shirked.

ANGELA CHAMBERS

Nativism and hybridity in Aimé Césaire's poetic vision

Since Raphaël Confiant's[1] attack on Césaire's fidelity to the African heritage as the fundamental element in Caribbean cultural identity, it has become commonplace to underestimate his relevance in the context of contemporary postcolonial literature,[2] running the risk, as Rosello points out, of consigning his major work, the *Cahier d'un retour au pays natal,* 'to the museum'.[3] In the postcolonial context of the twenty-first century, in which writers focus on the present and accept the hybridity of their cultures, Césaire's continuing emphasis on the importance of the history of his race may appear to signal a refusal of hybridity and a decision to seek refuge in the rediscovery of a pre-colonial past, real or imagined. The aim of this study is to examine aspects of the writer's work in order to discover what light they can shed on this issue, with reference not only to the *Cahier,* which has received the major part of the critical attention devoted to Césaire, but also to the other poetic works and the ideological and

---

1   Raphaël Confiant, *Aimé Césaire: une traversée paradoxale du siècle* (Paris: Editions Stock, 1993).

2   The term 'postcolonial' is used here not in a chronological sense, but to refer to 'toutes les strategies d'écriture déjouant la vision coloniale, y compris durant la période coloniale'. Jean-Marc Moura, *Littératures francophones et théorie postcoloniale* (Paris: Presses Universitaires de France, 1999), p.4. This definition is doubly suitable for the works of a writer such as Césaire, who wrote at a time when few colonies had won independence, and whose native island is now a French *département.* This usage is also common in postcolonial writing in English. (See Bill Ashcroft, Gareth Griffiths and Helen Tiffin, *The Empire Writes Back: Theory and Practice in Post-colonial Literatures* (London and New York: Routledge, 1989), p.2).

3   Mireille Rosello, Introduction to A. Césaire, *Cahier d'un retour au pays natal* (Newcastle upon Tyne: Bloodaxe Books, 1995), pp.9–68 (p.13).

aesthetic writings. A study of Césaire's ideological writings on the role of the writer in the process of decolonisation reveals a grandiose vision of the artist as a prophet-like, demiurgic figure whose task is the creation or re-creation of a culture destroyed by the process of colonisation. For Césaire this process, exemplified in the *Cahier d'un retour au pays natal*, took the form of a return to a mythical African civilisation and formed the cornerstone of negritude. For postcolonial critics such as Edward Said, Césaire, Senghor and the négritude movement have come to epitomise nativism alongside the work of the Irish poet W. B. Yeats. In a short text on Yeats which contains several references to Césaire, Said asks if Yeats can be seen as 'a particularly exacerbated example of the *nativist* (e.g. négritude) phenomenon, which has flourished elsewhere as a result of the colonial encounter'.[4] As nativism is closely associated with, if not synonymous with, nationalist revival, it is particularly ironic that the label should be used to describe a poet from the Caribbean, an area where nation-building and the development of a common, composite culture have been highly problematic. Indeed, Césaire's Caribbean heritage seems to position him more accurately for a place in the ancestry of the concept of hybridity, defined as 'the blending of different cultural influences, an upfront and active syncretism',[5] leaving Senghor, Yeats and others to re-imagine the history of the land from which they write. The question thus arises if Césaire's poetry can be read in a way which, while recognising his explicit nativist stance, can also be seen as relevant in a multicultural world in which nativism is no longer valid.

It is easy to understand why Césaire is almost always included in the pantheon of what Said calls 'the great nationalist artists of de-colonisation and revolutionary nationalism' (Said, p.8), as well as in the category of 'theoreticians, militants and insurgent analysts of imperialism' (Ibid.). Césaire's prolific political and theoretical writings on colonisation and decolonisation are of particular interest here, in that they include works devoted specifically to the ideological

4   Edward W. Said, *Nationalism, Colonialism and Literature: Yeats and Decolonization* (Derry: Field Day Theatre Company, 1988), p.14.
5   Elleke Boehmer, *Colonial and Postcolonial Literature* (Oxford and New York: Oxford University Press, 1995), p.203.

context of literature, such as the debate with René Depestre on the concept of national poetry[6] and the two lectures on culture and colonisation delivered at the first and second Congresses of Black Writers and Artists in Paris in 1956[7] and Rome in 1959.[8] The second of these forms the most complete statement of Césaire's ideological views on the writer's role in the process of decolonisation, clearly justifying his claim to a place among Said's list of insurgent analysts of imperialism. Césaire explains that, since the relationship of coloniser and colonised is not only one of master and servant, but also of creator and consumer, literary creation must reverse the historical process by restoring the initiative which has been forcibly removed:

> Quand Sekou Touré, leader d'un pays libre, affirme fièrement: 'Je suis le descendant de Samory', il ne s'agit pas d'une puérile vanité généalogique. Cela signifie: 'J'assume Samory' et ce faisant il fait une grande chose: il rétablit l'histoire, il remet les choses à leur place. Il dit: la colonisation ce n'est pas l'histoire, ce n'est que l'accident, et il rétablit le 'continuum' historique. Il réaffirme ou réinvente la continuité historique rompue par l'intrusion coloniale.

> Ce n'est pas autre part qu'il faut chercher notre devoir à nous écrivains et artistes noirs: il est de rétablir la double continuité rompue par le colonialisme, la continuité d'avec le monde, la continuité d'avec nous-mêmes (Ibid., p.121).

By stating the need to pass from the status of consumer to creator, and by doing so in the language of the coloniser, Césaire is taking the first step in recognising his syncretic identity; but by refusing to recognise colonisation as historical fact, by identifying taking back the initiative with re-establishing continuity with the pre-colonial past, he is simultaneously refusing to accept that syncretic identity. This continuity, a fundamental concept of negritude, has received considerable and well-known critical attention and will not be further examined here. What is relevant to mention here is that it led to a focus on a race and on its

6   Aimé Césaire, 'Sur la poésie nationale', *Présence africaine*, 4 (October–November 1955), 39–41.

7   'Culture et colonisation', *Présence africaine*, 8–10 (June–November 1956), 190–205.

8   'L'Homme de culture et ses responsabilités', *Présence africaine*, 24–5 (February–May 1959), 116–22.

past, a mythical Africa in Césaire's case, which is criticised as accepting the imperialist distinction between coloniser and colonised and as having no relevance for the future of the communities involved:

> It is the first principle of imperialism that there is a clear-cut and absolute hierarchical distinction between ruler and ruled. Nativism, alas, reinforces the distinction by revaluating the weaker or subservient partner. And it has often led to compelling but often demagogic assertions about a native past, history or actuality that seems to stand free not only of the coloniser but of worldly time itself. [...] To leave the historical world for the metaphysics of essences like negritude, Irishness, Islam and Catholicism is, in a word, to abandon history (Said, p.15).

It is ironic that the realisation of the broken continuum and the expression of that realisation in French, implying the acceptance of the syncretic, lead only to an impossible search for a 'pure' idealised past. Maryse Condé made essentially the same point as Said when she declared that 'le nègre n'existe pas. L'Europe soucieuse de légitimer son exploitation le créa de toutes pieces'.[9] The conclusion of Condé's well known article aptly summarises the implications of this critique for Césaire's reputation, giving him credit as the author of the *Cahier d'un retour au pays natal*, 'le plus beau poème peut-être, écrit par un colonisé' (Ibid., p.419), before condemning it as irrelevant for the future of colonised communities.

However, Césaire has written more than one work, and a study of his œuvre which situates the *Cahier* in the context of the considerable body of works published after it may shed more light on this question. Although Césaire's fidelity to the fundamental importance of the African heritage is unchanging throughout his career,[10] there is a marked development in the attention explicitly devoted to it in his poems, which goes hand in hand with a marked change in the style of

---

9   Maryse Condé, 'Négritude césairienne, Négritude senghorienne', *Revue de Littérature Comparée*, (1974) 409–19, p.413.

10   For example, several decades after the publication of the *Cahier*, he described himself as 'un poète africain'. Mwabil a Mpang Ngal, *Aimé Césaire: un homme à la recherche d'une patrie* (Dakar: Nouvelles Editions Africaines, 1975), p.143.

the poems. The reason normally cited for this change, namely Césaire's discovery of surrealism through his encounter with André Breton when the latter passed through Martinique on his way to the United States in 1941, is surely insufficient. The obscurity which became dominant in Césaire's poetry after 1941 was already there in the *Cahier*, and deserves much more critical attention than being seen as the result of the passing visit of a European intellectual. The progression of this obscurity is easy to document. His first work, the *Cahier*, in which the term negritude was coined, is a clear and exemplary expression of nativism, with its very title now used at times to describe what has become a literary genre in its own right, returns to the native land.[11] While the images in this first work are often obscure, there is nevertheless a series of clear and confident statements on the cultural alienation caused by colonialism, the poet's revolt against it and the vision of liberation based on the discovery of negritude. This extreme clarity of expression does not entirely disappear from the later works. The poem 'Hors des jours étrangers',[12] in which the poet addresses 'mon peuple' as in the *Cahier*, as if referring to a clearly definable, monoracial and monocultural, unchanging group, appears towards the end of *Ferrements*, first published in 1960, the last of a series of collections published after the *Cahier* and marking the end of Césaire's most intense period of creativity as a poet. However, with a few notable exceptions such as this, the tone of Césaire's poetry changes markedly in the poems written after the *Cahier*, and the focus becomes much more introspective and searching, with few of the confident expressions of leadership and representativity which characterise the latter part of the *Cahier*. 'Viscères du poème' (Ibid., p.286), for example, provides an anguished statement of the difficulties besetting the poet both writing in and creating a new cultural context:

11   See, for example, Gerise Herndon, 'Returns to the native land, reclaiming the other's language: Kincaid and Danticat', *Journal of International Women's Studies*, vol.3, no.1, November, 2001.

12   Aimé Césaire, *The Collected Poetry*. Translated with Introduction and Notes by Clayton Eshleman and Annette Smith (Berkeley and Los Angeles: University of California Press, 1983), p.348.

Angoisse tu ne descendras pas tes écluses dans le bief de ma gorge

Peur dans l'écheveau fou je n'aurai que faire de chercher en tremblant
le fil rouge de mon sang de ma raison de mon droit
le dur secret de mon corps de l'orgueil de mon cœur
une étoile de toujours se lève grand'erre et sans laisser de lie
s'éteint pour mieux renaître au plus pur
si tranchant sur les bords qu'Eclipse tu as beau faire infâme
moi le bras happé par les pierres fondrières de la nuit
je refuse ton pacte sa fureur de patience
et le tumulte debout dans l'ombre des oreilles
aura vu pour une fois sur la blancheur du mur
gicler la noirceur de viscères de ce cri sans oubli

The lines representing the nativist solution come early in the poem (ll.3–4), while the overall emphasis is on the poet's difficulty in expressing and realising this aim. The focus on the poet's fear of the blank page – or the white wall in the case of this poem – can be read in terms of the Mallarméan influence on Césaire, but can also be seen as an expression of the impasse in which he finds himself. This is not just an explosive statement of the cultural alienation caused by colonial oppression, but also an expression of the impossibility of realising the nativist solution.

This is not to suggest that Césaire is in any way rejecting negritude, as many statements in interviews and other works testify to the contrary, in addition to clear indications in the poems themselves, but rather that alongside the ideological certainty of negritude one finds in his poetry a less confident persona, attempting to piece together an identity from the incoherent pieces which the colonial heritage has given him. It is as if the contradiction implicit – and unrecognised – in his 1959 lecture is emerging in the poems, leading to reiterations of the theme of the *Cahier,* but significantly in ever more obscure forms. The obscurity, the explosive imagery bringing together contradictory elements can be read as a potential expression of hybridity and syncreticity, while the thematic of negritude simultaneously denies that identity. At times, usually in very short poems, the expression of displacement and revolt dominates the entire poem. The vision of destruction in 'Entre autres massacres' (Ibid., p.168) for example, forms the entire poem, without any nativist reference, while in other poems the contradiction between the hybrid poetic identity and the impossible nativist solution is clearly expressed. The striking image of alienation and displacement at the start of 'N'ayez point pitié', which is a potent expression of a fractured identity:

les images rupestres de l'inconnu
Vers moi détournent le silencieux crépuscule
De leur rire (Ibid., p.105)

is followed later in the poem by the return to the past as solution:

Et la pureté irrésistible de ma main appelle
De loin de très loin du patrimoine héréditaire
Le zèle victorieux de l'acide dans la chair de la vie (Ibid.).

One can conclude that hybridity and syncreticity are not absent from Césaire's poetry; they are present but denied, a fact which may well explain the vehemence and the increasing obscurity of his style alongside the passionate revolt against colonialism.

The detailed and perceptive analyses by a number of researchers of the expression of negritude in the collections after the *Cahier* reveal how far this obscurity has gone, at once expressing and concealing the theme. Critics have shown how negritude is still central in the later works, how despite their lack of explicitness, they are an internalisation of the process of discovery of negritude which forms the development of the *Cahier*. As Steins[13] has pointed out, the narrator of the *Cahier* discovers his vocation as a poet at the moment when he celebrates the receptivity of his race to the natural world: 'ils s'abandonnent, saisis, à l'essence de toute chose'.[14] Steins notes that this receptivity, close to Senghor's view of emotion as African in contrast to European reason, reveals the influence on Césaire of the ethnologist Leo Frobenius's view of African civilisation, in which this receptivity is the basis of culture. This thematic is explicit in the *Cahier*, but, while still present, it is expressed through the focus on the natural world in the later poems, where the prevalence of key images

13   Martin Steins, 'Nabi Nègre', in Mwabil a Mpang Ngal and Martin Steins (eds), *Césaire 70* (Paris: Editions Silex, 1984), pp.228–72.
14   Aimé Césaire, *The Collected Poetry*, p.68.

such as 'arbre' and 'fleuve', symbolise the continuity of heritage and future, but often without any of the explicit clarity of the expression of negritude in the poet's first work.

Alongside the less explicit tone of most of the poetry after the *Cahier*, there is clearly an even stronger focus on the role of the poet. Steins has analysed the religious references in the first work, the glorification of suffering, the union of man and nature as an archetypal religious experience, as an expression of the poet's prophetic role in leading his people out of decline to a future in which their values will be a source of renewal in a decadent Western civilisation (op. cit.). While the religious references in the *Cahier* are reminiscent of Christianity, in the later poems myths such as Prometheus[15] and the phoenix[16] are either explicitly referred to or evoked through references to birds and rebirth after destruction by fire. For Arnold, this is all part of the search for identity through an exploration of the past:

> For the founders of negritude, their relation to history and myth was to form the decisive intellectual problem. In Frobenius they discovered an apparent legitimisation of their blackness, even though the Caribbean writers could experience the black soul, or paideuma, only in distorted, fragmented or residual manifestations. But for Césaire and many others of his generation, the survival of remnants of an African culture in the midst of a modern technological civilisation suggested a quest for origins. Thus the first phase of negritude [...] involved an increasing reliance on various approaches to myth and a concomitant refusal of the claims of rationalist and empiricist historical writing.[17]

Once again we can recognise in the act of bringing together myths from different sources an expression of the syncretic, of the hybrid nature of the poet's origins, upbringing, education and poetic expression, all in marked contradiction to the impossible quest for origins which is expressed through those references in the very same poems. It is tempting to imagine that Maryse Condé, had she devoted an article to this subject, might have presented the withdrawal into a world of myth as even further distanced from the struggle against

15   See, for example, 'Ferment', Ibid., p.312.
16   See, for example, 'Tam-tam 1', Ibid., p.134, and 'Spirales', Ibid., p.268.
17   Arnold, A. James, *Modernism and Negritude: The Poetry and Poetics of Aimé Césaire* (Cambridge, MASS: Harvard University Press, 1981), p.50.

exploitation which she sees as much more crucial in her study of the negritude of Césaire and Senghor (Condé, p.419). Indeed, Césaire himself decided to abandon poetry after *Ferrements* to seek a more direct form of communication with his public through his theatre.[18] And 'Hors des jours étrangers', with its sudden return to simplicity and clarity after four collections of complex and obscure poetry, can be seen as a final cry of exasperation by the nativist Césaire. Nothing hybrid or syncretic here, just a *cri de cœur*:

> mon peuple
>
> quand
> hors des jours étrangers
> germeras-tu une tête bien tienne sur tes épaules rondes[19]

The final line of the poem, however, is not the optimistic 'demain plus haut plus doux plus large', but rather the more complex two lines which follow:

> et la houle torrentielle des terres
> à la charrue salubre de l'orage.

Even here, the impossibility of Césaire's quest emerges, but the poem remains his anguished (although not his final) farewell to the genre in which he was trying in vain to promote nativism as the solution to his hybrid, syncretic identity.

Despite his fidelity to negritude, it is interesting to note that several aspects of Césaire's work, that is to say the approaches which he adopted in his quest for identity, have characteristics in common with those adopted by later generations of postcolonial writers and

18 'Effectivement je donne ma preference à la forme théâtrale, je crois que les événements extérieurs y sont pour quelque chose. [...] dans le siècle où nous sommes, la poésie est un langage qui nous paraît plus ou moins ésoterique. Il faut parler clair, parler net, pour faire passer le message. Et il me semble que le théâtre peut s'y prêter – et il s'y prête bien.' From an interview in *Magazine Littéraire*, no.34, novembre 1969. Quoted in Lilyan Kesteloot and Barthélémy Kotchy, *Aimé Césaire, l'homme et l'œuvre* (Paris: Présence Africaine, 1973), p.131.
19 Aimé Césaire, *The Collected Poetry*, p.348.

which are now described in the research as characteristic of hybridity. For example, Césaire has been criticised for writing in the language of the colonial master, but, as Ashcroft, Griffiths and Tiffin point out, in the context of the English language:

> Syncretic views of the postcolonial distance themselves from the universalist view of the function of language as representation, and from a culturally essentialist stance which might reject the use of English because of its assumed inauthenticity in the 'non-english' place.[20]

Césaire himself is unapologetic for his choice of French, explaining that:

> Mon désir, [...] tout en me servant du français, c'est de transformer le français, d'en faire une langue à nous, de lui imposer notre marque. Par conséquent ce n'est pas un acte de soumission à une langue; il y a en même temps la volonté de refaire une langue, de reforger une langue. Evidemment cela rejoignait en un certain sens la démarche poétique que l'on connaît en France depuis Rimbaud, Mallarmé et plus encore les Surréalistes. Il y a là une rencontre, en partant de points différents.[21]

Even Confiant, Chamoiseau and other exponents of *créolité* in later generations, share with Césaire their use of French as an expression of their hybrid identity.

Ashcroft, Griffiths and Tiffin also, when listing models of hybridity and syncreticity, mention the importance of 'imaginative escape as the ancient and only refuge of oppressed peoples',[22] recalling Césaire's attraction to poetry and to Surrealist images as 'armes miraculeuses'. Furthermore they highlight the importance of place in all models (Ibid., p.37), a feature which certainly applies to Césaire's poetry, with its many references to the island (of Martinique) in the present on the one hand, and on the other its simultaneous evocation of the absent place (Africa), representing the past. Ironically, the researcher seeking evidence of hybridity in Césaire once again dis-

---

20   Bill Ashcroft, Gareth Griffiths and Helen Tiffin, op. cit., p.42.
21   In an interview with the present author, 3 April 1974.
22   Bill Ashcroft, Gareth Griffiths and Helen Tiffin, op. cit., p.35.

covers the opposing concepts of hybridity and nativism existing side by side.

Finally, Ashcroft, Griffiths and Tiffin also mention as a feature of hybridity and syncreticity the '"rewriting" of canonical stories' (Ibid., p.97), recalling *Une Tempête*. In similar vein, Moura cites Césaire's tragedies as examples of the appropriation of genres from Western literatures (Moura, p.137), seeing this appropriation as a sub-category of the hybridity of genres which categorises postcolonial literature. Indeed, Césaire's work provides an even better example, going beyond the concept of genre itself:

> La première chose que j'ai écrite, c'est le *Cahier*. J'ai dû le faire assez lentement, vers 1936, en des strates différentes, mais en gros, je l'ai certainement commencé vers 1936, comme un cahier. Un cahier, parce que j'avais renoncé à écrire des poèmes: toute la métrique traditionnelle me gênait beaucoup, me paralysait. Je n'étais pas content. Un beau jour, je m'étais dit: 'Après tout, fichons tout en l'air'. Puis je m'étais mis à ecrire sans savoir ce qui en sortirait, vers ou prose. Il m'importait de dire ce que j'avais sur le cœur. C'est pourquoi j'ai pris un titre extrêmement neutre: cahier. Il est devenu en réalité un poème. Autrement dit, j'ai découvert la poésie à partir du moment où j'ai tourné le dos à la poésie formelle.[23]

Césaire goes even further than this, describing the *Cahier* as an 'anti-poème':

> Le *Cahier*, c'est le premier texte où j'ai commencé à me reconnaître; je l'ai écrit comme anti-poème. Il s'agissait pour moi d'attaquer au niveau de la forme, la poésie traditionnelle française, d'en bousculer les structures établies (Ibid., p.69).

It is not only in the first work that this hesitant approach to genre is evident. Of *Et les chiens se taisaient* Césaire comments: 'Cette première pièce, je ne la voyais pas "jouée"; je l'avais d'ailleurs écrite comme un poème.'[24] Thus from the very beginning of his literary career many of the essential characteristics of hybridity are exemp-

---

23 Quoted from an interview with Césaire by Mwabil a Mpang Ngal, op. cit., p.64.
24 'Un poète politique: Aimé Césaire. Propos recueillis par François Beloux', *Magazine Littéraire*, no.34, novembre 1969. Available at http://www.magazine -littéraire.com/archives/ar_césai.htm

lified in Césaire's literary output. 'La reconnaissance d'un moi pluriel, issu d'une négation permanente entre l'origine et la culture dominante et l'examen de son expression littéraire constitueraient une nouvelle direction des études postcoloniales.' This account by Jean-Marc Moura (p.155) of the future of postcolonial criticism in the context of world literature is also an accurate description of the task of the researcher on Césaire's work.

This is not to suggest that in Césaire's work one can see the direct ideological origins of these models of hybridity and syncreticity which characterise postcolonial literatures. The above references to the models described by Ashcroft, Griffiths and Tiffin also contain clear statements that in these models 'hybridity in the present is constantly struggling to free itself from a past which stressed ancestry, and which valued the "pure" over its threatening opposite, the "composite"'.[25] By existing alongside a nativist ideology, hybridity can never be fully realised in Césaire's work. Not only does it lack the acceptance of that identity which postcolonial writers and critics stress, but it simultaneously harks back to an impossible past. As Boehmer points out:

> post-independence writers again relied on hybridity – that is, the blending of different cultural influences, an upfront and active syncretism – to unsettle the inheritance of Europe. Indeed, they had no other option but to be syncretic. No matter how determined were writers' efforts at reclamation, in a postcolonial society coming to terms with the corrosion of tradition during colonial occupation, cultural purity was not on offer (Boehmer, p.203).

It is ironic that a poet like Césaire who embodies not only the displacement which is the starting point for much postcolonial writing in a way which Senghor never could, but also the syncretism of postcolonial writing, should be seen as – and should have declared himself to be – a major exponent of nativism through his fidelity to the importance of Africa in Caribbean identity. While nativism is presumably consigned to the museum, Césaire's poetry need not necessarily join it there, despite condemnation by Condé and others. It can now be read as an expression not only of a clear illustration of

25   Bill Ashcroft, Gareth Griffiths and Helen Tiffin, op. cit., pp.35–6.

nativism, but also as an example of the contradictions inherent in it, particularly in the works of a poet in Césaire's situation where, as in the case of his postcolonial counterparts, 'cultural purity was not on offer' or, to use Césaire's own words, the historical continuum, once broken, could never be fully re-established.[26] Such a reading offers a fuller explanation of the explosive quality of his images than to read them simply as a nativist's three-decade expression of anger at the colonial past, seeing his poetic works rather as an expression of cultural hybridity which was at odds in many ways with negritude and which was only to become accepted in later generations.

26 See 'L'Homme de culture et ses responsabilités', p.121.

EDWARD J. HUGHES

'Sous un signe double': language and identity in Assia Djebar's *L'Amour, la fantasia*[1]

> Toute écriture de l'Autre, transportée, devient
> fatale, puisque signe de compromission
> (AF, p.44).

Assia Djebar's *L'Amour, la fantasia* functions as a form of cultural hybrid at a number of levels. Classified as a *roman*, the text also operates as part-autobiography, part-history of colonial Algeria. In structural terms, the central axis linking the nineteenth and twentieth centuries sees the reader shuttle between the eve of the French colonisation of Algeria in 1830 and the postcolonial late twentieth century. We see the initial colonial accounts of French rule in Algeria stitched in alongside the testimonies of those who resisted the French, both in the early days of empire and in the Algerian War of Independence over a century later. The splicing effect that this creates is also reflected in the overlaying of public and private histories. The imbrication of Djebar's autobiography and the lives of early French conquerors and Algerian *maquisards* and *maquisardes* of the 1950s accentuates this. As narratives converge, a significant slippage occurs at a pronominal level: the pronoun *je*, which initially designates the autobiographical subject, mutates in order to accommodate the identities and voices of a series of Algerian women whose accounts of the War of Independence are resurrected in the third part of *L'Amour, la fantasia*, entitled 'Les Voix ensevelies'. The exhumation of these buried voices ensures that the testimonies of witnesses of trauma are incorporated into the collective memory and that the conflicts in

---

1   Assia Djebar, *L'Amour, la fantasia* (Paris: Albin Michel, 1995 (1985)), p.12. Abbreviation: AF.

Algeria that span two centuries reverberate stereophonically across national and linguistic boundaries.

Djebar highlights zealously the way in which the colonial conquest of 1830 spawned a great flurry of writing. She works from an archive of almost forty testimonies, virtually all of which are works penned by French conquerors; on the side of the besieged there are only three accounts, those of the *mufti* Ahmed Effendi, the secretary to the *bey* Ahmed and a German prisoner in Algiers (AF, p.55). In an arresting concertina movement, the narrator connects the sense of a 'fièvre scriptuaire' which she picks up reading the archive sources with what she terms 'la graphorrhée épistolaire des jeunes filles enfermées de mon enfance: écrire vers l'inconnu devenait pour elles une manière de respirer un nouvel oxygène' (AF, p.56). There is an irony in Djebar's analogy. For if the young girls write *towards the unknown*, there is a powerful sense in which the conquerors' accounts deliver precisely a rebuttal of alterity and of the culturally different. In a very real sense, the triumphalism of empire required this. Yet the provocative linking of colonial 'adventure' to the frenzied writing of adolescent Muslim girls of her own generation is one of the many ways in which Djebar chooses to articulate the difficult connection between autobiography and colonial history.

This splicing also operates at a microtextual level: section II of Part 1 ends with reference to a sudden 'explosion' of love in the Narrator's private life, while section III begins: 'Explosion du Fort l'Empereur, le 4 juillet 1830, à dix heures du matin' (AF, pp.38–9). The trans-lation or 'carrying over' effect delivered by the lexical clip 'explosion' connects present to past, adolescent female to adult male, North African to European, and civilian to soldier, and thereby demonstrates how Djebar's text sits astride cultures.

The curiosity about the Other extends to Djebar's imaginative reconstruction of the manner in which early colonial reports resonated in the Paris of Louis-Philippe. She attributes to metropolitan audiences of the day a greedy desire for vicarious pleasure-taking: 'Mais que signifie l'écrit de tant de guerriers, revivant ce mois de juillet 1830? Leur permet-il de savourer la gloire du séducteur, le vertige du violeur?' (AF, p.56). The explicitly linguistic nature of the conquest is underscored by Djebar:

Le mot lui-même, ornement pour les officiers qui le brandissent comme ils porteraient un œillet à la boutonnière, le mot deviendra l'arme par excellence. Des cohortes d'interprètes, géographes, ethnographes, linguistes, botanistes, docteurs divers et écrivains de profession s'abattront sur la nouvelle proie. Toute une pyramide d'écrits amoncelés en apophyse superfétatoire occultera la violence (Ibid.).

While in part seduced by the archival material, Djebar also identifies how erudite nineteenth-century textual production masks what is at root a legacy of colonial violence.[2]

Translating a message of love

Language not only lies at the heart of Djebar's reflection on the workings of history but also shapes her understanding of familial love, which itself cannot escape entanglement in the colonial legacy. Her story of the relationship between her parents is regularly couched in metalinguistic terms and provides a key to understanding the cultural interstices that her narrative works within. Traditionally her mother refers to her father using the personal pronoun in Arabic that corresponds to 'lui'. Thus her use of the third-person singular where no specific subject is identified inevitably denotes the father. (Djebar adds that this was true of all the married women of her town between the ages of fifteen and sixty, the exception being that husbands who had gone on pilgrimage to Mecca might also be designated as 'Hadj' (AF, p.46)). Yet in spite of the 'règle de la double omission nominale des conjoints' (Ibid.), a culturally significant shift emerges: little by little Djebar's mother learns French from her husband and from the spouses of her husband's colleagues most of whom hail from France.

2   The ambiguous combination of enthusiasm and wariness which Djebar experiences in relation to the archive corroborates Walter Benjamin's celebrated observation that cultural treasures regularly occlude a legacy of barbarism. See W. Benjamin, 'Theses on the Philosophy of History', in *Illuminations*, trans. Harry Zohn (London: Fontana, 1992), p.248.

The cultural translation into French means that, however slow and faltering the transition, the mother learns to refer directly to her spouse. This awareness of the mother working her way over into another language provides Djebar with a powerful memory: 'Je retrouve aisément le ton, la contrainte de la voix maternelle; le tour scolaire des propositions, la lenteur appliquée de l'énonciation sont évidents' (Ibid.). While lovingly dramatising the ponderous steps of her mother's own acculturation, Djebar shows how the mother tongue comes slowly to be supplanted by the language of the Other.

In the first-person narrator's projection, the effect on the mother of this moving into French is of a potentially perplexing trans-formation in affective terms:

> Une écluse s'ouvrit en elle, peut-être dans ses relations conjugales. Des années plus tard, lorsque nous revenions, chaque été, dans la cité natale, ma mère, bavardant en arabe avec ses sœurs ou ses cousines, évoquait presque naturellement, et même avec une pointe de supériorité, son mari: elle l'appelait, audacieuse nouveauté, par son prénom! Oui, tout de go, abruptement allais-je dire, en tout cas ayant abandonné tout euphémisme et détour verbal. Avec ses tantes ou ses parentes plus âgées, elle revenait au purisme traditionnel, par pure concession cette fois: une telle libération du langage aurait paru, à l'ouïe des vieilles dévotes, de l'insolence ou de l'incongruité... (AF, pp.46–7).

The mother, then, occupies this transitional, hybrid space generated by awareness of a second language and culture. Djebar goes further, seeing in the explicitly linguistic emergence or crystallisation of the father a welcome individualisation, in contrast with the 'anonymat du genre masculin, neutralité réductrice' (Ibid.) into which her male relatives are conventionally subsumed. In singling out the father (whose first name, moreover – Tahar – means 'pure'), the mother in turn singles out herself: 'je pensais qu'une distinction nouvelle éclairait le visage maternel' (Ibid.).

In this departure from what we might term, adapting Djebar, modes of cultural periphrasis, Djebar playfully celebrates the emerg-ing directness. Hence, when the father sends the mother a postcard, he address it to Mme (accompanied by the family name) and her children. The marvel for Djebar and the shame for her traditionalist Muslim neighbours (including the male postal worker who must handle the correspondence) is that the family should be designated in these explicit terms: 'or, tout autochtone, pauvre ou riche, n'évoquait femme et enfants que par le biais de cette vague périphrase: "la maison"' (AF, pp.48). In this masculinist order, the naming of a female Other translates, in Djebar's terms, into a declaration of love.

Djebar is also alert to awkwardness and slippages in intercultural contact. Recounting the warm relations between two women, one of them Arabo-Berber, the other a woman originally from Burgundy now married to the French policeman of the village, she scrutinises their hesitations, the way they swop recipes and converse seriously, and their body language as they take leave of each other:

> La Française finissait par tendre gauchement le bras et avancer la main; l'autre se haussait en sautillant dans son large saroual [...] et, malgré le bras tendu, elle plantait deux baisers rapides sur chaque épaule de la Française. Celle-ci, chaque fois surprise et le visage empourpré, claironnait à la ronde: – Au revoir, mes sœurs! (AF, pp.30–1).

The stilted, culturally conditioned reaction of the French woman and the North African woman's no less conventional embrace become an occasion for playful, whimsical comment among the Muslim women and girls gathered in the house. Alert to the cultural negotiations in play, they ask what is wrong with adopting European customs such as sitting on chairs or saying hello in the French way. However fleeting these moments of intercultural contact among women may be, they allow Djebar to celebrate the cultural interstices of everyday life in the colony. In this way, she nudges the narrative beyond the memory of violent colonisation and shows how a redemptive alternative to past antagonisms can be imagined and indeed practised.

Yet even the micronarratives of European lives prompt serious cultural reflection. Hence when the Muslim girl narrator hears the policeman's daughter, Marie-Louise, parading her love for her French-officer boyfriend by addressing him uninhibitedly as 'Pilou chéri', the narrator concludes that love is to be situated beyond these hackneyed words and gestures. The effect of the 'Pilou chéri' is to induce aphasia in the young North African: 'une aridité de l'expression s'installe et la sensibilité dans sa période romantique se retrouve aphasique' (AF, p.38). The hilarity caused among Muslim girls in the

village by the public words of affection serves as a prelude to the
narrator's altogether more serious conclusion that in matters of love
she developed a form of autistic relationship to the French language:
'pas le moindre de ses mots d'amour ne me serait réservé' (Ibid.).

By the same token, constructing her autobiography in French
entails for Djebar, 'sous le lent scalpel de l'autopsie à vif, montrer
plus que sa peau. [...] Les blessures s'ouvrent, les veines pleurent,
coule le sang de soi et des autres, qui n'a jamais séché' (AF, p.178).
To speak of herself beyond the language of her female ancestors, she
observes, triggers a form of self-mutilation and a retrospective com-
plicity with the violence imposed by colonial rule in the previous
century:

> Or cette mise à nu, déployée dans la langue de l'ancien conquérant, lui qui, plus
> d'un siècle durant, a pu s'emparer de tout, sauf précisément des corps féminins,
> cette mise à nu renvoie étrangement à la mise à sac du siècle précédent (Ibid.).

The death of the translator

The tense shuttling between the languages of the coloniser and the
colonised connects fundamentally with the constitution of identity in
Djebar. Seen against this background, rendering or translating the self
can equate to self-betrayal. The paradigm of translation as cultural risk
is already the subject of pure melodrama in one of the early vignettes
in *L'Amour, la fantasia* in which Djebar evokes the fate of the elderly
colonial emissary Brasewitz. In the stand-off between the French
military leaders and the *dey* of Algiers in July 1830, Brasewitz finds
himself at the centre of a drama of a specifically linguistic kind. One
clause in the surrender document written in French is unclear to the
dey, namely the condition that he and his people should 'se rendre à
discrétion'. Brasewitz, whose career stretches back to his days of
service with Napoleon in Egypt, is sent into the city to translate. As
the first member of the European invasion force to enter Algiers, he

faces a tirade of abuse from its inhabitants. Djebar narrates how the anger of the assembly rises as Brasewitz translates each of the clauses but that he drinks a ceremonial refreshment with the *dey* before leaving the city. Yet as the contemporary account of J. T. Merle explains, the trauma of the translator's perilous mission together with his advancing years had a powerful impact:

> L'interprète contractera [...] une maladie nerveuse dont il mourra quelques jours après. Comme si l'éclaircissement de cette hautaine expression 'à discrétion', venue spontanément à l'esprit du chef français, devait faire au moins une victime: le porteur même de la missive! (AF, p.53).

Djebar savours the drama of the moment. The interpreter Brasewitz is depicted as the dutiful carrier of the word-in-transit: 'En assurant au mot le passage dans la langue adverse (langue turque du pouvoir vacillant ou langue arabe de la ville maure, je ne sais...), Brasewitz semblait devoir payer cela de sa vie' (Ibid.). The tense convergence of three lexicons (the language of waning Ottoman rule, that of the newly emerging colonial power, and the Arabic of Algiers) encapsulates not only a diplomatic and military power-struggle but also the intensely private plight *in extremis* of the linguistic go-between. His mission completed, Brasewitz returns to the French positions: 'Le dey abdiquera par écrit, le lendemain matin' (AF, p.53).

To the tale of the interpreter-victim Brasewitz, Djebar adds the case of the elderly native Algerian who randomly approaches the French troops, providing them with their first close-up view of an Arab. Some suspect him of being a spy, others see him as a lone figure with no special mission. He dialogues with De Bourmont, at the end of which the French leader hands him sheets of paper on which his plans, 'ses intentions pseudo pacifiques' (AF, p.44), are written in Arabic. But when he goes back to his own people, the text-bearing North African is killed on suspicion of being a spy:

> Ainsi les premiers mots écrits, même s'ils promettent une fallacieuse paix, font, de leur porteur, un condamné à mort. *Toute écriture de l'Autre, transportée, devient fatale, puisque signe de compromission* (Ibid.; my italics).

The lessons of history which Djebar here recounts with operatic intensity exercise a narrator who converts the risks entailed by the culturally hybrid position she occupies into the building blocks of her own autobiographical narrative.

Writing as transgression

The censorship on expression which these vignettes enact finds resonance in another area of Djebar's text. Cautioning the Western reader not to assume uniformity of behaviour among women who wear the veil in her native Algeria, she notes the condescension that such women traditionally reserve for any of their number who shout and scream: 'la seule qui se marginalisait d'emblée était celle qui "criait"' (AF, p.228). But whereas the refusal to moderate the voice is conventionally viewed as an act of indecency, Djebar adopts it as a prefigurement of her own transgressive activity as a writer in French. Writing in a foreign language, in the language of the adversary of old, 'hors de l'oralité des deux langues de ma région natale – le berbère des montagnes du Dahra et l'arabe de ma ville – […] m'a ramenée aux cris des femmes sourdement révoltées de mon enfance, à ma seule origine' (AF, p.229).

The contact with French situates Djebar in a liminal cultural space. Her *révolte* triggers a form of cultural and linguistic disorientation in which she is confused about her 'langue mère disparue' (AF, p.240). She problematises the status of French: 'le français m'est langue marâtre' (Ibid.). There are sacrifices to be made in the cultural transition to this 'stepmother' tongue. Hence Djebar contrasts both the Andalusian refinement that speaks of the erotic body and the Muslim mystic's hunger for God with what she sees as the aridity of the French language that she uses. Indeed the identitarian conflict ensuing from linguistic transplantation is conveyed as a rerun of the drama of colonisation itself, with imperial pride and native resistance locked in antagonistic positions:

La langue française, corps et voix, s'installe en moi comme un orgueilleux préside, tandis que la langue maternelle, toute en oralité, en hardes dépenaillées, résiste et attaque, entre deux essoufflements. Le rythme du 'rebato' en moi s'éperonnant, je suis à la fois l'assiégé étranger et l'autochtone partant à la mort par bravade, illusoire effervescence du dire et de l'écrit (AF, p.241).

The *rebato*, Djebar explains to her reader, goes back to the days of Spanish settlements in North Africa long before 1830 and designates the point from which counter-attacks were launched in a series of regular skirmishes between natives and raiders.

At a linguistic level, there is the persistent conflict between the perceived imperium of French and the essential orality of African languages that nineteenth-century Eurocentrism saw as a mark of their inferiority. The denigration of oral culture provided the necessary flip side to the celebration of European cultural achievement. In the decade when France was embarking on the colonisation of Algeria, French and, more generally, European intellectul life reflected a mood of confident superiority, providing a cultural corollary to conquest. Philarète Chasles, lecturing at the Athénée in Paris in 1835, spoke of 'the grand civilising moment' and asserted that France was 'the most sensitive of all countries [...] what Europe is to the world, France is to Europe'.[3] Coincidentally, one of Djebar's chosen epigraphs is drawn from Barchou de Penhoën's *Expédition d'Afrique*, also of 1835, in which de Penhoën reports that the French guards were learning to 'distinguer du pas et du cri de l'Arabe, ceux des bêtes fauves errant autour du camp dans les ténèbres' (AF, p.9). Djebar succeeds in turning European denigration and ignorance of local culture into a serious reflection on the *cry* as, crucially, a repository of powerful cultural identity.

The tension between a discarded orality and the prestige of the written is nicely captured by Djebar when, late in the text, she rewrites the 'L'Amour s'écrit' section of the Part 1 title of her text. As the *s'ecrit* merges with its homophone *ses cris*, so

---

3   Quoted by Susan Bassnet in her book, *Comparative Literature: a Critical Introduction* (Oxford and Cambridge, MASS: Blackwell, 1993), p.20. I am indebted to Michael Sheringham for pointing out the relevance of Bassnet's work in this context.

the autobiographical narrator's body is described as reconnecting with 'le hululement des aïeules sur les champs de bataille d'autrefois [...] il ne s'agit plus d'écrire que pour survivre' (AF, p.240). Ancestral cries, then, accentuate the notion of a transgenerational sorority, even if paradoxically Djebar enshrines memory of her tribe through the process of writing in French. The suggestion that this writing process should itself perform an intensely vital role further complicates the affective response to the French language:

> Langue installée dans l'opacité d'hier, dépouille prise à celui avec lequel ne s'échangeait aucune parole d'amour... Le verbe français qui hier était clamé, ne l'était trop souvent qu'en prétoire, par des juges et des condamnés. Mots de revendication, de procédure, de violence, voici la source orale de ce français des colonisés (AF, p.241).

In the collective memory of the colonised, French stands inexorably as the vehicle for encounters with a punitive colonial law. Freighted in this way, it can only problematise the narrator's writing medium as she seeks to negotiate her way through a history of conflictual relations: 'Sur les plages désertées du présent [...], mon écrit cherche encore son lieu d'échange et de fontaines, son commerce' (AF, p.241).

Djebar also grounds the urge to write in tribal memories of nineteenth-century persecution. In a self-mythologising vein, she converts 1842 – the year when Saint-Arnaud's forces destroy the *zaouia* of Djebar's native tribe, the Beni Ménacer – into the year of her birth. Before finding her own voice, she hears the voices of her imprisoned tribespeople: 'ils assurent l'orchestration nécessaire. Ils m'interpellent, ils me soutiennent pour qu'au signal donné, mon chant solitaire démarre' (AF, p.243).

Interment in the language of the Other

The affirmation of tribal allegiance further accentuates Djebar's sense
of treason caused by the cultural evolution she has undergone. This is
captured dramatically in an arresting image of the French language:
'Cette langue était autrefois sarcophage des miens; je la porte aujourd'hui comme un messager transporterait le pli fermé ordonnant sa
condamnation au silence, au cachot' (AF, p.241). Within this hub of
both powerful self-recrimination and self-incrimination, the sarcophagus awakens memories of ancient imperial civilisations (Greek,
Roman, Egyptian) while etymologically the idea of a flesh-consuming
edifice recalls the murderous legacy of French colonial rule that is
evoked elsewhere in the text in accounts of nineteenth-century massacres. Djebar's anxiety stems in part from the uneasy suspicion that
she herself might be assisting in a process which encases the native
North African within a French legacy. Yet she consoles herself by
identifying illustrious predecessors who, she speculates, faced potentially similar dilemmas. In a self-dramatising gesture, she posits as a
celebrated North African precursor St Augustine of Hippo, who, she
notes, wrote in the imperial language of the Roman Empire, in the
language of writers and generals like Caesar or Scylla from an earlier
'Guerre d'Afrique'. In Djebar's pantheon of cultural *transfuges*,
Augustine is joined by the fourteenth-century philosopher and
historian Ibn Khaldoun, who writes the story of his life's adventures in
the language of another conquering culture, that of the Arabs who
colonised his native North Africa. As Djebar endorses imaginatively
the plight of Ibn Khaldoun writing his autobiography in exile in
Egypt, she projects on to his writerly activity the sign of death
foregrounded in the earlier image of the sarcophagus: '[Ibn Khaldoun]
obéit soudain à un désir de retour sur soi: le voici, à lui-même, objet et
sujet d'*une froide autopsie*' (p.242; my italics).

The aesthetics of life-writing in these interstitial spaces acquires
a life-and-death urgency made palpable in the images of the sarcophagus and of autopsy. Yet the translation over into the other language
is a gift ironically offered by the narrator's North African father:

> La langue encore coagulée des Autres m'a enveloppée, dès l'enfance, en
> tunique de Nessus, don d'amour de mon père qui, chaque matin, me tenait par
> la main sur le chemin de l'école. Fillette arabe, dans un village du Sahel
> algérien... (AF, p.243).

The father's gift effectively frames the narrative in *L'Amour, la
fantasia* in that it both initiates and concludes it (AF, pp.11, 243). He
himself is a figure of hybridity: a local teaching in the French school,
he wears a fez and European-style suit. He is commended by the
narrator for having preserved her from 'la claustration', that is, the
restrictions on her social appearance that adherence to a more traditional Muslim code would have entailed. Djebar observes ironically:
'Mais les princesses royales à marier passent également de l'autre côté
de la frontière, souvent malgré elles, à la suite des traits qui terminent
les guerres' (AF, p.240). The autobiographical subject here becomes,
like the princesses of history, a pawn in a necessary but always
conflictual cultural exchange. Djebar's text thus functions according
to a logic of translation, of working from and into cultures that a
colonial legacy has drawn into antagonistic proximity.

Sisters across cultures

In addition to summoning up Augustine of Hippo and Ibn Khaldoun
as exemplary ancestors who write in the language of the enemy,
Djebar evokes an obscure precursor whose legacy she is nevertheless
moved to champion. Returning to voices from the nineteenth-century
archive in the closing part of her work, she focuses on the figure of
Pauline Rolland, one of ten French women who in June 1852 were
moved to North Africa from the Saint Lazare prison in Paris where
they had been held for their part in the 1848 revolution. The government's twin strategy was to populate Algeria and rid the capital of
militant dissidents. Well over a century later, Djebar raises to epic
status the discarded figure of Rolland. But whereas the dissident
quarante-huitards become for Albert Camus, for example, a reposit-

ory of French Algerian identity, Djebar works towards a specifically gendered history of militancy for her own ends.[4] In a transcultural switch, Rolland, a revolutionary of her day, is mythically adopted by Djebar as an ancestor of the women of Algeria who in the mid-twentieth century resisted French colonial rule. This assertion of transnational sisterhood spurs Djebar on to imagine the women of North Africa uttering, in Rolland's honour, 'le cri de triomphe ancestral, ce hululement de sororité convulsive!' (AF, p.250). The loop enables Djebar to connect with women's proactivity and militancy. She transcends national identities by attributing to herself and Rolland a common linguistic identity: 'dans la glaise du glossaire français, elle et moi, nous voici aujourd'hui enlacées' (Ibid.). If Djebar finds authentication and acceptance in this projection of primitive bonding, the French language, elsewhere seen as the *step*mother tongue – the 'langue marâtre' (AF, p.240) – now becomes the medium of communication for dissident sisters. In that sense, evocation of a buried feminist militancy from the 1848 revolution becomes redemptive and maps out for Djebar a terrain of cultural belonging. The effect of sisterhood is to transcend national cultures in conflict and to spawn a redemptive *lingua franca* that works as a counter-discourse to male, Western colonialism.[5]

4   In his posthumously published *Le Premier Homme* (Paris: Gallimard, 1994), Camus hails the rebels of 1848 as the naive settlers of nineteenth-century Algeria and as the precursors of the politically isolated *pieds noirs* of the late 1950s. By drawing gender into the frame, Djebar opens out a different angle on the traditionally manichean depiction of coloniser/colonised relations.

5   Yet if Pauline Rolland provides a French antecedent with whom Djebar senses a powerful cultural connection, the narrator's experience attending a French school draws her into contact with a metropolitan world that can only ever be exotic. Hence the depictions of French school life, along with the celebration of European flora and fauna and cultural data from twentieth-century France (all of which are integral to the cultural message mediated by the French school in the colonial situation), have an unreality about them in the eyes of the young Algerian narrator. The sense of dislocation triggered by images of modern France contrasts with the capacity of the nineteenth-century archive to throw up a testimony such as Rolland's which transcends coloniser/colonised antagonisms.

Extending her reflection on the role of women in colonial relations, Djebar suggests that woman's scope for autonomy in twentieth-century Algeria operates at an essentially linguistic level. Whereas men may be legitimately polygamous, Muslim women of Djebar's generation have, she suggests, four languages in which to express their desire: 'le français pour l'écriture secrète, l'arabe pour nos soupirs vers Dieu etouffés, le libyco-berbère quand nous imaginons retrouver les plus anciennes de nos idoles mères' (AF, 203). The fourth language is that of the body, 'le corps qui, dans les transes, les danses ou les vociférations, par accès d'espoir ou de désespoir, s'insurge, cherche en analphabète la destination, sur quel rivage, de son message d'amour' (Ibid). If Djebar's text is a search for a language in which to express love, the body becomes an ultimate repository of that impulse. The body, which houses the *cry* that Djebar so values, is also the privileged medium of commemoration as her depiction of the dead victims of colonial history confirms.

In *Amour bilingue*, the Algerian critic Abdelkebir Khatibi writes of the affective impact on the colonised of writing in French, the language of the enemy. He reflects on the orthographic proximity of the words *mot* and *mort*: just one letter, as he says, separates the terms for word and death.[6] In an analogous way, the search for identity in *L'Amour, la fantasia* entails a dual reflection on writing and on death. The two are conflated most spectacularly in Djebar's excavation of colonial accounts of conquest and in the traumatised voices retrieved from the Algerian War of Independence. In triumphalist nineteenth-century accounts, the word is a harbinger of violence, as we have already seen: 'le mot deviendra l'arme par excellence' (AF, p.56). Yet for Djebar, writing 'sous un signe double' (to refer back to my title) means that her work carries the ambiguous allegiances of the *transfuge* and does not map tidily on to any predictable partisan position. She confesses to being spellbound by the thought of the colonisers violently subjugating the local population: 'je suis étrangement hantée par l'émoi même des tueurs, par leur trouble obsessionnel' (AF, p.69). Indeed her delving into the French archives often verges on the

6   Abdelkebir Khatibi, *Amour bilingue* (Paris: Editions Fata Morgana, 1983), p.4.

celebratory to the extent that the tales of conquest that she unearths convey a rhetoric that not only seduces the nineteenth-century European reader but also appears ambivalently to mesmerise Djebar.

One of the most haunting of these accounts involves the asphyxiation by the French of the native Ouled Riah tribe who had taken refuge in caves situated on the plateau of Kantara in June 1845. Fifteen hundred tribespeople perished. Djebar is transfixed by the report of the officer-writer Pélissier, the 'bourreau-greffier' (AF, 92). Yet however much Pélissier intended his document to be a conventional military account, he has become for Djebar 'l'émouvant arpenteur de ces médinas souterraines, l'embaumeur quasi fraternel de cette tribu définitivement insoumise…' (AF, p.93). The metaphorical preservation of the bodies of the tribespeople by their executioner exerts a hold over Djebar, who receives Pélissier's report as a palimpsest on to which she will inscribe 'la passion calcinée des ancêtres' (Ibid.). Djebar thus *carries on from* Pélissier while also *carrying him over into* the memory spaces of the native Algerian.

In a coda entitled 'Biffure' that marks the end of Part One of *L'Amour, la fantasia*, Djebar provides a reflection on the superimposition of French and Arabic, on how the strange-looking letters of the French language written on a cave wall mutate: 'l'inscription du texte étranger se renverse dans le miroir de la souffrance, me proposant son double évanescent en lettres arabes, de droite à gauche redévidées; elles se délavent ensuite en dessins d'un Hoggar préhistorique…' (AF, p.58). For the narrator, the connectedness of these languages and the link back to North African prehistory clarify her task, which is to excavate histories, accounts and utterances that work across languages and to reconstruct the details of what she terms '[une] géologie sanguinolente' (Ibid.).

Jean-Charles Vegliante

In dream I see a friend, a young man dead
afar, *angelic* as from a Wenders film,
heading towards me on an unmapped road,
along the edge. 'How can this be, oh friend of mine ?'

Repeated twice in the dangling air. Why
thunderstruck like this, I wonder once
    the tears which wake you in the night had welled :
    the unforeseen, that's what I was for him perhaps,
    incapable of speech on those haggard shores,
in that fork in time where our target lies.

                            (translated by Peter Broome)

Je vois en rêve un ami, un jeune mort
distant, angélique à la façon Wenders,
venant vers moi sur une route égarée,
au bord. 'Mon ami, comment est-ce possible ?'

Deux fois le redit l'air suspendu. Pourquoi
cette stupeur, je me le demande après
les larmes qui vous éveillent dans la nuit :
l'imprévu, peut-être étais-je moi pour lui,
ne pouvant parler sur ces rives hagardes,
dans le temps divergent où est notre cible.

Draught of night

Little sibyl of our dreams
always and never uttering —
finding amusement in that time, I'd say
which never changes for you,
never answers to one's love ;
to spare us also
     victims
far too fast of finalizing
muffled words.
     We live then on your lack.
With no betrayal you deceive, and succour us.
       (translated by Peter Broome)

Gorgée de nuit

Petite sibylle de nos rêves,
toujours tu dis et tu ne dis pas —
je crois, pour t'amuser dans ce temps
qui jamais ne se change pour toi,
qui jamais ne répond si l'on t'aime ;
et par pitié de nous
                              qui avons
trop vite des mots définitifs
et sourds.
                    Donc nous vivons de ton manque.
Sans mensonge tu nous trompes, tu nous aides.

Index

(Critics are indexed only where they form part of the substantive argument.)